ENGAGING FAITH:
MY STORY IN GOD'S STORY

ENGAGING FAITH:
MY STORY IN GOD'S STORY

Jay J. Shim

DORDT PRESS

Cover design by Julia Visser
Layout by Carla Goslinga

Copyright © 2024 Jay J. Shim

All quotations from Scripture are taken from The New International Version® NIV®. Copyright © 1995, and newer versions are used throughout the book. Used by permission. All rights reserved worldwide.

Fragmentary portions of this book may be freely used by those who are interested in sharing the author's insights and observations, so long as the material is not pirated for monetary gain and so long as proper credit is visibly given to the author. Others, and those who wish to use larger sections of text, must seek written permission from the publisher.

ISBN: 978-0-932914-27-9

Printed in the United States of America.

Dordt Press
700 7th Street NE
Sioux Center, Iowa 51250

www.dordt.edu/DCPcatalog

The Library of Congress Cataloging-in-Publication Data is on file with the Library of Congress, Washington, D.C.

Library of Congress Control Number: 2024931275

Acknowledgement

As I am gathering the chapters into a book, I wish to express my heartful gratitude to my teachers who shaped my theological mind, and to my colleagues with whom I have worked side by side and shared the theological vision. I want to thank Dr. Justin Bailey and Dr. Gayle Doornbos, who have read my manuscript and advised me. I also thank Dr. Channon Visscher for his publication administration, and Ms. Carla Goslinga for the layout of the book and Ms. Julia Visser for the cover design. My special thanks should be given to Dr. Mary Dengler, who so painstakingly edited this book into a readable format.

Jay Shim

CONTENTS

Forword i

1. Introduction 1
2. The Bible as God's message in human language 9
3. Good creation as the archetype of salvation 17
4. Humanity as God's image in the world 29
5. Sin as transgression of God's will 39
6. The plan for salvation as restoration of the created world 47
7. The whole story of salvation 55
8. Patriarch: the foundation of God's people 63
9. Exodus: liberation as the beginning of Israel 73
10. Covenant and law: the means of salvation 83
11. The Promised Land 93
12. Ruth: the salvation of nations 101
13. Prophets: the judgment and promise of restoration 109
14. The Messianic expectation 121
15. The gospel: who Jesus is and what he accomplished 129
16. The way of righteousness 141

17. The kingdom of God we live in 153
18. Christian spirituality and worldview 163
19. Practicing spirituality and worldview 175
20. Foretasting the eternal life here and now 189
21. Epilogue: My story in God's story 199

Foreword

This book, *Engaging Faith: My Story in God's Story*, is a culmination of Dr. Jay Shim's many years of teaching Biblical studies and Christian theology both to Dordt University students and Christian faculty members in overseas universities. It also is the fruit of lifelong study through which he has pondered the Christian grounding for our lives and an understanding of redemption that encompasses all of God's creation. Dr. Shim's writing honors Biblical revelation from Genesis through Revelation as a wholistic story of salvation; and he expands his theological ideas with contributions from Augustine, Calvin, Kuyper, Bavinck, and contemporary sources. He writes that "Religion does not simply deal with one aspect of life; instead, it motivates the whole of human existence because it determines one's view of reality." In a God-created world where all of reality is sacred, the author believes our calling as ambassadors of reconciliation and renewal is an effort of freedom and joy. Dr. Shim understands that when the world is the theater for God's glory and Christ's renewal, it is our Christian place for faith, learning, and service. In his book, he is eager to share this message with his readers.

Dr. Shirley J. Roels
Executive Director
International Network for
Christian Higher Education

Chapter 1

Introduction

For many years, my mind toiled over the question of what it means to be a Christian. I sensed a missing link between faith and faith's relevance to life. What is God doing when he saves us: is salvation just a matter of making us believe in him? Is faith solely a matter of changing our spiritual status before God, with the goal of allowing us to escape suffering and go to heaven? If so, the Christian religion would be a private matter only, neither related to nor mediated by our lives. Then, questions arose regarding the object of salvation: does salvation work or make sense at the core human existence—in who we are and what we do? Is salvation real in a life situation? How would salvation help us live a good life in the world? It is absurd to assume a dualistic view of salvation's reality, in which life in the world, reason, and work are severed from salvation. It is absurd because the dualistic view in effect restrains God's absolute sovereignty over his creation and denies the wholistic nature of human beings. As I thought my way through various approaches to Christianity, I was blessed to experience diverse perspectives on theology and diverse modes of Christian thinking and living. It was an encouraging experience to witness and be a part of the church, where many commit to godly living with common faith. It was, at the same time, a puzzling experience, because the common faith and zeal for a godly life often yields diverse theologies and spiritualities, which are sometimes contradictory to one another.

When only a partial sum of the gospel is taken as a whole, the gospel is distorted. An account that renders a full recognition of the gospel and a wholistic redeemed life is the biblical framework of salvation that is analogous to creation and achieves its goal in the new creation. Salvation by grace, through faith, is not something foreign to be added to the world, but is God's way of accomplishing his creational ordinance. What is new is the ineffable sacrifice that Christ offered to restore fallen humanity. Christ redeems believers and establishes them as the new humanity in his reconciling world to himself. In such a framework, personal salvation embraces its public and even cosmic relevance. As the godly identity and work of humanity was integral for the management of the created world, God renews and re-establishes the new humans for the redeemed world.

In God's grand act of salvation, we find a full scope of reality—where grace restores nature and where the spiritual and natural and faith and so-called worldly activities such as public life, education, and work are integrated in Christian life. Faith engages life, for it is an engaged faith. Theology aims at shaping the habits of the Christian heart and mind so that believers may live the Christian life in everyday setting out of joyous responsibility, with the doxological goal.

My story in *God's* story

In the biblical scheme, human salvation is not singled out as a stand-alone act of God, detached from his other acts, as if it takes place against the background of the creation, but is a major act of God that will fulfill all his acts for the created world. Within the broad perspective of God's will for the creation are found the need and purpose of human salvation. As the message of salvation in the Scripture progresses, the eschatological force of God's creational ordinance is clearly revealed. God intended for humans, his representatives on earth, to nurture the world and to realize its goodness. In fact, the brief introduction to human nature—being made in God's image—is instituted in such a way as to lead to humanity's ruling responsibility. Within the grand scheme of God's management of the world, human acts, either good or bad, affect the world. Human sin corrupted the world as well as humans themselves. God's salvation renews humans and gives them a vision of the restored world. From the creation through sin and redemption, human identity and life are known by their engaging with the created world. Such a broad biblical scheme of human existence anticipates personal salvation as being essentially related to the restored creation.

The micro perspective of human salvation, which is understood as a transfer from a sinful to a redeemed status, is to be seen within the macro perspective of God's acts that move creation from its fallen condition to its redeemed condition as the new creation. The broad scheme of biblical salvation does not obscure the nature of Christ's redeeming work; rather, it underlines the true nature of his redeeming work. It does not conceal or reduce the centrality of personal salvation; rather it places personal salvation in the right place and role in God's saving and restorative work.

Since God's act of salvation was unfolding over a long period of time in diverse cross-cultural settings of the world, it is important for us to acquire an integrative perspective of God's salvation, understanding its parts and progression in light of the whole. When we study a map, it provides us with a big picture of the land as well as its details, such as roads, mountains, and rivers, and with that knowledge we can make our trip plan. The map shows where we are, where we go, what route we should take, and what kinds of terrain we are going through. In the same way, our trip through the Scriptures starts at a certain point and moves through certain courses in order to reach the destination. We can take a trip without a map or without the ability to read the map. However, it is not hard to imagine the differences between taking a trip guided by a map (or even a GPS) and a trip with no map or understanding of a map.

Let us look at Romans 10:9-13, which is popularly presented as a sum of the gospel—as an example to show the importance of the big picture of the Bible. In verse 9, Paul presents the gospel that if you confess Jesus as Lord, you will be saved. What does he mean by saying Jesus as Lord? How does salvation work with our confession of him here and now? The presentation of the gospel is founded on God's work, which was progressively known from the past to the present. The gospel of verse 9 is the sum and conclusion of the one plan of God's salvation, which started long ago in the Old Testament. Paul provides the big picture—that salvation is achieved by receiving God's righteousness, that is, becoming right with God through faith in Jesus Christ. His presentation in verses 1-13 moves as follows:

- Israel pursued God's righteousness by keeping the law in a misguided way.
- Christ fulfilled the law to save all who believe in him; that is, righteousness is by faith.
- Gospel is: "if you confess with your mouth, 'Jesus is Lord,' and believe in your heart that God raised him from the dead, you will be saved" (v. 9).[1]
- The way of becoming righteous by faith is the same for all people, with no difference between Jews and Gentiles.

Revisiting the Old Testament history of Israel is essential for Paul's presentation of the gospel. He deals with the requirement of the law, which goes all the way back to Moses, is misdirected in its keeping, is fulfilled in its requirements by Christ, is gained through the faith that confesses Jesus as Lord, and provides the common way of salvation for all people. Paul presents the gospel of salvation by faith in Jesus Christ, a gospel that is rooted in his work as "the end of the law." Christ obediently fulfilled God's Old Testament plan of salvation. That obedience was the right way of receiving God's righteousness, unlike the old Israel's seeking after their own righteousness in their own way (v. 3). Since Christ fulfilled the requirement of the law, he can transfer that righteousness to all who believe in him, regardless of race. Thus, salvation by faith in Jesus Christ is the conclusion and sum of God's work of salvation, which progressed from the Old Testament. The way of salvation by faith is not contradictory to keeping the law and does not do away with it; instead, it fulfills the law's requirement. Paul's presentation of the gospel testifies to the integrated history of salvation, which implies that we must read the

Scripture as the history of God's salvation for one people of God.

The same Paul presents a broad picture regarding the nature of Christ's saving work. In Romans 8, he includes the sin-damaged creation as the object of God's salvation act: "For the creation was subjected to frustration… [in order that] the creation itself will be liberated from its bondage to decay and brought into the glorious freedom of the children of God" (vv. 20-21). As the creation became corrupt through human sin, it joined human corruption and need for redemption. The one redemption that embraces humans and the created world finds its first expression in God's salvation revealed through Noah's flood. There God made his covenant with all living creatures not to destroy the world with water. In Colossians 1, Paul defines Christ's achievement by his crucifixion as the reconciliation of all things. The *all things* refers to the whole creation that Christ created, as emphatically described in verses 15-17. Human reconciliation is a part of the broader cosmic reconciliation (vv. 20-22). In the Scriptures, humans are identified in their relationship to the world in both creation and redemption, never as being above the created world. God's creational ordinance for the place and role of humanity in and for the world is to be achieved in the new heaven and new earth. In Revelation 21-22, the vision of humanity's place and role is found as parallel to that of God's salvation plan in the Old Testament, with an example of Isaiah 65:17-25. The correlated description of the creation and re-creation that is found in the creation account of Genesis 1-2, Isaiah 65, and Revelation 21-22 suggests the continuity of God's cause and purpose for the creation and its culmination in the new heaven and new earth.

The key to finding the Christian identity and life lies in the integration of personal salvation and the vision for cosmic renewal. Personal salvation and the cosmic vision, though distinguishable, are not different tracks to salvation or different modes of the Christian life, as if the latter is an intellectual appendix to the former. Rather, they are the source and power of the new life and the ultimate goal for the Christian life. Personal piety toward God expresses its power through participating in the reconciliation mission of God.

The benefits of reading the Scriptures with an overarching picture are many. Just as salvation is personally affected by individual experiences of suffering and the anticipation of deliverance, Scripture-reading and faith-forming may be influenced by human concerns. A common difficulty is the temptation to fit the Scriptures into one's situation, instead of trying to live by what the Scriptures teach. We are to face the blunt truth that the gospel is God's message to us, not something that is born within us. We are to learn to be surprised by it and to be humble before it. Another temptation is to focus on selected parts of the gospel that sometimes are claimed to be the essential gospel. Often the essential aspect of the gospel is selected for personal need.

When one takes salvation as merely personal forgiveness of sin and the consequential transfer to heaven, one reduces the cosmic scheme of the Bible to an appendix to or historical background for personal salvation. In that case, the creation remains a remote background that had been created good but now is hopelessly sinful. When the creation is not seen in its essentially eschatological stance, it remains indifferent to human eyes, and the redeemed life does not have much to do with the world. As a result, the Christian life restricts itself to the "religious" sphere, agreeing with the scientific worldview, which severs the religious/private life from the secular/public life. Such a Christian view reduces one's sense of responsibility for society to one's membership in the church and reduces one's moral engagement in the world to one's moral engagement in the church community. The big picture of salvation in the Bible can correct the personal, self-centered interpretation. In the broad scheme of salvation, the Christian life is essentially a public matter; God worked with creation and re-creation openly in the world and for the world. The Church, individually and communally, is not an isolated island in society, but exists in the world as its light.

An ethnocentric reading of the Scriptures similarly keeps the readers from understanding God's intention for the gospel. Often, Christian communities shape an us-against-them attitude toward others, an attitude that limits both the Christian life and the hope of others. We need to face the truth—that God is the Creator of all peoples, and he worked the gospel for all peoples and within multi-cultural contexts. God started his work of salvation by choosing a pagan man and woman from Ur and formed Israel from their descendants. The overarching scheme of his salvation reveals the movement from Israel to the Gentiles. God sent Israel to serve as the priestly nation for the sake of other nations. Forming Israel aimed at incorporating all nations to God's people. Israel, however, misconstrued their identity of the holy nation when they understood the law only in terms of a distinguishing mark from others. They were chosen as a holy nation to serve as the model people of God. As Israel was located in the narrow bridge-land between world powers, her people were to engage other nations with the law of God. God continuously moved his people to and from pagan cultures so that they—his people—could be shaped as God's people and serve as his witness to others. Their engaging with others, due to their unfaithfulness to their God, was painful, resulting in defeats and exiles. Israel herself became divided by ethnic backgrounds and theologies. The gospel of salvation, as a result, was formed out of the cross-cultural contexts that frequently produced prejudices and conflicts among diverse people groups.

God does not show favoritism toward any particular nation; instead, he shapes his people out of all nations. The idea of the chosen people and the holy nation is to be seen from God's intent of using them for the sake of other nations. The benefit of Israel as God's holy nation carries a responsibility, not something to take pride in as being an exclusive attitude toward others. God judges all sinful nations and calls them to salvation. God called the Egyptians, along-side the Hebrews, to recognize him as the true lord. Isaiah recorded God's broad vision of his people: "blessed be Egypt my people, Assyria my handiwork, and Israel my inheritance" (19:25). Paul presents the movement of the gospel from the Jews to the gentiles: "accept one another, then, just as Christ accepted you, in order to bring praise to God. For I tell you that Christ has become a servant of the Jews on behalf of God's truth, to confirm the promises made to the patriarchs so that the Gentiles may glorify God of his mercy" (Rom. 15:7-9). The gospel comes with a strong moral message. The message of God's salvation as redemption and reconciliation was shaped within concrete and painful interactions among peoples. All peoples and cultures of the region were involved in forming the message of the gospel. The message of salvation demanded, and still demands, God's people to be reconciled to God and also with and among neighboring peoples. The confession, founded on the body of Jesus Christ, demands the church to adopt a new attitude toward others. In fact, Christ does not demand the church to work hard to achieve that unity; rather, he demands that the church practice and further the already-attained unity.

My story in God's story

God communicates to humans in human ways. Having been made in God's image, humans were endowed with the gift of self-consciousness, with which they could recognize and understand their existence and their relationship to God in the world. They were able to accept and understand God's will in their finite settings. To fallen humanity, God graciously accommodated his message in the Scriptures to their finite and sinful level. God's Word regarding spiritual matters comes to us in an analogical form, being rendered into terms rooted in human affairs. The flip side of God's accommodated communication is humanity's responsibility to process God's Word in human terms. By "human terms," I do not mean a human-centered assessment of it, but a "human" understanding of it. When we read the Scriptures guided by human wisdom, we tend to judge the messages and tailor them according to our wish. However, when we read them within the context of the triune God's work, we listen to God's living voice communicated through his Spirit. Through the work of the Holy Spirit, human faculties are restored to the effect that human rationality is no longer contradictory to spirituality; instead, they work together within faith. Faith does not repudiate so-called human or worldly faculties; instead, it restores them in the renewed human being. The intrinsic human faculties—spiritual, rational, emotional, and physical—are renewed and work in harmony with faith. In the renewed human being, the Christian can figure out what God's message means and eventually live it out.

Just as the Second Person of the Trinity is incarnated in Jesus Christ, who died and rose from the dead for us, and just as his Spirit works for us in the world, so too must we see to it that the message of salvation is incarnated in us, that our faith and its practice are visibly worked out in our life. Christian realism is essential for forming and practicing faith. We are to find what kind of salvation God is working in and around us, what is meant by faith, how it works in our concrete life situations, and even what conflicts of faith we experience in life. Experience is an essential aspect of the Christian faith, even to the point that it brings us to faith when reason fails. When experiences are examined through the lens of the Scripture, either for conformity or conflict, they become a significant validation of the gospel truth. Experience has a constitutive role, as it constantly seeks further support in everyday life to strengthen the gospel of salvation.

Let us go back to the text of Romans 10 and see what Paul means by salvation by faith. After pointing out Christ's fulfillment of the law, Paul reaches the conclusion as to the way of salvation. It is by confessing that Jesus is the Lord. Jesus who died as ransom for sinners and resurrected is actually the God of the Old Testament. How does the historical knowledge of Jesus—which is objective information—save us subjectively? Paul answers: "it is with your heart that you believe and are justified, and it is with your mouth that you confess and are saved" (v. 10). We are affected by Jesus' work through our confession of faith. Believing Jesus in our heart and confessing him with our mouth signify that we believe him with our whole human dedication. In verse 11, Paul delineates the belief as trust. Trusting what Christ has done for *me* relates the effect of his saving act to me personally. This gospel, "the word" Paul calls it, "is near you; it is in your mouth and in your heart" (v. 8). The message of salvation is not esoteric knowledge; it is God's message available to us so that we can process it in our human heart and mouth.

Outline of the book

I have organized this book around the biblical account of salvation that God is working for us and around us, and consequent spirituality and worldview for living Christian life. In order to achieve the goal, I will review the overarching framework of God's salvific acts from creation, through the fall and the work of Christ Jesus, to the consummation in the new creation, with examination of relevant biblical texts. As we move along the progressive development of God's salvific work, I will discuss how God's requirement of faith of Israel regarding living with covenant and law applies to our present theological context. The relevance of salvation by faith to our life will be discussed under the headings of spirituality and worldview. As this book is dedicated to such a goal, not all subjects that are significant for Christian theology are discussed in this book.

The reader is advised to pay attention to the following summary of the biblical framework of salvation: first, salvation is creation-analogous-inclusive throughout the Bible. The obvious feature that the Bible begins with the creation of heaven and earth and ends with the new heaven and new earth serves as a significant pointer to the nature of salvation that is disclosed in the following history. Only by God's creational will for his world can anything in it be assessed. Based on God's will for a good creation, sin can be judged as disobedience, and salvation can be anticipated as restoration. Creation is essentially teleological for its future blossoming and is eschatological for the salvific goal of history.

Second, the Bible reveals one integrated act of God's salvation and consequent formation of one people of God. God's use of covenant and law for shaping Israel to be his people in the Old Testament was coupled with his requirement of faith. The good news of salvation began with God's forming faith in the hearts of Abraham and Sarah, and Christ accomplished God's salvation plan, which works by faith. Discontinuity from the Old to the New Testament is found in the new way of satisfying the requirement of law to fulfill the covenant relationship—that is through Jesus Christ. Since salvation history is framed in this typologically progressive movement, the nature of Christ's salvation is properly understood in light of God's previous acts in the Old Testament.

Third, God's act of salvation culminates in Christ's kingdom in the world. In Christ is known the full reality: seeing and living in the world can be summarized by Christian spirituality and worldview. This reality includes what the redeemed believe and know, and how they see their identity and calling in their lives. The present Christian life is characterized by the unique period we are living in—between "already" and "not yet" of salvation's effect. We are called to live faithfully to salvation with the hope of future full salvation. Faith engages life, for it is not a static status; instead, it means being relational with God and is to be lived out before God.

Endnote

1. The New International Version of 1995 and some newer versions of it are used throughout the book.

Chapter 2

The Bible as God's message in human language

This book offers an introduction to the biblical message and is a tool through which further insights into the Scriptures can be developed. Before we get to that point, however, we must first understand the nature of the book we are about to delve into, the Holy Bible.

Scripture is God's communication to us.

Set apart from all other literature, the Bible is God's message to us. The Lord reveals himself in other settings and through other means, such as visions and nature, but only in Scripture do we find a clear offering of knowledge about God and humans and the world, knowledge that enables us to live a redeemed life for God's glory with grateful joy. Only in Scripture do we find words and teachings so powerful as to rightly transform the lives of those who read it. The unimaginable greatness of our God makes us undeserving of this knowledge and power, but he graciously offers us his words.

The Bible is God's self-revelation. God shows himself and speaks to us through the written form of his Word, the Bible. He had to come down to our human and sinful level of understanding. Were God, who is holy and perfect, to attempt communicating with us limited and sinful creatures in his own terms, we would not understand or learn anything. In fact, God has accommodated his message to our sinful and finite level of understanding, and that is exactly the way the Bible was written. It is as if God is "lisping" to us. How then did God offer his Word in human language? God inspired the human authors, through his Spirit, so that they could record the perfect message of God in imperfect human language. The process is called *God's inspiration*. Apostle Paul calls the process of inspiration "God-breathed:" "All Scripture is God-breathed and is useful for teaching, rebuking, correcting and training in righteousness" (2 Tim. 3:16). It is like God's seal on the message written in human language. The human aspect of the Bible is not a problem, but a necessary means of proper communication from God to us: "For prophecy never had its origin in the will of man, but men spoke from God as they were carried along by the Holy Spirit" (2 Pet. 1:21). Thus, the Bible is God's

Word, inspired by his Spirit and accommodated to our level of understanding.

While the human writers of the Bible were "carried along by the Holy Spirit," they did not lose their own characters as they wrote. Each human author of the Bible contextualized his own writing even as he was inspired by the Holy Spirit. This way of inspiration, called *organic inspiration*, means that each author wrote the message of God in his own language as well as within his own context of custom, culture, and historical background. God could have inspired the writers of the Bible alternatively, revealing his truths in ways that take no particular context, but doing so would have reduced the accommodative nature of the Scriptures. Humans exist within history and know how to communicate only within history. We approach every piece of information, knowing it comes from a particular time, place, and perspective through which it should be understood. In addition, the inclusion of historical and cultural influences on Scripture helps communicate significance and meaning where it might not otherwise be understood. God has revealed himself to humans through his organic inspiration that is accommodated in human form.

Because we believe the revelation in the Bible to be inspired by the Holy Spirit and thus the Word of God, we also believe this Word to be infallible. The Bible is completely trustworthy and reliable, offering us the truth as God intends to reveal it to us. This distinguishes it from all things without divine nature. The Bible as the inspired Word of God is "more precious than gold" and "sweeter than honey" (Psa. 19:10), and thus can be used for growing and shaping the people of God, as explained in the cited passage above.

The Scriptures can be described as inerrant as well as infallible. Inerrancy characterizes the divine nature of the Bible as being without error in a factual sense. This inerrancy is meaningful within the given historical and literary contexts. For example, the feeding of the 5,000 (Matt. 14, Mark 6, Luke 9, John 6) tells a story of Jesus feeding more than 5,000 people. As Matthew mentioned, this number did not include women and children, and Mark and Luke noted the presence of 5,000 men. Does this create a problem in the truthfulness or accuracy of the Bible? This should not surprise us because the episode was written within the cultural context in which women and children had little significance. God's Word was written in specific historical and cultural backgrounds, and its truth is expressed against those backgrounds—again, it is the means of God's meaningfully communicating to us.

Through his Word, God meets us and speaks to us. In his speaking, we find who we are and how he reconciles us to him. In his speaking, we interact with and respond to him. This communication is made possible through his Spirit. The Holy Spirit, who inspired the writing of the

Scriptures, illuminates those words for our understanding. When we are reading the Bible, it is as if we are listening to the original author, God's Spirit, who is the true author, illuminating its meaning to our hearts. However, the Bible does not teach all things or answer every question. Though it provides sufficient knowledge about our salvation and living a redeemed life, it is not offered as a science or a history textbook. It does provide some understanding of the world, like the divine creation and God's providential rule in the process of history, but it does not intend to offer scientific or historical information about the world. This does not imply inaccuracy of the Bible about science or history. It simply means that the Bible was written for a religious purpose in a pre-scientific age. It deals with the most important matters for every human in every time and every place. In defining the purpose of God's message in the Scriptures, we look to the Scriptures themselves:

> But these are written that you may believe that Jesus is the Messiah, the Son of God, and that by believing you may have life in his name. (John 20:31)

> You diligently study the Scriptures because you think that by them you possess eternal life. These are the Scriptures that testify about me. (John 5:39)

> From infancy you have known the holy Scriptures, which are able to make you wise for salvation through faith in Christ Jesus. All Scripture is God-breathed and is useful for teaching, rebuking, correcting and training in righteousness, so that the man of God may be thoroughly equipped for every good work. (2 Tim. 3:15-17)

As we encounter God in his word, his Spirit leads us to a saving faith in Jesus Christ. The first two passages cited above illustrate the purpose of the Bible from a religious standpoint. The third passage expands the biblical meaning of "eternal life" to a fuller level—living the redeemed life in "every good work." The Scriptures reveal a fuller scope of salvation than forgiveness of sins for believers. Salvation pertains to living a new life as well as receiving it. The full story of salvation will be discussed in later chapters. Now, let us get to the point—that the Bible provides meaningful application in our lives today. As the infallible Word of God, the Bible is the ultimate authority for Christian faith and practice. The work of the Spirit, combined with the inspired and accommodated truth of the Scriptures, transforms our souls and teaches us to know and live the truth so that we can forever glorify God and enjoy the fullness of his blessings: "For the Word of God is alive and active. Sharper than any double-edged sword, it penetrates even to dividing soul and spirit, joints and marrow; it judges the thoughts and attitudes of the heart" (Heb. 4:12). Even as the messages in the Bible judge our sinful ways, within those messages lies hope. Our response to biblical correction and teaching should not be sorrowful but joyful. When the message of Christ dwells among people, even their teaching and admonishing can be done in joy and gratitude (Col. 3:16). The words of the Lord are to be our joy and our heart's delight (Jer. 15:16):

> The precepts of the LORD are right,
>   giving joy to the heart.
> The commands of the LORD are radiant,
>   giving light to the eyes. (Psa. 19:8)

Living in faith and according to the Scriptures, the way humans were created to live, we experience joy that can never be diminished.

Issues of the infallible Bible

When we look to the Scriptures for truth and for guidance in our lives, we are not looking at those documents that were originally inspired by God. Those documents, autographs, no longer exist. The Bibles we use today have been translated from Greek and Hebrew texts into many languages, including English. Even within the English language, tens of diverse translations exist. Considering this, we will explore on what basis it is still right to refer to the Bible as the infallible Word of God. We will also look at different types of translations and appropriate uses for each.

Thousands of years and many interpretations separate our present Bibles from the original manuscripts of each book of the Bible. So, what connects our Bibles, diversely translated, to the inspiration of the Holy Spirit in the human authors, and what allows us to claim that our Bibles are still the infallible Word of God? We will apply the argument that we made above, namely the intrinsic bond between the Word and the Spirit. We suggested following the traditional church doctrine that the same Spirit of God recorded the Word in the past and now illumines its meaning to us when we read it. The Spirit of God is the Lord of the process of recording and illuminating, thus securing Scripture's divinity and truthfulness. In other words, the Word and the Spirit stay and work together when we read and use the Bible.

The intrinsic bond of the Word and Spirit may also answer this question: Which Bible out of diverse translations is the infallible Word of God? This is a vexing question theologically as well as practically when we face differences among translations. The work of the Holy Spirit as the Lord of the Bible extends to the issue of biblical translation, as we discussed earlier. It is definitely part of the providential care of God for the preservation and use of his Word in all times. Though the Spirit did not inspire the translations, we see how God used the translations of the Bible for his church. When the Hebrews lived in international cultures after the exile, they needed to translate the Hebrew Old Testament into the popular Greek. That Greek translation is called the Septuagint, made from the third to second century BC. When the New Testament authors cited from the Old Testament, they did so from the Septuagint. God is using many translations of his Word. He wants his people to read his Word in their own languages. We need to be reminded of the basic idea of revelation: communication. Allowing diverse translations is another aspect of God's accommodation of his Word for the sake of proper communication.

How then shall we understand the issues of different translations? Are they all, though different, the same infallible Word of God? Shall we agree that all the translations are the true Bible as long as the Holy Spirit is illuminating? This view emphasizes the Spirit aspect of biblical divinity and may promote the danger of subjectivism. It overlooks its Word side. For we concluded that the divinity of the Bible is founded on the intrinsic bond of the Word and the Spirit. The Word aspect of biblical divinity demands better texts to be produced. We are reminded here of the historical situations in which God's Word was written, translated into diverse languages, and preserved throughout ages. The history of Bible translation shows how newer excavations of the biblical texts, such as the Dead Sea Scrolls in the 1940-50s, helped the church produce better, closer-to-the-original translations. Along with the work to produce faithful texts, the church also works to translate the texts relevant to the culture of the contemporary church, which is ever-changing. With this history of the church, we confess that the Spirit guides the whole process of preservation and use of the Bible for the church.

Translations and use of Scripture

Because the Holy Spirit works in and through translators, we can trust that the Scriptures remain true. Even so, it is important to consider the need of diverse types of translation. The process of translation involves changing the language of the text, but this can be done in many different ways. In translating from one language to another, differences in words, grammar, expressions, culture, and history must all be considered. The way in which all these things are transferred from one language to the next can be separated into three types of translations: literal, dynamic equivalent, and free. Here we consider the English translations.

Literal translations are made to stay as close to the original words and grammar contexts as possible. Even when contemporary words of an understandable language are used, their meaning can be unclear because common expressions and cultural references unfamiliar to us remain in the text. The goal of a literal translation is to maintain the original meaning in its literary and cultural contexts.

Free translations are written in a different fashion. Maintaining words and grammar in the original contexts is of less concern, as a free translation is an attempt to communicate concepts and ideas to the receiving audience. While a free translation makes more sense to contemporary people, there is some risk in using such translations. Translators may render ideas they wish were being communicated in the text rather than those that truly are. If ideas are faithfully reflected in a free translation, they can offer a refreshing and stimulating look at a familiar text.

The third type of translation is called *dynamic equivalent*. These translations take on a form in-between those of literal and free translations. While attempting to be faithful to the intended meaning of the text against its historical and literary contexts, translators change the wording, grammar, and expressions to reflect the contemporary language and culture. Dynamic equivalent translations are rendered to communicate what was intended in the original language in a way that is consistent with what it would mean in a different and contemporary language.

Knowing what type of translation we use helps us best understand what we are reading and how it may differ from the original text and the intent of the original text it was made to reflect. In any case, using two different translations to be compared with one another may help us get a fuller picture of the original text.

Interpretation of Scripture

Do we need to interpret the Bible? Isn't reading the Bible enough? First, every reading is an interpretation. Consciously or unconsciously, we all interpret the biblical text when we read. Diverse interpretations are gleaned even for the same text, as each person brings into reading a different spiritual perspective and different theology that may alter understanding of ideas, or even words. Readers are often under the impression that their understanding of a Bible passage is the true meaning that the passage is intended to communicate. Because all of us bring our own background with us every time we interpret the Bible, this may often not be the case. Secondly, the historical means through which the Bible was written and came into our hands demands interpretation. As discussed above, the Bible was written within the particular times, places, and cultures of the long past, and in the voices and literary styles of human authors. The contrast of an ever-relevant message written under conditions so different from ours gives us reason to interpret and to do so faithfully. Does the need of biblical interpretation imply that every believer should engage a serious study of theology? While theological study will surely reward, it is worth remembering that each individual interprets the Bible within common interpretive principles and confessions; for reading and interpreting the Bible is basically a communal practice.

Simply put, the task of interpretation may be illustrated like this: as it was written, so should it be read. This principle of reading is a consequence of the way the Bible was written—organic inspiration and accommodation. For a deeper understanding, this principle can be broken down into two steps. For these steps, one probably needs some scholarly assistance. The first step is to see what meaning was intended for its original audience. In order to properly do this, one must consider the content of the text within its literary and historical context. Understanding the context involves learning about the time and place it was written, along with factors such as the political and cultural environment. Gaining an understanding of the historical context also means having an idea of the occasion and purpose of the author as he addresses his audience. Understanding a passage also requires taking the literary context into consideration. The meaning of each word is determined by the sentence in which it lies, and the meaning of each sentence by the sentences that surround it. Considering literary context means following the author's sequence of thoughts to understand the point he is trying to make. We must also give thought to the genre in which the author was writing, as this will affect how we interpret the intentions of his writing. The Bible was written in literary styles including narratives, letters, poetry, proverbs, and prophecy. Even as the Word of God, the Bible is accommodated to the writing styles of humans and is to be understood within these. The final consideration is the content itself. To understand the intentions of an author, we must know how the words being used are defined and how clauses and phrases relate to each other within each sentence.

After learning what a biblical text meant to its original audience, we can move on to the second step of interpretation. The purpose of this step is to discern the relevance of the meaning for our contemporary life. Because the Holy Spirit, who inspired the original text, can never contradict himself, we can trust him to help us both understand the intent of that original text and apply it to our own lives. It is necessary to first know the original meaning of a text before we can apply it to our life.

While the many steps involved in reading Scripture—such as understanding its nature, how it came into our hands, and how it ought to be interpreted—may seem like a daunting task, the important thing to remember is this: God wants to communicate his will to us. The way that God recorded his Word, namely through organic inspiration and accommodated means, and the way he preserved it, namely through a series of copies and translations, attests to his intent of communication. The doctrine of Scripture, that Scripture is the infallible Word of God and has the ultimate authority for Christian belief and practice, should be understood within the historical origin of the Scriptures. In that way the doctrine is not a static declaration but a dynamic means to help us see God talking to us in Scripture. God is talking to us by way of the intrinsic bond of the Word and Spirit.

The goal of our reading Scripture is to grasp its natural, intended meaning. In the Scripture, the spiritual message is written in the historical context. We attempt to extract the intended meaning "out of" the text, not read our meaning "into" the text. The common mistake we make in reading it is to glean comfortable ideas from the Bible texts. We need to be aware of our own bias in reading, such as our cultural or theological backgrounds. While we attempt to be sensitive to the illuminating work of the Holy Spirit, we should also seek help in regard to the aforementioned steps of interpretation.

Discussion Questions:

1. The Bible is God's Word, written in human languages. Do the double aspects—divine and human—pose a problem for maintaining its divine authority?
2. It has been said that the literal meaning is the intended meaning of the biblical text. Share what the literal meaning may mean in diverse literary genres of the Bible.
3. The illuminating work of the Spirit is essential for our understanding and applying the Bible messages. Share with one another the ways we keep ourselves from being subjectively biased and remain faithful to the messages.

Chapter 3

Good creation as the archetype of salvation

People come to Christ with penitent hearts when they realize their lives are miserable because of sin. With the guiding work of the Holy Spirit, they accept Jesus Christ as Savior and become regenerated. They begin the Christian life with their personal relationship with God regarding sin and salvation, but as they mature in the Christian life, they find that the Christian story is bigger than a personal story of salvation.

The fuller story of God, revealed in the Bible, begins with God's creation of the heavens and the earth and ends with his completion of the new heaven and new earth. Within the "envelop" structure, with the creation as beginning and the new creation as ending, are found all the stories of humans in the world, who they are, their joys and pains, their problems with God, and how God responds to them. The full story is summarized in the framework of creation → fall → redemption → consummation. Since the full story is about salvation, it is called *a history of salvation*. In the cosmic lay-out of the history of salvation, Jesus Christ is not simply a savior of the church. In the Bible, God is first the Creator, who created all and later came down to save his sin-damaged world. God loves the world and thus saves the world because he created it. Creation is not subordinate to the doctrine of salvation as if creation simply serves as the background in which salvation takes place. Rather, the idea of creation directs the nature of salvation. This structure of the Bible does not devalue the significance of Christ or his salvation, but establishes them to their proper places so as to reveal that God accomplishes salvation in the creational scope. In this structure, the creation account sets God's will for his world, which implies his teleological perspective toward the world—his joyous expectation to see the blossoming of the creatures. The divine teleological concern is continuously seen in his providential care of the world, which guides the coming salvation after the creation became corrupt through human sin.

To properly understand the message of God's creation, we need to consider its historical background. For no literature, including the Bible, is born in a historical or cultural vacuum. A common difficulty that people experience in reading the Bible is conflict between a modern scientific mindset and ancient faith. The proper answer to the problem is not to find harmony between the two but to find how ancient faith had been shaped. The human authors of the Bible "addressed their contemporaries concerning issues that were at stake in their day and in the language, conceptual modes, and literary forms familiar to their original readers."[1] Within the culture that was characterized by conflict between the Israelite monotheism and popular pagan polytheistic religions on the one hand, and the political image of king on the other, the text of creation was written in the format of a king proclaiming from his holy temple to his people. As a result, the Israelites pulled their identity from it. Two prominent literary aspects of the creation account that reflect the religious issue and conceptual mode of the day are the kingly and the functional language.

Kingly language

"Let there be light," the Creator commanded; and light was made. The Bible is God's accommodated message to our limited and sinful level of understanding. Thus, biblical literature used human terms that were popularly received by the first audiences. Describing God as the great king is the most significant example of God's accommodation. The Bible is permeated with metaphors of king, kingly rule, and kingdom to describe God's acts of creation and redemption. God's making by commanding, conferring names to what he made, assigning their roles, and judging what he has made as good reflect kingly authority. Creation of humanity in God's image and likeness reflects the political act of kings who ruled vast territories by erecting their images and assigning a ruling authority to lesser kings. The completion of his creation and blessing on the creaturely world on the seventh day also reflects kingly authority. The intended message of the creation account is that the God of Israel is the Lord over all.

God is the Lord as Creator and Law-giver. The God who created light by separating it from darkness determined it was good. His will that light and darkness are not fused becomes the law with which he rules the world. The Creator determines what is good and true in the world. The issue of lordship held a striking significance to the ancient Israelites, for the pagans at that time worshipped deities that were fashioned in the images of the sun, sky, river, stars, and even animals. The God of the Israelites, who created what so many believed to be gods, belittled the power of those gods and the thought that they could even be considered gods. In this conflicting situation, they were informed of the fundamental truth about God—the monotheistic God, who created all and is Lord over all—that gave Israel an identity and mode of life. The sovereign God, who was proclaimed in the creation account, would prove himself publicly over all the powers of the world in the story of Exodus.

Functional language

Functional language augments the sovereignty of the Creator and elaborates it in concrete reality. The text demonstrates the Creator's lordship by showing him bestow his order on the world with the goal of completing his sacred place. In this way, the creation account highlights "for what" God created each creature in the created system rather than "how" the material creatures came into being. The functional terms are familiar to modern thinking, but they are religiously functional more than materially functional. Though the two were not separate, the ancient Near Eastern conceptual mind saw the material function through a religious view of reality. Within such an ancient mindset, "to create something" meant "to give it a function or a role within an ordered cosmos."[2]

Genesis 1:2 describes the earth as being "formless and void" before God's acts of creation. The Hebrew terms are used to describe unordered chaos or wilderness, wasteland, and the result of destruction. The chaotic situation was symbolized by the presence of water. If read from a material and scientific standpoint, it would mean that God created the world out of pre-existing materials. But the point of the text is to show God's sovereignty, which is demonstrated by his bestowing order on the unordered universe.

On the first day of creation (Gen. 1:3-5), God made light by separating it from darkness. The separation of the two and the corresponding functions of the day and night find full description in the creation of the sun, moon, and stars on the fourth day. Note the functional terms: "Let there be lights in the expanse of the sky to *separate* the day from the night, and let them *serve* as *signs* to mark seasons and days and years…[,] the greater light to *govern* the day and the lesser light to *govern* the night… to *govern* the day and the night, and to *separate* light from darkness" (vv. 14-18). The text reflects the Creator's orderly organization of his placing functional objects in it.

The creation of humanity shows a unique parallel to the creation of light—to the point that as God made light to govern the day and night, God made humans to rule the world. It is no coincidence that Christ, who is the Light himself, identifies the redeemed people as the light of the universe. The structure of human creation, "Let us make man in our image… so that they may rule…" (Gen. 1:26), reveals an unmistakably functional concern. The functional creation of mankind will continue in the next chapter.

God's cosmic house, our home

God's creative act is described in terms of his building his holy temple, separating spaces, filling them, and making them habitable environments for all creatures. The early writers wanted readers to understand creation in terms of its origination as a holy temple, a dwelling place of

God rather than a material house. We may compare the effect to walking into a room of a house and wondering, first of all, who made it and what purpose it serves and who spends time there, rather than wondering how it was made and with what material. The importance lies in the order and harmony of the creatures, which eventually leads to the ultimate goal of creation, shalom under God's rule. This idea is exemplified in the symmetrical and progressive structure of the text, which directs all God's creative acts toward his rest on the seventh day.

In the first three days, God prepared spaces. On the first day, God separated light from darkness, making day and night. On the second day, God created a space by separating the waters above from the waters beneath and called the space "sky." On the third day, God gathered waters below together, making land and sea. And God let the land produce vegetation. In this way, God prepared a livable environment, which we recognize as time, weather, and habitats. A unique feature of the creation structure is that God named the creatures in a way that gave them purpose and function. Naming in the ancient culture symbolized the exercise of authority, and the authority was expressed in terms of assigning a particular function and role that a creature would serve in the creation. On days four through six, God was creating in a different way—he was filling those prepared spaces. The separation created in the first day made room for the stars, planets, and moon, created to fill space on the fourth day. The separation of the waters on the second day allowed for the creation of the sea creatures and birds, created on the fifth day. The gathering of the waters apart from the dry land on the third day created a space to be filled with land animals and humans on the sixth day. The structure of the creation account shows God, first, building a house and, second, filling his house. God made his holy temple our home to live with God.

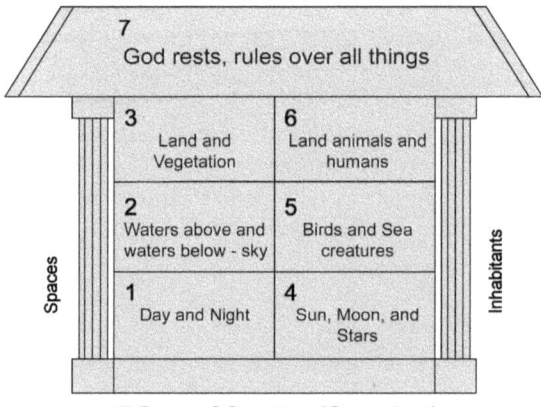

7 Days of Creation (Genesis 1)

The order of creation is functionally progressive, shaped by the ancient religious conceptual mind, but still understandable to modern readers. God made spaces and filled them, created living creatures suitable to the food chain, created all but human living creatures "according to their kinds," created humans "in God's image," and more significantly, moved from all acts of creation toward the Creator's rest.

God's rest on the seventh day signifies the completion of his acts of creation and the inauguration of his rule over the created world. God applies the idea of rest in the creation account to the order of the world because God made a specific rhythm of work and rest to the world functions. The creator God is now enthroned as the King and proclaims that all is good, according to his creational decree. Now the perfect order is set, and shalom is achieved in his creation. It is important that we understand the correlation between work and rest from God's creational ordinance and not from human sinful experience. God does not rest from work and call us to rest because work is hard and afflicting. God rested from his holy work of creation, which is never hard and afflicting. Work in our life is affected by sin and therefore arduous and oppressing. Resting is very important for maintaining godly life in the situation. God called humans to follow his pattern of working for six days and resting on the seventh day (Ex. 20:8-11). God's command was a complete rest, not only of the Israelites but also servants, animals, and even foreigners. They could rest with full knowledge that God is completely ruling over them. The moral and physical rest is made possible with their trust in God's rule. Childlike reliance on God's promise is required for us to have rest. When we take rest from work, we remember God's faithfulness to his creational ordinance, and we show the world that our identity comes from God rather than the work that we do.

The idea of rest as completion of God's creational will and rule over the created world continues to shape the nature of salvation. In the Old Testament law, rest was celebrated at certain designated times and spaces. As the meaning of sabbath was fulfilled by Christ, the timely and spacial distinction has ended, to the effect that God's people may now enjoy his rest in all places and at all times. The present experience of rest is like a foretaste of the complete rest that God's people will enjoy in the new heaven and new earth. In the meantime, the question is how we rest in working: by acknowledging God's faithful carrying out of his salvation in the past and by trusting his promise to accomplish it in the future.

Our sovereign God's good creation

The message of the creation account is that the sovereign God made his world good. To the ancient Israelites, it proclaimed that the God who made a covenant with their ancestors and saved them is the Creator, who made all in the heavens and the earth. Imagine the religious situation in which the Israelites heard the message of creation: they lived as a minority tribe in the mainline pagan culture. Their belief regarding creation was the lordship of their God, from whom they pulled their identity, over all pagan gods. It is not that they had a religious issue with life, as in a modern view of religion that severs religion from life, but that they saw all from the religious standpoint. The belief in God's lordship, proved in creation, served as a spiritual foundation upon which Israel was established and as the prologue to the following history of the world: "His intent was to proclaim knowledge of the true God as he has manifested himself in his creative works, to proclaim a right understanding of humankind, world, and history that knowledge of the true God entails—and to proclaim the truth concerning these matters in the face of the false religious notions dominant throughout the world of his day."[3]

The functional language helps us understand God's will for his creation that is reflected in his affirmation of its goodness. God's affirming its goodness seven times in the seven-day creation symbolically highlights the idea that the creation was fully completed, as God had assigned to it his order and purpose. Even though the creation of light, for example, seems to indicate material and even scientific ideas of the role of light and the concept of time, it was judged good in its religious role and function. To separate day from night and to give light on the earth, the sun was meant to govern the day. Creation is good because the true God bestowed his order and function on it, in contrast to the pagan cosmogonies, in which gods were known as tyrant kings.[4]

The goodness was applied to the whole creation and to all times of its history. The whole creation was made as God's holy temple and dwelling place. Thus, any form of ontological dualism that separates sacred and secular is rejected. The fact that it was made also as a habitable home for all living creatures is highlighted by God's preparing an ecosystem and a food chain for them. Its goodness persists with the Creator's providential care; that is, he preserves the original roles and functions of the creation. The reason why light is still good today is because God made it and preserves its role and function, not because it was made materially durable. The same is true of God's benediction on the life of living beings. They are still being born because of his divine providence. God's providence is a continuation of his creational goodness.[5]

God then celebrated his good creation. He designed all living creatures with their unique natures, shapes, and niches to live, enjoy, and serve. He satisfied their need of food. And he blessed them with the blessings of life when he said, "Be fruitful and increase in number" (Gen. 1:22, 28). God's joyful celebration of the completed world must accompany the meaning of God's rest on the seventh day. God created the world out of his free, sovereign pleasure. He was not forced to make anything; he did not need others' service or fellowship. But out of his love,

God wished to have a community of genuine love and fellowship. The creation account's unique corresponding parallel between the first and second three days points to God shaping his house as a community. God invited every creature into his community to occupy its unique niche and serve in its unique way, i.e., dragonflies in their insectological way, the natural law in its physical way, and humans in their human ways, together in an organically formed community, eventually glorifying the Creator. They are all invited to the fellowship, joy, and love of the Creator God, as I learned in childhood.

When I was about five years old, my family lived by a river. Every autumn I played with my friends on the bank along the river. Of many things to play with, I enjoyed the dragonflies the most. One afternoon when the golden sun was reclining in the western sky, tens of dragonflies flying above my head dazzled my youthful mind. Their two sets of subtle wings reflected light at the sides of their glowing red, long, slender bodies. For hours and hours my friends and I played with them. Because we were preoccupied with play on the bank, oftentimes I returned home late for dinner. One evening when I came back home very late, I saw everybody sitting around the dining table waiting for me—I was the youngest in my family. I had to hurry, but I had a handful of dragonflies in my tiny hand. I didn't want to lose them. I found a little carton box nearby, quickly threw them in it, tossed it into my humble small room, and rushed to eat. Then I forgot about them because I had so many other things to play with. Days later I found the box in my room and wondered what it was. Completely forgetting what I had done, I opened it with much curiosity. And guess what I found there! I saw—no, actually I met—tens of tiny, baby dragon-flies coming out of the box, buzzing around my head and filling my small room. It was a different sensation from what I used to have with them flying in the air. While the familiar sensation dazzled me, the new experience with the baby ones made me wonder. I forgot this memory of my youth for many years. Suddenly, when I was reading the creation account in the Bible, the long-gone memory came alive in my mind. The first word that flashed in my adult mind to represent the memory was joy, joy of life, followed by wonder and awe of God, creating living beings. A living being is great, but living beings giving life to other living beings requires a higher plane of thought. How had I lived for so many years without such great joy and wonder of God that I once enjoyed? I wonder what joy God experienced when he thought about and actually created all living beings. I wonder what blessing God felt and intended when he gave the command of life: "Be fruitful and increase in number and fill the water… and earth."

Though this good creation became corrupt because of human sin, even today the sovereign God upholds his creation. He created it, and he came down to save it, and he will reign till the creation is fully redeemed:

"For from him and through him and to him are all things. To him be the glory forever!" (Rom. 11:36).

Creation provides a teleological perspective of the world.

The truth regarding God, humanity, and the world is foundational to understanding the unfolding acts of God's salvation. We are challenged—since it was written within the ancient Near Eastern conceptual mindset—when we relate it to our Christian life, which has been formed in a modern scientific and materialistic culture.

The author's use of Hebrew terms to indicate God's act of creation in the unique structure of the creation account shows the idea of our reality. Among the Hebrew terms, *bara*, usually translated as "to create," denotes only divine acts of creation, supporting the idea of God's sovereign act. It signifies "the incomparability of the creative work of God in contrast to all secondary products and likenesses made from already existing material by man."[6] It was used at the beginning of the creation account in the form of a title (1:1), at its concluding statement (2:3-4), in creation of great sea creatures that were considered as objects of pagan worship (1:21), and three times in the creation of humanity in God's image (1:27). The author's placing of the term in this unique structure, along with expressions like "In the beginning" and "the heavens and the earth," establishes the principal idea of creation as God's sovereign act.

The idea of God's sovereign creation complements other occasional events of making material entities. Several other Hebrew verbs were used to refer to God's act of creation such as *asah*, meaning "to make," and *yatsar*, "to form." These two verbs and *bara* are used to describe God's act of creating humans: God created humans in his image (1:27), formed man from dust of the ground (2:7), and created and made man (5:1-2). As in the latter text of the creation of humanity, *bara* and *asah* are also used interchangeably in creation of material objects, such as the celestial objects, great sea creatures, and heaven and earth. Most texts that use *asah* express the functional aspect of creation rather than the material origin in the Old Testament. The functional terms, like "to do," and terms that designate material origins, like "to make," though conceptually distinct in modern language, were considered more inter-connected in the ancient mind.[7] Though the ancient Israelites considered the sky as immaterial space and did not realize the celestial objects as real physical entities, they indeed did realize material reality. For they felt heat from the sun and ate food grown by its light. The text that shows space and time, reflected in the symmetrical and progressive movement from the first three to the later three days, was structured in terms of function; however, the functional structure would not function without assuming the physical reality of creation. Thus, the principal idea of creation as God's sovereign act complements the creation and existence of physical reality.

The Old Testament theology of creation was developed in the New Testament teaching that Christ the Redeemer is the Creator God. There, the sovereign lordship of the Creator includes the material origin of the world. John 1:3 teaches that the Word, Christ, made all things, and "without him nothing was made that has been made"; Colossians 1:16 says that Christ created all things; and Hebrews 11:3 reads that the universe was formed at God's command. The idea of *creatio ex nihilo*, creation out of nothing, that was developed later to capture the material origin of the world, should be based on the concrete idea of God's lordship rather than from a speculative idea.

The sovereign creation, described in kingly and functional language, provides a teleological perspective of seeing the history of the world. Creation neither is isolated from salvation nor simply functions as a background in which salvation takes place; but by setting out God's will for creation, the author anticipates achievement of God's will through the unfolding history of salvation. In other words, creation guides the nature of salvation. God's sovereign creation is reinstated in the first sign of the gospel message, the Flood. God judged the sinful world by water and re-created it by separating the land from water. To the re-created world, God conferred the same creational blessing on the living beings. And he made the covenant not to deluge the world with water again, a decree to continue his purpose of the original creation. Salvation was illustrated in terms of re-ordering the world, and the motif of God's order continues throughout the history of salvation to point out that the Redeemer God is the Creator God. Peter summarizes salvation in terms of God's creational Word working out in the world, connecting creation through the Flood to the future consummation of salvation: "By God's word" he created the earth "out of water and by water." After judging the earth with water, "by the same word"—that is his sovereign creational Word—he will judge and cleanse the world with fire as he did before with water (2 Pet. 3:5-7). It is God's sovereign creational Word that created, maintains, and restores the world into the new heaven and new earth.

Paul teaches that the redeemed are given a godly responsibility to participate in Christ's ministry of reconciling the world to God (Col. 1:20, 2 Cor. 5:17-21). God does not forgive and save his people for the sake of salvation—as God did not simply create mankind for the sake of making them into beings—but reshapes them so that they may accomplish the original mandate God gave at their creation. Now the redeemed are sent into the world with the mission of being Christ's ambassadors; and Matthew reflects the same role with his reference to "light of the universe" and "salt of the earth" (Matt. 5).

The new heaven and new earth are described in the language that originated with creation and was accomplished throughout the history of salvation: the New Jerusalem comes down from heaven and merges with human dwelling, and there is no night or sea, and God's people are called from all nations. The earth will be remade as the sacred place for God's dwelling with mankind. God's creational will for separating light from darkness, and land from water, is extended to the spiritual realm in the history of salvation and will be accomplished in the new heaven and new earth. The non-existence of night and sea symbolizes the idea that the creational Word, the term Peter used to refer to God's creational sovereignty, rules completely, and there is no evil power against it. Then God's original purpose of ordering his world is complete, and God's people live in shalom. There, all are light, God and his people, which is highlighted by the jewelry that decorates the new heaven and new earth. The Creator God's inauguration as the sovereign ruler on the seventh day of creation is reinstated in the new heaven and new earth.

In summary, the idea of the completed world that runs according to its God-given function and order reveals the teleological and eschatological perspective of seeing and living in the world—teleological, in the sense that God is expecting with great joy to see the blossom of the world; eschatological, in that God is directing, after the fall into sin, the whole world toward the goal of restoration. The teleological and eschatological perspective set by the creation suggests Christian responsibility in the world.

Discussion Questions:

1. What major points of the creation account do you find?
2. What do you feel when you hear that God invited you to his fellowship in his house?
3. Does the good creation as the beginning of the world suggest to you any different image of the present world?
4. Where do you see or not see God as the sovereign Lord today?

Endnotes

1. John H. Stek, "What Says the Scripture?" in *Portraits of Creation: Biblical and Scientific Perspectives on the World's Formation* (Grand Rapids: Eerdmans, 1990), p. 206.
2. John H. Walton, *Ancient Near Eastern Thought and the Old Testament* (Grand Rapids: Baker, 2006), p. 181; *The Lost World of Adam and Eve: Genesis 2-3 and the Human Origins Debate* (Downers Grove: IVP, 2015), Propositions 1-2; *NIV Cultural Backgrounds Study Bible* (Grand Rapids: Zondervan, 2016), comments on Genesis 1-2.
3. John H. Stek, "What Says the Scripture?" p. 230.

4. While pagan stories of creation considered kings as images of gods and humans as slaves to serve kings, the God of the Bible made all humans in his divine image to rule over creation. While pagan stories considered certain places like temples as sacred, God made the whole of creation good and holy. More comparison between pagan cosmogonies and the biblical creation account is found in John H. Stek, "What Says the Scripture?" pp. 230-31.

5. John H. Stek, "What Says the Scripture?" pp. 246-48.

6 Karl-Heinz Bernhardt, "bara," *Theological Dictionary of the Old Testament*, vol II (Grand Rapids: Eerdmans, 1975), p. 246.

7. John H. Walton, *Genesis 1 as Ancient Cosmology* (Eisenbrauns), pp. 134-135.

Chapter 4

Humanity as God's image in the world

While the previous chapter includes some details about the place and life of humans in God's creation, this chapter provides an in-depth examination on the nature of humanity. By gaining a biblical understanding of human nature, we will be able to better understand how we experience, think, and live as God's images in his world.

Aspects of human nature

The creation account provides three fundamental aspects of human nature. The first is that God created humans in his own image. The text, by comparison to the way God created the rest of living beings, namely "according to their kinds" (Gen. 1:21, 24, 25), highlights the astonishing way of creating humans: "Then God said, 'Let us make man in our image…'" (Gen. 1:26). The divine-image aspect of human nature is given in functional terms. The structure "Let us make… so that they may rule over…" finds its parallel in God's creating light sources. The function of the luminaries in the sky is "to govern" the day and night. A similar functional term, "rule over," was used to describe human life on earth. God set the lights in the sky—the Bible will say "God is Light"—to govern it, and he placed his images on earth to rule over it. God established the ruling system of his kingdom, "the heavens and the earth," by placing his royal representatives respectively.

The creation account emphasizes God's sovereign rule over the creation in his using his royal representatives. However, since humans' spiritual status becomes an essential concern in the subsequent history of salvation after the Fall, we need to mention the spiritual wholeness of human beings at the creation. The spiritual wholeness of human beings is implied and reflected by their identity as the image of God. Being made in the image of God means that, since God is holy and righteous, humans were created to be holy and righteous. Human holiness is also reflected in the granted mandate to rule. It is a required attribute to be God's royal representative, to communicate with him, and to fulfill his will. It is also assumed retrospectively by the fact that they were banished from God's presence when they became fallen. Living in the presence of

God highlights their spiritual status.

The unique identity of humans in the world is clarified through the political connotation of the kingly language used to describe them: "God created mankind in his own image" and commanded them to "Be fruitful and increase in number; fill the earth and subdue it. Rule over the fish in the sea and the birds in the sky and over every living creature that moves on the ground" (Gen. 1:26-27). In the ancient Near East, kings established images of themselves in conquered lands and along important borders to declare their ruling presence in the territory. Employing the then popularly received way of ruling, the text describes the Creator as the Great King and signifies his ruling presence in the world. That is, God rules the world through his images, the humans. Humanity, then, represents God's existence and his ruling authority in the world. The Hebrew words that have been translated to "subdue" and "rule" come with the meaning of "trample on." God sent humans to his world to do his own work, trampling or walking on the creation as good kings. The mandate to exercise the ruling authority as good kings may be rendered in modern English as "to bring it into service."[1] We see a couple of implications of the mandate. First, the rulership that was granted to humans is delegated authority; it is not innate in human nature. In obedient relationship to God, humans are to represent him and serve him in the manner that is consistent with his will and authority.

Secondly, the human-delegated ruling does not duplicate God's rule in any automatic or programmed way in human life, but instead works through humans freely and creatively conforming to his will. Free, voluntary choosing to serve God is essential for genuine worship. The free and creative aspect of the human-ruling mandate requires moral and aesthetic motivation as well as spiritual and religious motivation for life in the world. An example of such ruling is found already in the creation account. While God himself named the creatures in the earlier days of creation, he assigned Adam the task of naming the animals on the sixth day. In the ancient Near Eastern culture, naming signifies the authority of lordship. Naming is not a programmed act, as if human obedience naturally produces God-approved names, but a free, creative act, using all the knowledge and reasoning that humans acquire in the world. Being made as God's image, they were able to communicate and conform to his will; being given a unified existence, they were able to wholly dedicate life to him; and being made from dust, they were able to apply their knowledge in the world. Adam gave names to living creatures, and God recognized them (Gen. 2:19-20). The significance of delegated authority is seen in that God named Adam and delegated him to name other creatures. The delegated authority means a joyful responsibility, rather than a prerogative, that makes humans accountable to God. They are to know creatures, with their natures and characters, in the organically inter-woven creational system, in order for both humans and creatures to flourish and fulfill their potential, eventually bringing shalom to the creation and glory to the Creator God. The ruling mandate necessarily involves learning about the world, which will be discussed later.

Being God's images, humans are created as "*nepes*," in the Hebrew language: "And the Lord God formed man from the dust of the ground and breathed into his nostril the breath of life and man became a living being" (Gen. 2:7). Infused with the breath of life, the molded clay became Adam the "living being" (*nepes haya*). While the term is sometimes translated as "soul," looking at its use throughout the Old Testament allows us to understand that *nepes* actually means the "whole living being." Unlike our common, contemporary tendency to think of humans as embodied spirits, those reading the original text understood humans as complex, unified beings. *Nepes* denotes a human's personal identity—the human person is *nepes*, not having *nepes*. When Deuteronomy 6:4 commands "love the Lord your God with all your heart and with all your soul (*nepes*) and with all your strength," it doesn't mean that we are to love God with only our soul, the inner part of a human being, but to dedicate the whole human being to God. Such totality of the human *nepes* is stressed by the combination of three terms: heart, *nepes*, and strength.

The Old Testament teaching on human nature as referring to the unified whole being should correct unbiblical dualistic, reductionistic understandings of human beings. For example, Greek dualism has left a long-lasting impact on the present Christian reading and thinking. Under this influence, humans are embodied souls. Though the Bible employs the terms body and soul, it does not use them in a dualistic way, as the embodied soul implies:

> The breath which God breathed into molded clay at the creation represents the principle of life; and the soul [*nepes*] that resulted is the human person as a whole. Thus man does not *have* a body; he *is* a body—a psychophysical unity. The body is the soul [*nepes*, the whole human being] in its outward form.[2]

The human body is an essential aspect of the human *nepes*; it is not added to the internal, more essential part. The Hebrew mind did not know the dualistic distinction of body and soul but knew the human being as a unified whole being, having diverse parts. The Greek language in which the New Testament was written was the popular language of the dualistic culture. An apparent dualism is found in the New Testament text, such as, in its literal translation: "For those who are according to the *flesh* set their minds on the things of the *flesh*, but those who are according to the *Spirit*, the things of the *Spirit*" (Rom. 8:5). The life according to the spirit (*pneuma*) is in contrast to the life according to the flesh (*sarx*). Though using the then-popular dualistic terms, Paul teaches a Christian message of human life. He never used "body" or "flesh" with the connotation of inherent sinfulness or wickedness. What we should overcome to live a godly life is not the body per se but the sinful lifestyle that the term represented in the culture.

The wholistic concept of a human being, which is implied in the creation account, becomes significant for understanding the completed human life in the new heaven and new earth. What will be the fulfilled mode of human life? The answer hinges on the re-unification of eternal life with the resurrected body. As the body was created as an essential part of human nature, the resurrection that takes place following death re-institutes the full human existence. Death is the God-arranged door by which the core of a human being enters to enjoy eternal life by being united to the resurrected body.

The third aspect of human nature is the material origin, the dust of the ground. When God breathed the breath of life into *adamah*, dust of the ground (Gen. 2:7), the mass of soil dough that was inanimate and lifeless became *Adam*, a human being. The Hebrew root of the name shows that Adam is basically "earth-man." Though created uniquely as God's image, humans are not unique in their material origins. Humans consist of the same raw material as the animal kingdom, though animals did not receive the breath of life from God (Gen. 2:19). What makes *adamah* in *Adam* valuable is God's gift of breath. It is God's life-giving spirit to humans, but it never becomes the property of humanity. This life remains God's possession.

The material source of humanity has often been thought to denote humanity's lowly origin and even sinful status. It continues with the idea of the body. Such a consideration has risen from the idea that the dust in Genesis 2 is the judgment of sin and death in chapter 3. The text of Psalm 103:14, "he remembers that we are dust," has been popularly associated with sin-caused death, as in sermons at funerals. The practice of Ash Wednesday during Lent, defined as a season to remember guilt and penance, reinforces such reading. In this reading, "remember you are dust" sounds fearful. However, there is a reading different from the popular association of dust with sin and death and faithful to the biblical texts. First, the dust in the creation account was used with no connotation of sin, lowliness, or death of humanity. It was part of the good creation. The root meaning of Adam, the "earth-man," has no inherent meaning of sin, lowliness, or death, but instead is known as physical existence, valuable enough to be united with the breath of life to become human *nepes*. It is proper to read the dust in other biblical texts in light of the creation account, rather than imposing the post-fall consequence to the creation account. As a result, the text "for dust you are and to dust you will return" (Gen. 3:19) simply refers to physical death. The text of Psalm 103, "he remembers that we are dust," is situated in the context of singing God's compassion and grace to humans. Up to verse 13, the psalmist praises God's fatherly compassion toward those who are aware of their sins: "so the Lord has compassion on those who fear him" (v. 13). From verse 14 he sings for God's compassion for another reason:

> For he knows how we are formed, he remembers that we are dust.
> As for man, his days are like grass, he flourishes like a flower of the field;
> the wind blows over it and it is gone, and its place remembers it no more (vv. 14-16).

God's compassion is offered to those who are aware of their creatureliness, their feeble form of life. The double formula affirms the idea that humans may exist only with the Creator's gracious care. Since human beings are "earth-creatures," subject to all the realities and limitations of materiality, they belong with, to, and for the earth. This reminds us that we cannot initiate life on our own. Since we are dust, we remain lifeless and inanimate unless we belong to the Lord of life.[3]

The psalmist sings "[God] remembers" rather than instructing us to remember. In God's remembrance of us, we remember who we are. God's remembering invites us to appreciate our origin; and through the remembering of this fact, we remain in awe and humble submission to our Creator. God's remembering also gives us great comfort that he knows who we are and cares for us exactly because of it.

Relational and social aspects of the image of God

God's creation of humans in his image implies the extension of divine fellowship to human relationships. This does not mean the emanation or duplication of God's nature in humanity. Humans are not made with a divine nature; rather, they are made in his image. The image of God suggests that God used his own internal triune existence and fellowship as the model for his creating humanity. God is known as one being in three persons, a unified community enjoying perfect fellowship and love. The divine unity and fellowship are modeled in creating human beings with the consequence that man and woman form one body. This social understanding of the image of God defines the relational nature of human beings: two parts united by loving fellowship. Such beautiful unity in humanity is illustrated in Adam's naming Eve woman: "this is now bone of my bones and flesh of my flesh" (Gen. 2:23). The unity and fellowship between man and woman determines the ground of marriage. Such an intimate relationship serves as a model for all human relationships, such as family, friends, and society. The way that human living is defined by this basic intimate relationship is found in the Decalogue. The commandments in the second half were given in a negative way for the sake of sinful human inclination. The conversion of these laws to a positive form should be the proper way of living in unity and fellowship. As Christ summarized the law, it all points to love. God, who is love, created humanity in his own image so that they can love one another.

Human life consists of three basic types of relationships in which humans are called to act in love. The first is a human's relationship with God. The fundamental human identity is defined by their origin as having been created by the Creator God. The Creator-creature distinction defines proper human living: that is, to enjoy and worship the Creator God by obeying his will. The worship and obedience are not something that has to be done in grudging or mechanical ways. Any kind of reluctant attitude toward God is a consequence of misunderstanding the Creator-creature relationship. We humans are not on an equal, not even close to it, level with God. The creation account teaches that God, who is love in himself, made us humans in his image. This truth should lead to the human attitude that we are to worship him freely and creatively. God desires his images to love and worship him in a true and genuine way. It is also the only way that humans can live with joy and happiness. In order for them to live such a blessed life, God lavished them with abundant gifts, such as spiritual wholeness, independent consciousness, and the will and need to communicate with him and obey his will. As God loves, humans are capable of choosing love and putting their choice in action.

The second type of relationship defining human life takes place among fellow humans. Humans were created as relational beings. This corporate nature means that one cannot stand alone but needs others to live properly. God judges, "It is not good for the man to be alone" (Gen. 2:18). The proper human existence is found and realized in community. Humans are to live and work in complementary fashion, synthesizing their abilities to do the work of the Lord and loving each other all the while. Life with fellow humans is to be based on the social connotation of the image of God as discussed above. While some English translations describe woman's creation as being from "one of the man's ribs," the Hebrew term translated to "rib" is most often translated elsewhere in the Old Testament as "side" or "side chamber" and is nowhere else translated to "rib."[4] The text does not describe the material origin of woman as being a specific anatomical part, but describes the religious origin of woman as made from a half or side of man. God took an entire side of Adam to create Eve, with the consequence that only when they were united, they were a full human. Although they were equally human, they were created to be in a complementary relationship with one another, to complete each other. Neither man nor woman is complete without the other, but when they unite, they become one full unit and one complete person.

A significant emphasis is also placed on the equality and human dignity of all humans, regardless of gender, race, skin color, nationality, and character of life. The creation account makes it very clear: "So God created man in his own image, in the image of God he created him; male and female he created them" (Gen. 1:27). The proper human relationship is realized in Christ. In Christ, God brings in the new creation, in which "there is neither Jew nor Greek, slave nor free, male nor female, for you are all one in Christ Jesus" (Gal. 3:28). The social context in which Paul brought this revolutionary message was full of political enmity and religious prejudice among social groups. Salvation as explained in the Bible demands much more than spiritual change from sinner to child of God; it should reflect that spiritual change in actual living. Salvation means re-creation of humans in God's re-created world, by God's restoring humans to their original sinless status. Salvation demands human responsibility, both spiritual and moral, for the present human life, just as in the creation account God mandated humans to live as his image.

The third human relationship defines their life in the world. Human relationship to the world is a celebrated responsibility. Being made as part of the world, humans are suitable rulers of it. With common physicality, humans can identify with the world and know their creaturely situation, which is essential for their ruling. The ruling mandate is given as the mode of human life in the world. Humans are to dedicate their entire existence to the goal of ruling in a way that worships God. There are diverse spheres and works in the world, and they are organically interwoven in God's creational system. All human acts are to be done according to the mode of human living—nurturing others and stewarding resources to reach their full creational potential. Working and making money are to be done to reach that goal and to create justice and shalom. Fragmentation and alienation are typical effects of sin that permeate every part of modern culture. Consequently, religion is considered a private sphere that is severed from public matters: Worship is considered something you do at church and should not affect your work, and vice versa. Satan's strategy is to isolate believers in the church so that they cannot live as God's people in the world. Insofar as church is severed from the world, God's kingdom is not fulfilled, and his sovereignty is damaged. We should learn the integrated life system and make it work in our life.

The ruling mandate requires humans to learn about the world. Christian education aims at shaping and establishing God's people by providing them with knowledge of the world from the vantage point of the history of salvation. That is, we try to know the world from the perspective of what God created, how it became fallen, and what kind of salvation he is working in and around us. From this history of salvation, the present world, though still sinful and distorted, is the object of God's love and process of reconciliation. What we teach and learn of the world is not simply "worldly" things, but the objects of God's love and redemption. Learning about the world provides deep motivation for further exploration of the world and gives us joy. Using our knowledge for the benefit of all creation is our task and leads to a positive attitude toward work and civilization.

Humans as created persons

Bequeathed with God's image, empowered by his breath of life, and physically enabled beings made from the dust, humans are creatures. As much as humans are endowed, they are dependent on the Creator. Human creatureliness means humans must focus on God—in humility and adoration. Having been created, humans are "created persons." They were endowed with an individual consciousness, freedom of desire, and reasoning capacity. With individual self-consciousness, humans were able to recognize their glorious status before God and among others, and their calling in the world. The freedom of desire made it possible for them to desire what God desires and the joy of serving him. Endowing creatures with freedom of choice and ability to think is an adventure, so to speak, on God's side. For with such gifts, they could reject God and act independently from God. Though it is absurd to postulate that creaturely humans could challenge the Creator God, surely the idea of human freedom leads to the question of why God created humans with such freedom to choose. Freedom is an essential attribute with which humans could stand before God as his image in its most genuine sense. For freedom evokes the attitude of voluntary obedience and worship. Without freedom, humans would become efficient robots that involuntarily obey but are not able to love or worship. As much as humans are endowed, they are still accountable to the Creator.

Were humans created as perfect beings? No, they were not, especially in the absolute sense of the term, for such meaning can only be used to refer to God. Along with the three prominent aspects discussed above, human nature may be characterized by the moral combination of capable freedom and divine-imposed limitation that is found in the second chapter of Genesis. The text reveals the unique human condition of being free to choose or reject God, not to automatically achieve the God-intended life. It shows that humans were fully capable of fulfilling the God-intended life in a voluntarily worshipping way.

Were humans created in as fully a *mature* mode as humans can reach? The period from the creation to the time when they misused their freedom was called the probationary period in traditional theology. The probation is God's invitation of humans to live out a blessed life in the world. It reflects God's joyful expectation for humans rather than an impersonal test to check how the human condition works. The key for interpreting the probationary period is that of moral accountability. Unfortunately, Adam and Eve did not meet God's expectation in their use of gifts. The human act of rebellion left a devastating impact on the whole created world and eventually resulted in God's making a radical turning point.

Discussion Questions:

1. What do you feel when you hear you are God's image, not just the bearer of his image?
2. What does the reflection of the holy Trinity in human relationships tell us about the modern crisis of gender and sexual choices?
3. If God made humans in his own image, why did they become sinful?
4. Does God require us to carry out the ruling mandate today?

Endnotes

1. John H. Stek, "What Says the Scripture?" p. 251.
2. Robert H. Gundry, *Soma in Biblical Theology with Emphasis on Pauline Anthropology* (Grand Rapids: Zondervan, 1987), p. 119.
3. Walter Brueggemann, *Remember you are dust* (Eugene: Cascade Books, 2012), pp. 77-89; Arthur Weiser, tr. Herbert Hartwell, *The Psalms* (Philadelphia: Westminster Press,1962), on Psalm 103:14-16.
4. "Lexicon:: Strong's H6763 - tsela`." blueletterbible.org. https://www.blueletterbible.org/lang/lexicon/lexicon.cfm?t=kjv&strongs=h6763 (Accessed May 17, 2019)

CHAPTER 5

Sin as transgression of God's will

While we expect to find the story of a blessed human life after the creation account ends, the story turns radically different from such expectations, and we find a talking serpent approach Eve. The fall into sin took place in the context of the garden, the creation account in Genesis chapter 2. While in the first chapter the Great God (*Elohim*) created "the heavens and earth," the whole universe, and created humans in his image and then placed them in the world to rule over it, in the second chapter the same God, identified as the relational God (*Yahweh Elohim*), created "the earth and the heavens" in the form of a garden and formed humans from its dust and placed them in it to take care of it. The two creation accounts complement each other to form a fuller story of God's creation, like the four gospels in the New Testament. The creation account in chapter 2 ends with human identity as one body composed of man and woman. The unity of man and woman is related to the common working mandate.

God furnished the garden with all delightful things, necessary for living creatures to live abundant lives, such as "all kinds of trees… pleasing to the eye and good for food;" rivers, another source for life; and gemstones. There, God put Adam and Eve to "work it and take care of it" (2:15). This working mandate echoes the ruling mandate of the first chapter. The working mandate is quickly followed by the limitation God places on them: "you are free to eat… but you must not eat from the tree of the knowledge of good and evil" (vv. 16-17). Human life is characterized by God's command that captures a unique combination: "you are free… but you must not…." Human life reflects the ability (surely a gift) to desire and act freely, on the one hand, and the limitation to live under God's law, on the other. The limitation is not ontological, meaning that they could not act against God's law, but moral, implying voluntary obedience. The combination of human freedom and accountable responsibility indicates God's expectation for humans.

What happened

That begins a series of temptations and an act of sin. To find the meaning of sin, we need to closely look at what happened. First, we need to note the type of literature in which the story of sin is described. People ask, "can we trust the story of a talking snake and form a doctrine out of it?" The story of sin was written in a pre-scientific culture, which was obviously quite different from our modern culture. We need to read it within its own cultural situation as much as we can (Remember the organic inspiration of the Bible?). The creation account was structured with a number of communicating tools of the age: symbolic numbers, symmetry, repetition, and a particular type of language that is rooted in the culture. These were borrowed from the cultures of the age to record who the true King is and how he is the Lord of all, by way of creation. A popular way of recording the acts of the great kings was hyperbole, and it was their way of recording historical incidents. Another popular technique was the personification of power in the form of human actions.

What is described in Genesis 3 is simply a short story of eating forbidden fruit, in spite of its heavy subject, sin. It even sounds like a trivial matter. One may wonder whether or not God unjustly condemned all humans out of it. Satan tempts humans with distorted truth and lies. When tempted, Eve began to desire in line with the distorted truth. She added to God's commandment, thus distorting it: "You must not eat fruit from the tree... and you must not touch it" (v. 3). The former is true, but the latter is not, for God did not say it. Once humans are caught in this snare, Satan intensifies the force of temptation by moving from a trivial matter to a more significant one, from a matter of eating fruit to the hubris of becoming like God. The verse 5 reads, "when you eat of it your eyes will be opened, and you will be like God, knowing good and evil." Temptation works because it assures a sweet but undeserved promise to the entrapped mind, and the sweet promise prevents the mind from working with truth. Now Eve's pride would not be satisfied with her given situation in the world. From this dissatisfaction comes a desire to covet something that is not her own, something she believes she deserves. The trees in the garden looked "pleasing to the eye and good for food" (2:9) in their innocent mind, but to the tempted mind, it looked "also desirable for gaining wisdom" (3:6). Pride is strong enough to ensnare the human mind, to tempt those made in the image of God to fly along with the tempting vision to become like God. The impossible vanity of humans to be like God suddenly made good sense and became reinstated as wisdom in the distorted mind. The story of sin pays much attention to the spiritual and psychological change in Eve's mind, signifying that her act of sin was only an external expression of her sinful internal disposition.

Nature of sin

Sin is commonly known as an act of disobedience, a legal transgression. Where and how does sin begin? Are we innocent until we commit a sinful act? The story of sin is rooted in the background of the accountable responsibility of humanity in the world. It is described in the text "You are free to eat from any tree in the garden, but you must not eat from the tree of the knowledge of good and evil, for when you eat of it you will surely die" (2:16-17). God's command not to eat from the tree is neither his arbitrary will nor a trivial law, for it reflects God's good nature and is rooted in the very nature of human beings. The human condition is determined by the creation ordinance: God is the Law-giver, and humans are given freedom and accountable responsibility. God determines good and evil. Humans are equipped with the ability to know the good, freely choose it, and carry it out. At the bottom of sin is deliberate misuse of the gifts of freedom and responsibility. Being triggered by their pride, Adam and Eve deliberately chose to disobey God's command. Though the matter of taking and eating forbidden fruit seems trivial, under the surface of the disobedient action was their desire to take over the authority of God in the matter of deciding what is good and evil. It is as if they were proclaiming their independence from God, saying "stay away and leave the matter to us, for we can handle it on our own." It is as if they were playing God, as if they had become like God. It is noteworthy that temptation comes in the form of wisdom, something noble and admirable that we all should pursue. Sin is capable of disguising the matter, distorting truth and beautifying the lie.

God reacted to their disobedience: "The man has now become like one of us, knowing good and evil" (3:22). Now humans were deciding good and evil in the way they thought they knew them. They were made as God's images to desire the good as God determines and to live a happy life in that way, but sin forfeited their native innocence, and they came to desire beyond their limit and ability of handling the good. The distorted desire made humans mistakenly imagine, as if their eyes were opened, that they knew the difference between good and evil. Now they had to take the responsibility of knowing good and evil in a disobedient and distorted way. First, they were prevented from approaching the tree of life, for they could not live forever in that way. Second, they were banished from the garden "to work the ground from which he [Adam] had been taken" (3:23). The seemingly trivial desire left an immeasurable impact on humanity.

Can humans blame Satan or temptation for their sin? Eve tried to justify her action: "The serpent deceived me, and I ate." She tried to blame the occasion of temptation as if arguing, "If Satan had not tempted me, I would not have committed such a sinful action." The problem of sin is not primarily evil temptation, but the desire of the mind. Created in God's image, humans were capable of desiring God and resisting evil when tempted. The issue of sin is what to desire with the given ability to think and will. Adam and Eve misused the gifts of freedom and reasoning ability, and thus they could not blame Satan.

Sin does not exist alone but takes up human life like a parasite. Sin first affects human desire unnoticeably, like a cancer cell, but it soon permeates the whole person. Sin first warms up human hearts with undeserved promises, but soon it burns the whole life to total destruction. When the desire is directed away from desiring God and his law, it is already sin. Sin is in desire, thought, and will, long before it develops into action. Sin affects the process of brewing into action; sin is using all the God-given gifts, such as freedom, desiring, reasoning, and will, not for the purpose of serving God, but for serving Satan. The wholistic idea of sin can correct the popular but misguided idea of sin as disobedient action. Applying the modern idea of sin as a violation of laws in the Bible makes sin a trivial matter that we think we can easily handle or recompense. The Bible teaches that sin is not simply a violation of God's law but rebellion against God himself.

Consequence of sin

As Adam and Eve hid themselves from God's presence, God issued a series of judgments on those who were involved in human sin, beginning with the serpent, then moving to woman and man. The curse on man was not imposed simply on him but extended to the ground which he was to rule: the ground was cursed because of the man, the ground would produce "thorns and thistles," man would have to work hard to eat from the ground, and he would return to the ground. This series of curses on man can only be understood within the idea of the created world as community, which may be hard to recognize with a modern, individualistic mindset. God created the earth as an organically interrelated community. The parallel between the formation of Adam from *adamah* and the extension of man's sin to the ground highlights the nature of creation as an intrinsic community of which humans are part. When the rulers became fallen, judgement came upon the whole community, which is captured in the text as the curse of the ground. *Adamah* would rebel just as Adam had done. Now the comprehensive consequence of human sin in the world had radically distorted the creation. As Paul says in Romans, "Creation was subjected to frustration," and "the whole creation has been groaning as in the pains of childbirth" (8:20-22).

The comprehensive effects of human sin in the world may be illustrated in terms of threefold human relationships: with God, with others, with the world. The human relationship with God can be seen deteriorating as Adam and Eve chose to hide themselves from God. In claiming independence from their creator, they forfeited their blessings to be in the presence of God and maintain a relationship with him in the same way they had. Adam and Eve were cursed by God and banished from his garden.

The relationship among fellow humans was also severely inflicted by sin. Sin affected the human relationship with each other as well as with others. Adam and Eve realized they were naked, and, feeling shame, they lost the innocent stage of human life. The curse of self-alienation extended to the relationships among fellow humans. Adam and Eve were ashamed in front of each other, afraid to be vulnerable even in front of the one with whom they were created to be in unity. The problems in their relationship are again seen when God questioned Adam and Eve about eating from the tree: Adam blamed Eve for the disobedience. Within the curse given to Eve was another strain put on the relationship between man and woman: man's rule over woman. The implications of sin among humans is further described in chapter 4, where hatred and murder took place among brothers.

The human relationship with the world also was ruined; consequently, the world became damaged as well. As we have discussed above, the effect of sin is all-inclusive, including the whole world in our modern terms. Humans must now labor to eat and live in the fallen state of all they were to take care of and rule over. They have also become prone to abusing the rest of world. They wrongly esteem themselves over God's creation, using it only to take care of themselves and forgetting their creational responsibility to take care of it. In doing so, they wreak havoc upon the order that the Creator God decreed on his creation. God's plan of managing the world became thwarted because of human sin. Work is not a consequence of sin, but hard work is. Humans were created to do the work of the Creator God: to subdue, rule over, work, and take care of the world. Doing God's work and living human life were one and the same in the original pattern of human life. While doing ordinary daily works, they were to serve the world, neighbors, and eventually God. Now, the natural integrity between God's work and human life had been destroyed. The glorious work, which they were to accomplish with great joy in daily life, became a difficult mission.

The most significant consequence of sin is death. Genesis 3:22 tells of this consequence when God said, "The man has now become like one of us, knowing good and evil. He must not be allowed to reach out his hand and take also from the tree of life and eat, and live forever." Adam and Eve did not immediately fall and die, but they were banished from the presence of the Lord of life, signifying spiritual death. Death as consequence of sin is recorded in Genesis 5. Paul, in the New Testament, notes this effect of sin in Romans: "Just as sin entered the world through one man, and death through sin… in this way death came to all people, because all sinned" (5:12). The death of humans can be seen in the following genealogy of sinful humanity.

Genealogy of Genesis 5

Genesis chapter 5 provides the "account of Adam's line," a genealogy of Adam's descendants. The genealogy does not intend to provide historical information of those who lived but, instead, delivers a story of how God responded to the crying of humans, who were suffering from the bondage of sin. Genealogy is a message. God's response to sin is structured in a unique combination of double accounts: the account of Adam's line in chapter 5 that lists descendants from Adam to Noah, and the account of Noah in the next chapter that narrates the Flood. This double-account structure was designed to show the "historical significance of a family"—Noah and his descendants.[1] The story of this significant family delivers a message of what God is doing to sinful humanity from the time of Adam, through the fall into sin, to the hope for the future through Noah.

The genealogy of Genesis 5 describes the progressive change of human status before God. It begins with Adam's original, past status as the image of God; moves to the present sinful status under sin; and ends with anticipation of future hope that is hinted through Noah and his descendants. This account of Adam's line serves as a major turning point in the overarching story of salvation in the Bible, turning away from the effects of sin in the world to the plan of God's salvation. It suggests what plan God has in mind for the sinful world. The first two verses summarize the creation of humanity in God's image, along with his blessing on them. Verse 3 describes a drastic change of human status from God's image to the image of sinful Adam. This change does not mean that those after Adam were no longer created in the image of God, but that they were the same as Adam, created in the image of God but now corrupt images due to the taint of sin. That change is followed by a description of the common pattern of sinful human life: the birth of a man, his living certain years and becoming a father of a son, his living more years and having more sons and daughters, and his death at certain age. The common pattern includes the first description of natural human death that is implied as consequence of sin. What did this pattern of man's life mean in the ancient Hebrew culture? It might have implied a livable life with many children because children were considered in the Hebrew Bible as gifts of God for an abundant life and security, but a life with a necessary ending of death. They lived with some joy, but they died. This same pattern continues up to Enoch, who "walked with God," but the genealogy does not say he died. The individual change found in Enoch from the common pattern escalates to a communal and universal change in Noah. It reads, "He will comfort us in the labor and painful toil of our hands caused by the ground the Lord has cursed" (5:29). The genealogy allows readers to taste the message of comfort in the story of Noah. It does not record Noah's death, as was the common pattern, but moves to the story of the Flood.

The Flood account is situated as a continuation from the account of Adam's line and the effect of sin in death, through God's act of judging sin on the entire earth, eventually anticipating future hope of restoration. As the first hint of salvation was situated in the middle of God's commanding curses (Gen. 3:15), so the hope of creation's restoration is found in the middle of God's judgment on the world.

Discussion Questions:

1. How might you define sin in one sentence?
2. Sin is generally understood in a legal term. Share how you think it affects the whole person, based on the story.
3. In what ways might pride, dissatisfaction, and covetousness precede sinful action?
4. Alienation and hatred are the immediate consequences of sin. Share the pains of injustice that take place in your society regarding gender, race, and social class.

Endnote

1. Sarah Schwartz, "Narrative *Toledot* Formula in Genesis: The Case of Heaven and Earth, Noah, and Isaac, *Journal of Hebrew Scriptures*, vol 16, art. 8, 2016, pp. 11-12.

CHAPTER 6

The plan for salvation as restoration of the created world

In this chapter we discuss the nature of God's salvation as reflected in the Flood account. The Flood account, uniquely structured within the genealogy of Adam and his descendants, gives a summary of human status from creation through the fall and in the subsequent sinful state. In this structure, the Flood story characterizes salvation in the language of creation, showing that salvation is significantly analogous to creation. First, humanity affects the destiny of the world. After Adam and Eve's sin corrupted the world, God called Noah to carry out God's mission of renewing the world—to be a progenitor of renewal. Thus, Noah is called the "comforter" to serve "in the labor and painful toil of our hands caused by the ground the Lord has cursed" (Gen. 5:29)—a description that alludes to the sweeping consequence of human sin in the world (Gen. 3:17-19). Second, salvation is described as restoration of the created world. The Flood account describes judgment of sin and re-establishment of the world by means of water, which signified the destructive power in the creation account. Salvation as restoration of the created world is epitomized by God's covenant that he made with all living creatures. The nature of salvation, described initially in the Flood account, gets further materialized in the history of Israel and is eventually fulfilled through Christ's reconciliation of the world.

The genealogy of Genesis 5 is interrupted by the story of Noah, after which the genealogy continues. The description of Noah's life stops at the end of chapter 5 and resumes at the end of chapter 9, which reads, "altogether Noah live 950 years, and then he died." This statement of Noah's death was made in the pattern of sinful human life in chapter 5. So, found within the broader account of Adam's line, the Flood story serves as the initial activation of "comfort" that Noah will bring to sin-oppressed humans. How could the story of the Flood deliver a message of comfort?

From the fall of Adam to the time of Noah, the world grew incredibly wicked: "Every inclination of the thoughts of the human heart was only evil all the time" (Gen. 6:5). God determined to cope with human sin by destroying humans along with all the animals, birds, and creatures that moved along the ground. But God found Noah to be a righteous man, who "walked with God," which is the sign of God's people, as is the case of Enoch in the genealogy of chapter 5. With Noah, God promised to make a covenant of salvation that would work through the Ark.

Judgement and starting over

God used water as his means of judgment of the world. It may not be easy to imagine water as a means of dreadful judgment and killing in modern culture. But when we realize that the story of the Flood was written in terms of the creation account, we can glean the implied meaning. The water that God used in the Flood is the water that signifies the situation of the formless, empty, dark, and deep chaos at the beginning of the creation account (1:2). Onto the formless state, the Creator God placed his order and created his kingdom. The source of the floodwater also alludes to the creation account, including "all the springs of the great deep," "the floodgates of the heavens," and "rain, [which] fell on the earth" (7:11-12). The flooding of the earth indicates the reversal of God's act of creating the sky and dry land in the creation account, for God made them by separating waters. By using water as the means of judgment, God shows that judgment of sin means plunging the earth into its pre-creation state. It is de-creation; it is not simply punishing sinful creatures. As the Creator God formed the earth "out of water and by water" (2 Pet. 3:5), he judged it by returning it to the status prior to creation. This water theme as the power of death continues in the story of salvation.

In the midst of the water, God saved the chosen living beings in the Ark. Noah and his family built the Ark to contain the eight humans of the family, along with "two of all living creatures, male and female… [and] two of every kind of bird, of every kind of animal and of every kind of creature that moves along the ground" and "every kind of food" for them (6:19-21, see also 7:14). The detailed description of the invited animals clearly shows that it is written in the language of the creation account to signify that the Ark was a microcosm of the creation. The same is repeated when they were led out of the Ark. The Ark was not a luxurious yacht to accommodate only humans; rather, it was God's cradle for the whole creation. This feature shows that the salvation provided by the Creator God at the very early stage of the history of salvation is a comprehensive salvation that includes all of creation.

New rules and new promises

The post-Flood description continuously shows the comprehensiveness of salvation by including a number of parallels to the creation account. After his judgment was over, God "sent a wind over the earth, and the waters receded" after "the springs of the deep and the floodgates of the heavens had been closed, and the rain had stopped falling from the sky" (Gen. 8:1-2). The emerging dry land is parallel to the result of his creation activity, when by separating waters, he created places for life. In the parallel between creation and re-creation, the post-Flood event signifies God's sovereignty over the water, which eventually points to his determination to continue his sovereignty over the recreated world. God invited "every kind of living creature" out of the Ark and re-committed his original blessing on life: "so they can multiply on the earth and be fruitful and increase in number upon it" (8:17). His blessing on the living animals is followed by his blessing on humanity, following the pattern of the creation account. This parallel between the post-Flood blessing and the original creational blessing signifies, first, that the Flood functions as cleansing as well as judgment and killing. God's judgment was not to destroy the earth, but to cleanse it of its evil so that it might become his own kingdom again. Second, by reissuing the creational life-blessing on the family of Noah in the re-created earth, God treated Noah as the new Adam, a renewed human race. This change of human status is significant against the genealogy of Genesis 5, which shows that Eve gave birth to Seth in Adam's sinful image but that Noah would bring rest to suffering humanity. Third, the parallel found in the Flood eventually leads to an extended meaning of salvation, in the Bible, as the re-creation of the earth after de-creation.

Next, we notice how God continued his original cause of the creation in the re-created world. God promised he will not "curse the ground because of man, even though every inclination of his heart is evil" (8:21). God did not treat human sin in a full sense through the Flood but continued his creation with sinful humans in it: "As long as the earth endures, seedtime and harvest, cold and heat, summer and winter, day and time will never cease" (8:22).

The text of 9:1-7 is a unit that emphasizes this continuity. The text is structured like an envelope, repeating the same, original blessing on humans in the front and back sections, and using the middle section for changes made in human life because of sin.

Genesis 9:1	Genesis 9:2-6	Genesis 9:7
Continuation of the creation blessing:	Changes made in human life caused by sin:	Continuation of the creation blessing:
"Be fruitful and increase in number and fill the earth."	Animals will have "fear and dread" of humans. All the animals are given as food for humans; but humans are not to eat their blood along with flesh. God continued the image of God in humanity.	"Be fruitful and increase in number, multiply on the earth and increase upon it."

While the blessings and commands given after the Flood are found to be parallel to the creation account, some changes were made to suit the fallen creation. God still maintains humans as his images, but they are damaged images. Humans can still enjoy both God's blessing on life and their ruling the world, but only in a distorted way. Humans are still gifts of God's life blessing, but they are born in great pain, which explains the identity of sinful humans. And their ruling is challenged by the revolt of the ground and animal kingdom. Another significant change was made in regard to the blood of life. Here blood was considered the seat of life, which belongs to the Creator. Remember that all living beings as *nepes* are created by God and depend on God for living and life. God informed sinful, craving humans, that though they might eat animal flesh, animal life belongs to him. God also warned humans against killing one another: "Whoever sheds human blood, by humans shall their blood be shed; for in the image of God has God made mankind" (Gen. 9:6). The creator of life became the protector of life in the fallen world. The nature of salvation would be established on this principle of the life-blood.

The following text (9:8-17) shows God making his first covenant of future salvation as a corollary of his life-blessings. God promised "Never again will all the life be cut off by the waters of a flood" (v. 11). God made the covenant with humans, their descendants, all the living creatures that came out of the Ark, and the earth (vv. 9-13). The Noahic covenant, written in terms of creation, was made with all creation. God's promise for the future was as comprehensive as was the Ark a representative of God's creation. Just as the ground was cursed because of human sin, so the earth now received God's promise of salvation. And God established his rainbow in the sky as the sign of his promise. Just as the Spirit of God hovered over the chaotic waters at the creation, so now God's rainbow guarantees he will keep the waters from damaging the earth.

Within God's blessing given after the Flood, his willingness to provide for his dependent creation, even as it will continually act apart from his will, is also seen. Just as in the creation account God provided the food humans needed, he made known that he would continue to provide food for them. God also promised to maintain seasons, cold, heat, day, and night on earth for the remainder of its existence. The world he created would remain a livable home for all he put within it. Even as humans brought about disorder to his creation, he would maintain order in the world. Although God's creation was fallen, his plan of re-creation was not a deviation from his plan of creation.

After the flood

After the Noahic covenant was made, the text returns to the genealogy, bringing us from Noah to the time of the Tower of Babel in chapter 11. People, again, became full of sinful pride. They were building a tower that reached to the heavens, which was considered God's abode, in order to build a name for themselves. They hoped this tower would prevent them from being scattered over the earth (Gen. 11:4). As they sought to make a name for themselves, they were no longer living according to God's will but pridefully seeking their own glory. They were in direct opposition to God's command to Adam and Noah to "fill the earth" with God's will for the creation (Gen. 1:28, 9:1). Because humans had again pridefully chosen to rebel against God's commands, he intervened. God confused their language and scattered them over the earth (Gen. 11:9).

God continued the history of the still sinful world. After the story of the Tower of Babel, the text continues with a genealogy, this time taking us from one of Noah's sons to Abram. Abram would become the next man set apart by God and would become the father of God's people, through whom a true and final redeemer would one day come.

Seeing the story of Noah and the Flood in light of the creation account allows us to better understand God's purpose in sending the flood. The Flood was not simply a way of judging the sin of the world, but a means of renewing the world. In the re-creation of his world, God maintained his blessings on both humans and animals, not deserting or condemning his fallen creation. The story of the flood takes us back to God's creation of the world and brings us to anticipate the re-creation that would come through a descendant of Noah. This coming re-creation would not be a complete destruction of what had been made, nor would it be exclusive of any part of creation. Just as in the flood, God's plan of salvation was one of judgement, purification, and renewal—by de-creation and re-creation of all things. As his name suggests, Noah provided rest and comfort in bringing about a new creation and foreshadowing the truly new creation that will come to be.

Implication in the history of salvation in the Bible

The Bible reveals a single story of salvation throughout the Old and New Testaments. In order to properly understand the one history of salvation, we need to look at the early chapters of Genesis, for there was laid the foundation of the progression of salvation that follows. The early chapters present the nature of salvation and guide its direction until it is eventually accomplished by Christ Jesus. So far, we have studied the creation of the world, the human fall into sin, its effect in the world, and God's response to human calamity by way of judging sin and preparing the plan of salvation.

The Flood of Noah serves a unique function in the history of salvation. At the beginning of creation, water symbolized a chaotic situation that threatened the existence of life forms. From that chaotic state, God created order and thus created the world. Peter reflects the divine activity of creation: "long ago by God's word the heavens existed and the earth was formed *out of water and by water*" (2 Pet. 3:5). When sin corrupted the world, the Creator God sent the Flood to serve his justice by "de-creating" the world (returning it to the pre-creational chaotic status) so as to finally "re-create" it. According to Peter's perspective of salvation, the Flood served as the first purification process. The water of the Flood serves as the means of judgment, killing, and eventually as a refining process. It judged and condemned all the sinful effects in the world; and when the water dried up, the Creator God extended the original blessings of the created world. With the Flood, God did not do away with the created world, but renewed it. Peter considers the Flood as serving a significant role in the larger history of salvation that set the stage for, and anticipated the kind of, salvation to be fulfilled in the future. Peter continues, "by the same word, the present heavens and earth are reserved for fire, being kept for the day of judgment and destruction of ungodly men" (3:7). "By the same word" indeed refers to God's sovereign act of creation, which he previously mentioned in verse 5: "by God's word the heavens existed and the earth was formed out of water and by water." The same sovereign act of creation will still be working in the re-creation of the world by fire. The overarching pattern of salvation, Peter sees, is that just as the world was judged and purified first by water, so will it be judged and purified by fire. Water and fire are not used to literally "destroy" the world, but instead serve double functions for re-creation of the world—judgment and purification. The object of destruction by fire is clearly seen in verse 7: "for the day of judgment and destruction of ungodly men." What is going to be burned is the effect of sin, not the world itself. Such use of fire as a process of salvation is well reflected in Zechariah 13:9, Malachi 3:2-3, and Isaiah 1:31. The text of 1 Corinthians 3:12-13 shows the function of fire as "revealing" what humans build in life and "test[ing] the quality of each man's work."

Reflection

When God pronounced his decree to not judge the world with water again, he said, "As long as the earth endures, seedtime and harvest, cold and heat, summer and winter, day and night will never cease" (Gen. 8:22). The four sets of creation order that will endure in the still sinful world were implied in the first three days of creation, illustrated here in the reverse order of the creation account. They are the natural orders of food, weather, and time. They are God's gifts and necessary conditions for living beings.

Now, see how these natural gifts of God, necessary conditions for life, have been damaged by humans. People are dying out of hunger, not because of lack of food produced in the world, but mostly by the problem of its distribution. People are suffering with ever-increasing eating disorders such as gluttony and anorexia. The broken order, related to the boundary between human habitats and animal habitats, causes many viral diseases. Weather disorder is one of the most urgent worldwide problems. Global warming, by way of causing heightened sea-levels and more hurricanes and tsunamis and transforming tillable land to desert and changing food-chains, impacts all living beings in the world. Day and night are getting more and more confused in the pursuit of efficient mass-production, and pleasure-seeking is causing diverse physical and emotional disorders. All the God-bestowed order is still here with us, as God promised to maintain, but is altered and damaged by greedy human exploitation.

As the Bible teaches that salvation is related to the whole world, questions arise as to who and what God saves. And because we know we are saved when we put our faith in Jesus Christ, how is human individual salvation related to the world? We will deal with these questions as the Bible unfolds the progressive history of salvation, but now let us move to the whole picture of salvation in the next chapter.

Discussion Questions:

1. What does the parallel between the post-Flood account and the Creation account imply about the unfolding story of salvation in the Bible?

2. What do you infer when you find the change of human identity from the image of God (Gen. 1) to the image of sinful Adam (Gen. 5) to confirmation as the image of God (Gen. 9)?

3. What differences are seen between God's commands to Adam in a fully ordered creation and to Noah in the disordered world?

4. How does God show his care for all of his creation within the Flood account?

Chapter 7

The whole story of salvation

"For God was pleased to have all his fullness dwell in him, and through him to reconcile to himself all things, whether things on earth or things in heaven, by making peace through his blood, shed on the cross" (Col. 1:19-20).

Overarching theme of the Scriptures

The Christian religion originated in God's gracious offer of salvation. Saving sinners and shaping them as God's people is indeed a wonderful blessing of God and occupies the major message in Scripture. However, Scripture presents the gospel of salvation in a larger structure that moves from creation to re-creation and provides a unique view of reality: who God is, who humans are in God's world, and what is meant by the scope and goal of his salvation through Jesus Christ. Within this broad view of Scripture is found the *missio dei*, what God is doing in his world, which gives us a truer, deeper meaning of salvation. There, the Christian religion is not simply a way of getting God's favor to avoid our human predicament. If salvation is understood as limited to the change of spiritual status from sinner to forgiven citizen of heaven (however pious and spiritual it may be), it is a partial understanding of the gospel and reduces God's salvation to a personal need. Scripture presents the Christian religion as a mode of human life that provides accurate human seeing, believing, and living. Religion does not simply deal with one aspect of life; instead, it motivates the whole of human existence because it determines one's view of reality.

The overview of Scripture may be presented in four major movements: the creation, the human fall into sin, God's redirection of humans toward redemption, and the consummation of the redemption. The four-part movement of Scripture shows God's sovereignty over his entire world. The creation established the kingdom where the Creator king is ruling. Since the fall into sin, humans have been making futile claims of autonomy and power over the world, and Satan has been claiming his power over humans. God's acts for revealing his sovereignty defeated the evil power and set his people free from the bondage of evil to serve him. By restoring his people, the king re-establishes his kingdom. God's acts to prove his sovereignty in the Scripture may be summarized in his seven major acts:

(1) calling his people out of pagan culture
(2) moving them
(3) resettling them in the pagan culture
(4) competing with the pagan lords
(5) proving his lordship over all
(6) saving his people
(7) shaping them as his people

These seven acts of God began with his calling Abram and making his covenant with him and his descendants. God moved Abram and Sarai, situating them in diverse cultures and religions, himself competing with the pagan gods there, and saved them from dangers. After that, the pattern continued through Joseph and Moses, who both demonstrated the power of the God of the Hebrew people over the gods of Egypt while there. The subsequent history of the Old Testament continued the redeeming campaign of God against pagan lords and gods. His lordship was confessed by pagan people such as Rahab of Jericho, Ruth of Moab, and pagan kings of Persia. Even as the Hebrew people were in exile under the Assyrian, Babylonian, and Persian empires through the remainder of the Old Testament, the prophets testified that those times were God's way of judging and shaping his people. God used these pagan empires to train and reform his people. While God proved his cosmic sovereignty over world powers, he also proved who he is to his covenantal people. The way God judged the pagan lords and gods coincided with the way he proved his lordship and shaped the faith of his people. At the end of each episode of God's shaping his people, the Israelites realized that their God was different from pagan gods and were reminded of his faithful working of the covenant.

God's acts of proving his sovereignty only became greater, in the progressive revelation, as they reached completion in the New Testament. The following text summarizes the proven lordship of the triune God in the world. God proved his sovereign lordship over the creation, fulfilled in Christ, now working through the power of his Spirit:

> There is one body and one Spirit, just as you were called to one hope when you were called; one Lord, one faith, one baptism; one God and Father of all, who is over all and through all and in all. (Eph. 4:4-6)

God's lordship over all, working in Christ, is emphasized by his being the Creator and Redeemer:

> For by him all things were created: things in heaven and on earth, visible and invisible, whether thrones or powers or rulers or authori-

ties, all things were created by him and for him.... And he is the head of the body, the church... so that in everything he might have the supremacy. For God was pleased to have all his fullness dwell in him. (Col. 1:16-19)

God is the Lord over all in a double way: because he made humanity and because he purchased humanity back from sin by paying the price of his son's blood. The story of God's proving his sovereignty connects redemption to the creation. Christ came down to save humans because he is the Lord of them all, due to his creation. God vindicated Christ's acts of salvation and raised him to his own full deity, with lordship over all. The trinitarian formula of these texts signifies the progressive revelation of God's acts to prove his sovereignty in history. Faith in God includes belief in the trinity: that the God who saves is the God who created and the God who sanctifies here and now.

God's proving and demonstrating his lordship will reach its completion with the New Heaven and New Earth. It is significant to recognize that the Bible begins with the creation and ends with the new creation in order to reveal the overarching theme of the Bible—God's claim of his sovereignty over his creation and thus putting his world back to the original status of shalom:

> Then I saw a new heaven and a new earth.... Now the dwelling of God is with men, and he will live with them. They will be his people, and God himself will be with them and be their God.... I am making all things new. (Rev. 21:1-5)

Personal and cosmic redemption

It is suggested above that the salvation achieved through Christ is located within the overarching theme of God's claiming his sovereignty. In what sense does Christ's salvation work fit within the structure of God's claim of sovereignty? The answer to this question explains the goal of God's salvation act through Christ: what Christ has achieved through his obedient life, especially through his cross.

After the Fall, God responded to the human calamity by preparing a plan of salvation. The salvation had to work in such a way as to satisfy both God's justice and his love—in a way that sinful humans would be punished for their sin, but after which they would be restored. No sinful human could ever accomplish the act of salvation, but only the one who would never fall into the traps of sin. God's love found a way to satisfy his justice—in sacrificing Jesus, the second person of the triune God incarnated. Jesus lived a perfect, obedient life and suffered death as an innocent man. Jesus took upon himself the wrath of God, satisfying God's justice. God the Father approved Jesus' redemptive act by raising him from death, lifted Jesus to his right hand in heaven, and transferred Jesus' righteousness to believers who are united to him in faith. When believers repent of their sins and believe in Jesus' redemptive act, their sins are forgiven, and they are proclaimed to be righteous before God, as Jesus is.

Described above is the personal aspect of redemption. The term "personal" here is not to be understood in an individualistic sense, as if God is singling out certain individuals from people. Rather, God uses the covenant community to save and shape his people. God chose the means of Christ's bodily sacrifice and the resulting body of believers to lead us to salvation and replace our sinful character. The personal aspect of salvation means that individuals must believe in and confess Christ. The experience of personal salvation begins with the painful recognition of being a sinner and pouring out one's sin in repentance before God. As the sinner stands before God with a transparent and genuine heart, not simply accepting moral guilt or agreeing with church doctrine, he or she becomes totally vulnerable to God. Then the sinner receives absolution of sin, and that blessing shapes in the sinner a new life, the spiritual attitude of love, reverence, and dedication of life to God.

The personal and cosmic aspects of salvation are integrally combined to complete the reconciliation of the God-created world to God. The Scripture teaches that salvation begins with individual spiritual blessings but extends to a higher goal. As we have seen, salvation in the story of Noah was described in terms of creation, and God made his covenant with all living creatures. The Noahic covenant was followed by the Abrahamic covenant: "I will make you into a great nation" (Gen. 12:2). This covenant with Abraham may seem to have ended God's concern for all creation and to have begun focusing on saving Israel. That is not true. With one man in concrete history, God is dealing with sin to reverse the sinful effect that extended from one man to all. Abraham was called as the father of all nations, and his wife, Sarah, as the mother of all nations. Israel was chosen not only as God's people but also to serve others as the model of God's people: "I will keep you and will make you to be a covenant for the people and a light for the Gentiles" (Isa. 42:6). Isaiah explained the meaning of the light for the gentiles: "I will also make you a light for the Gentiles, that you may bring my salvation to the ends of the earth" (49:6). In other places, he envisioned a broader scope of salvation: "See, I will create new heavens and a new earth. The former things will not be remembered, nor will they come to mind (65:17).

The New Testament describes Christ's redemptive act as a cosmic renewal, in which are found the place and meaning of personal redemption. Christ, who is supreme over all creation, redeems all creation:

> For God was pleased to have all his fullness dwell in him, and through him to reconcile to himself all things, whether things on earth or things in heaven, by making peace through his blood, shed on the cross (Col. 1:19-20).

Paul's thesis in this text is that Christ created all things, and he reconciled all things to himself by his crucifixion. This thesis is structured in the double identity of Christ: Christ is the Creator and the Redeemer. Christ reconciles what he has created to himself. In this text, redemption is analogous to the creation. Creation is not simply the background in which redemption is taking place; creation is the object of redemption. The meaning of "all things" is unmistakably illustrated: "things in heaven and on earth, visible and invisible, whether thrones or powers or rulers or authorities." Even the highest political authority who was worshipped as god at the time, the Caesar, was included in "all things." Paul defines Christ's redemption as reconciliation. Reconciliation is a relational term. By choosing it, Paul summarizes the unfolding of God's plan of salvation from the beginning till Christ. The world was created as a good creation (good relationship), became fallen (broken relationship), and is now restored in Christ (reconciled relationship). Among the "all things" reconciled are the believing humans: "Once you were alienated from God and were enemies in your minds because of your evil behavior. But now he has reconciled you by Christ's physical body through death to present you holy in his sight" (vv. 21-22).

Connecting the Colossians text to the rest of the New Testament, we can conclude the plan of God's salvation as follows: as God promised to Israel in the Old Testament, Christ came and accomplished the reconciliation of the world to himself. Then he ascended to heaven and reigns on earth from there. When he returns, he will finally complete the reconciliation that he began on the cross. The completion of the reconciliation of the world will be realized in the new heaven and new earth, as in Revelation 21:1-5. There, the sovereign Lord of all claims, "I am making everything new."

God's claim of sovereignty is achieved by Christ's redemptive act when he proved his lordship over creation by reconciling it to God. What does Christ's cosmic reconciliation imply for believers' life?

Being reconciled, we live the life of reconciliation.

How is the reconciliation of all things (cosmic redemption) related to the salvation of individual believers (personal redemption)? Is Christ working for two different kinds of redemption? That cannot be. The latter is found in the broader redemption of the former:

> Therefore, if anyone is in Christ, the new creation has come; the old has gone, the new has come! All this is from God, who reconciled us to himself through Christ and gave us the ministry of reconciliation: that God was reconciling the world to himself in Christ, not counting men's sins against them. And he has committed to us the message of reconciliation. We are therefore Christ's ambassadors, as though God were making his appeal through us. (2 Cor. 5:17-20)

While in the Colossian text Paul describes Christ's redemption as the reconciliation of all things, here he applies it in the life of believers. Being "in Christ" suggests the redeemed status of individual believers in that they are united with Christ in his death and new life. The personal aspect of salvation is correlated to the cosmic salvation in verse 19: "God was reconciling the world to himself in Christ, not counting men's sins against them." God is working for the reconciliation of the world by reconciling his people to himself. In God's plan, personal salvation assumes and leads to cosmic salvation.

The text shows this integrated sequence at the beginning: "if anyone is in Christ, the new creation has come." The consequence of being in Christ is the new creation. While some older translations read it as "he is a new creature" or "he is a new creation," the new translation of the NIV reads, "if anyone is in Christ, the new creation has come." Christ's salvation does not simply transform the spiritual status of sinful humans and leave them in the sinful world. It brings his kingdom into the world, transforming the world itself. A new system of human life has arrived. In the presence of the kingdom, Paul exhorts believers to live the "ministry of reconciliation" by being equipped with the "message of reconciliation." This redeemed lifestyle is characterized by our living as "ambassadors" of Christ in reconciling the world. Though "we" in the text—the recipients of the mandate—may primarily refer to Paul and his ministry team, it should be extended to all believers, because the subject of living in the new creation includes all believers, as it reads, "if anyone is in Christ." It is as if Christ is sending us with this commission: "now that you are reconciled to me, go out and live the life of reconciling the world to me." For God is making his appeal to the world through the redeemed, the ambassadors. The committed lifestyle suggests that if believers do not live as ambassadors, God is not managing the world. This does not mean that God is incapable of managing his creation without the cooperation of his people. It means, rather, that God is pleased to manage the world through his redeemed people. Here we find a parallel between the mandate of the ambassador for redeemed humans and the original mandate for humans. The commission of the ambassadors is in fact a re-delegation of the creational ruling mandate. Salvation does not add to creation, but instead completes its purpose.

Living a redeemed life in the world today

We have now examined God's broad salvation. That broad salvation sends us to the world with responsibility. However, is not the world sinful and aren't we not of the world? Christ has defeated sin and death, but we still live in a time in which we face both. As to cosmic salvation, the reconciliation of all things has begun to work here and now, but God's claim of sovereignty over the world is not yet fully completed. The tension of living as "already" but "not yet" redeemed people determines the character of our present Christian life. Let us leave a fuller study of eschatological unfolding of salvation to later chapters and now see the Christian attitude toward the world.

The way we are to understand the world can become a bit confusing, as the term is used in different ways throughout the Bible. The 1 John text seems to be fully against the world:

> Do not love the *world* or anything in the *world*. If anyone loves the *world*, love for the Father is not in him. For everything in the *world*—the cravings of sinful man, the lust of the eyes and the boasting of what he has and does—comes not from the Father but from the *world*. (1 John 2:15-16)

Here John's view of the world seems to be in opposition to his view of it in John 3:16, where he says, "For God so loved the world that he gave his one and only Son...." God's love for the world is also found in 1 John 4:14: "the Father has sent his Son to be the Savior of the world." Verse 9 says almost the same thing. When we read the term "world" in these contexts, we find that these passages are not contradictory to each other. The passage of 1John 2:15-16 does not describe the creation itself, as do the passages in chapter 4 and John 3:16; instead, they refer to the things of the world that were never part of God's good creation. In the former passage, "world" means sinful lifestyle, such as cravings, lust, and boasting. We are to read the "world" from the historical progress of salvation, that is, from good creation, through its fall, to salvation. The Christian view of the world is well reflected in Christ's prayer to his Father:

> My prayer is not that you take them out of the world but that you protect them from the evil one. They are not of the world, even as I am not of it.... As you sent me into the world, I have sent them into the world. (John 17:15-18)

We live in God's world—which is the only home that God created for us, and which is in the process of being redeemed—to reclaim for God all that has been tainted by sin in it.

Reflection

What is the destination of reading God's Word in the Bible? Bible reading should be doxological—glorifying to God. Religion is born out of the benefits that God offers us. Calvin made the point: "I call piety that reverence joined with love of God which the knowledge of his benefits induces." Being assured of the benefit of salvation, believers are provoked to worship God: "Here indeed is pure and real religion: faith so joined with an earnest fear of God that this fear also embraces willing reverence, and carries with it such legitimate worship...."[1]

The benefit of salvation that provokes us to worship God is double-sided: personal salvation is offered for accomplishing the cosmic mission of God. Taking only the personal benefit of salvation reduces Christian piety to a personal, spiritual relationship to God that works in the private sphere only. Service is expected to be done for and within the church community, both domestic and abroad on the mission fields. With recognition of the full benefit of salvation, believers adopt a spiritual relationship with God that governs not simply personal but also public spheres. The public aspect of Christian faith and spirituality is not a supplemental but an essential aspect of faith. For God rules over the world through the newly established people of God—the believers. They are serving God by serving the world. Their services in life are all geared toward glorifying God. After expounding the Christian roles of salt and light in the world, Christ teaches, "In the same way, let your light shine before men, that they may see your good deeds and praise your Father in heaven" (Matt. 5:16).

Discussion questions:

1. What do you feel when you read that the broad salvation God is working in and around you?
2. Can you reiterate in your words how God works from the Old into the New Testament?
3. With what attitude should you approach the world and all within it?
4. What is your role in God's plan of redemption?

Endnote

1. John Calvin, *Institutes of the Christian Religion* (Philadelphia: Westminster Press, 1960), I.ii.1, I.ii.2.

CHAPTER 8

Patriarch: the foundation of God's people

What is God doing?

While God made his covenant with Noah, regarding the whole creation, in a negative way ("Never again will all life be destroyed by waters"), he made his covenant later with Abraham about his people in a positive way ("I will make you into a great nation"). What God promised in anticipation of the re-creation of the earth, he now begins to carry out by choosing one person in concrete human history. In the account of Abraham, we see that God is reversing what had happened in the Fall. As sin entered by one person and corrupted all, God is establishing a one-person foundation to eventually recreate his people. In that sense Abraham becomes the patriarch of God's people. Abraham foreshadows Christ because Christ would eventually overturn the effects of sin and establish his people.

The means that God used to establish his people out of sinful humans is a covenant. A covenant is a contract that creates a relationship, namely between God and his people, and, thus, the covenant shapes the identity of God's people. To continue the covenantal relationship, God required the proper response from his people, that is faith. Faith is defined in the context where God made a covenant with his people. God initiated the situation of Abram and Sarai, made his covenant with them, and shaped their faith in the covenantal context. It is notable that the nature of faith is illustrated in the early chapter of the first book in the Bible, since Abraham was to become our forefather, the model of faith. Later Paul, in the New Testament, formulated his theology of justification by faith based on the Abrahamic episode. The history of the covenant also illustrates the scope of salvation. God chose Abraham as the patriarch of his people, who were shaped first from Israel but eventually out of all nations. As the history of the covenant unfolded, we see how God saved and shaped his people and eventually led and leads all nations to the new creation.

We have said that the covenant shapes the identity of God's people. For the subsequent story of shaping God's people, we need to pay attention to, first, who Abraham was, for he would become the ancestor of all believers, and, secondly, for what he was chosen, for the scope of salvation depends on the nature of his calling.

Who is Abram?

The episode of Abram begins with God's calling him, in Genesis 12: "Leave your country.... I will make you into a great nation." God's purpose in calling Abram is contrasted to the plan of sinful humanity, represented by the Tower of Babel in Genesis 11. Fallen humanity attempted to build their own city with a tower "that reaches to the heavens, so that we may make a name for ourselves." The heavens symbolized God's presence. God thwarted their plan by confusing human language. While sinful humans attempted to build their city to make their name great, that is to be like God, God called a person to build, or make, his nation great.

As we consider the situation of Abram, we notice that God demands commitment from him. First, Abram was a pagan man from Ur. Joshua 24:2-4 shows that when his ancestors "worshipped other gods" in Ur, God called Abram out of from among them. Even though through family tradition, Abram might have retained some knowledge of the true God, Yahweh, he was born and raised in the pagan culture. Against the pagan spiritual background, when this God might have been a strange deity to Abram, God's command, "Leave your country, your people, and your father's household and go to the land I will show you" (Gen. 12:1), must have been a tremendous challenge. God commanded him to leave everything of the pagan culture, including their religion. Abram would become the father of the Jewish nation, thus called a patriarch, but he was not a Jewish man, only spiritually a pagan. Second, the Bible shows that Abram and Sarai were old and barren. Abram was seventy-five years old and Sarai sixty-five when they came out of Haran. Would not God need a young and healthy couple when he commands them to go on a long journey to a new land and become a progenitor of the coming nation? God's purpose of choosing an old couple, a point that is continuously reflected by reminders of the couple's age and Sarai's barren condition, guides readers' attention to the conclusion of the story. Third, Abram was not morally a perfect person. The twelfth chapter tells us that Abram told his wife Sarai to tell the Egyptians he was her brother. Staying in Egypt as poor foreigners, since they came to flee famine, must have made Abram vulnerable and fearful. His fear dramatically increased because the Egyptians saw Sarai as a beautiful woman. The situation tested Abram's character, and his moral quandary ended up with the Pharaoh taking Sarai as his concubine. Probably his fear made him forget his trust in God.

Why does the Bible record these seemly insignificant and disgraceful episodes of Abraham, who later will be established as the model of faith, the forefather of all believers? Is the life situation of Abram and Sarai's ages and barrenness necessary for God's making covenant with them?

The situation dramatically reveals the nature of God's covenant and the subsequent history of salvation. When Abram and Sarai were physically old and barren, unable to reproduce; spiritually pagan, having no relationship with the true God; and morally deficient, the sign of a sinner, thus having no merit at all in themselves to deserve to be chosen by God, God graciously chose them. The gospel begins right here with Abram. As a believing gentile, he was called and became the model of faith for us all.

Abraham's journey with the covenant

A covenant is a contract that involves command and promise. God tells Abram to leave his pagan culture, and he will be made the foundation of God's people: "I will make you into a great nation and I will bless you; I will make your name great, and you will be a blessing" (Gen. 12:2). As Abram and Sarai left in obedience, signifying their trust, and continued on the journey, they received confirmed promises: a promise of land—"all the land that you see I will give to you and your offspring forever"—and a promise of offspring—"I will make your offspring like the dust of the earth" (Gen. 13:15-16). By pointing out the coming of the heir, both promises aimed at the fulfillment of the great nation. The realization of the promises hinged on whether Sarai would give birth to a son. How did Abram and Sarai take these promises of God?

In Genesis 15:1-6, we see two sets of God's confirmation of the covenant followed by Abram's response. God's first confirmation of the covenant, "Don't be afraid, Abram. I am your shield, your very great reward," met Abram's distrusting response in verses 2-3: "what can you give me since I remain childless.... You have given me no children; so a servant in my household will be my heir." Abram here lacked faith and had no hope in the future. However, in the second promise, Abram responded with faith to God's confirmation of the great number of his offspring. God assured Abram of the promise with visual signs of the dust on the ground in the daytime and the stars in the sky at night. Dust and stars were things they saw all day long in their wilderness journey. They were continuously reminded of God's reassured covenant "I will make you into a great nation." We don't hear Abram's response directly from his lips, but the narrator assesses his reply: "Abram believed the Lord, and he credited it to him as righteousness" (15:6).

How shall we understand the dramatic change in Abram's faith, from distrust and hopelessness (vv. 2-3) to belief (v. 6)? Abram's response to God continues as the story unfolds. God responded to Abram's belief of verse 6 with a ritual of solemnizing his covenant. Abraham brought God animals, cut them into pieces, and placed them on opposite sides of each other, and then he fell asleep. It was customary that a lesser party, Abraham, was to pass through the cut animals, but he was in "a deep sleep, and a thick and dreadful darkness came over him." But "a smoking firepot with a blazing torch appeared and passed between the pieces." Fire often symbolizes the presence of God. The greater party, God, passed through the cut-pieces of the animals and fulfilled the ritual of the covenant for Abraham. This event signifies that God took on both sides of the covenant because humans could not fulfill their own side. The human side of the ritual included taking up the warning of blood of the animals, representing the punishment of death in case the party failed to keep their side of the covenant. When God passed through, he took on himself the required judgement and death. The ritual confirmed God's love for Abraham and assured that he would be faithful to the covenant. With the formal ritual made, there was a solemn declaration: "On that day the Lord made a covenant with Abram and said, 'to your descendants I give this land'" (v. 18). Now promises of both the number of people and the land were sealed.

Chapter sixteen begins with a reminder of Sarai's barren condition and of the ten years they lived in Canaan. It describes the birth of Ishmael from Abram and Hagar, Sarai's maidservant. Sarai and Abram tried to take matters into their own hands, probably out of good motivation, to make God's promise happen, but that was not God's direction. Sarai planned Ishmael's birth out of her firm belief in her body's condition and out of her disbelief in God's promise. This episode shows they could not wait until God fulfilled the promise. Disbelief works in impatience. The episode ends with Abram's age, eighty-six. The next chapter begins with Abram's age, ninety-nine, and God's confirmation of his promise. God assured Abram of his covenant by giving a sign of the covenant in his own body—circumcision. With the renewed covenant, Abram's name changed to Abraham. However, Abraham responded to God with laughter: "he laughed and said to himself, 'will a son be born to a man a hundred years old?" (v. 17). The chapter ends with another reminder of Abraham's age, ninety-nine, at the time of his circumcision. Chapter eighteen shows Sarah also laughing at the reassured promise of God, out of her disbelief. Both Abraham and Sarah laughed and doubted because they believed they were too old for such a miracle to happen. But God continuously remained faithful to his promise: "I will return to you at the appointed time next year and Sarah will have a son" (v. 14).

The description of Abraham's and Sarah's journey with God highlights God's continuous faithfulness to his promise in spite of their continuous distrust throughout the long progress that seemed impossible because of their ages and Sarah's continued barrenness. What God did for Abraham and Sarah and why are the keys to the story. Some challenges may be resolved in time and end up with desirable results. But the challenge of the conflict that Abraham and Sarah faced is a different kind. Sarah's physical condition deteriorated as she advanced in age, and Abraham knew it. The more time progressed, the less possible became the hope of achieving the promise. The reminder of their ages and barrenness dramatically underscored the conflict between God's promise and the reality they knew. They might have become wiser, but human wisdom could not handle the realistically impossible challenge that God was going to meet. The challenge was anticipated from the very beginning when God called old Abram and barren Sarai. Throughout the long time period, from Abram's seventy-fifth to his hundredth year, God continuously assured Abraham and Sarah of his covenantal promises and encouraged them to trust in him.

God's promise finally came true, and old Abraham and Sarah became parents: "Now the Lord was gracious to Sarah as he had said, and the Lord did for Sarah what he had promised. Sarah became pregnant and bore a son to Abraham in his old age.... Abraham gave the name Isaac.... Abraham was a hundred years old when his son Isaac was born to him" (Gen. 21:1-5). Out of his gracious faithfulness to his covenant, God guided Abraham and Sarah through their long struggling journey, as signified by the one hundred years of age, and Isaac was born. The name Isaac means laughter; God gave joy over the fulfillment of his promise to Abraham and Sarah in spite of their laughter of distrust. What a happy ending after so many struggles! The miraculous birth of Isaac should now confirm for Abraham and Sarah the truthfulness of God himself and his covenant. They now had firm evidence to believe and trust God. They still did not know what God was doing with them or why he was doing it, but they had become confident in trusting what God promised. Now the great nation God had promised would be realized.

The happy ending is followed by another, more excruciating, challenge for Abraham. God commanded him to sacrifice Isaac. This command, "Take your son..., go to the region of Moriah... [and] sacrifice him there," echoes his first command, "leave your country... and go to the land I will show you." God did not transform Abraham or his life immediately at the time of calling but provided him with an opportunity for processing the command while going on a journey. Abraham had to envision the commandment with its accompanied promises, but without knowing what God was doing. This challenging situation summoned him to trust God, surrendering all his human wisdom. The test of Abraham's faith in chapter twenty-two demanded more of him than simply trusting; now he was called to take action—sacrifice his son. On the way to the mountain, Isaac asked an innocent query: "...where is the lamb for the burnt offering?" Abraham's response, "God himself will provide the lamb," sounds as if he had acquired a firm trust from past experience, but he was quivering inside. He still did not know the reason for God's command. Abraham's trust in God led him to the mountain, and the time had come to prove it. When he was about to take the action, the angel stopped him and led him to sacrifice a ram instead. God approved his faith by saying, "Now I know that you fear God" (22:12). This testifies that Abraham had grown to a more mature faith, a progress from the earlier approval of his faith: "Abraham believed the Lord, and God credited it to him as righteousness." The test in chapter 22 is not to see whether he had faith, but whether his faith worked in action. Now Abraham was learning that faith is trusting God's promise to the point of putting it in action out of fear of the Lord. The fear of the Lord here does not imply God's threat of punishment in case Abraham disobeyed, but instead his worshipping attitude toward God, shaped by his experience of God as both the awesome, sovereign Lord over nature and the personally faithful lord to him. God's approval was followed by reconfirmation of his covenant:

> … because you have done this and have not withheld your son, your only son, I will surely bless you and make your descendants as numerous as the stars in the sky and as the sand on the seashore. Your descendants will take possession of the cities of their enemies, and through your offspring all nations on earth will be blessed, because you have obeyed me. (22:15-18)

It is notable that this passage mentions "because" twice: "because you have done" and "because you have obeyed me." With Abraham's faith that worked in action, Isaac was "reborn" and became the assurance of the coming great nation. Later James, in the New Testament, visits this episode to prove the theology that faith includes obedient action.

The covenantal nature of faith

God used the covenant as the means of salvation throughout the Bible. The covenant is like a string that includes many beads to form a single necklace. It organizes all ordinances, human figures, and institutions in such a way that all are directed toward the completion of God's Kingdom in Jesus Christ. A covenant is a contract which both parties must faithfully keep in order to achieve the intended consequence. In order to faithfully keep the covenant, the lesser party, Abraham and his children, needed to trust the greater party, God. The covenant history began when God made the covenant with Abraham and formed faith in him. Faith is trusting God and his covenant. Abraham was called as an individual, but he was chosen to become the foundation, the Patriarch, and the father of all nations. As God's covenant anticipated the coming of his great nation in the future, his covenant extended from Abraham to his descendants. Therefore, God's name is characterized by his faithfulness throughout generations: "I am the God of your father, the God of Abraham, the God of Isaac and the God of Jacob" (Ex. 3:6). The birth of Isaac as an offspring of old Abraham was a critical condition for the coming nation. As the covenant extended from Abraham, so faith followed after his faith.

Faith is believers' response to God's covenant, a genuine response in real-life situations, as we have seen in Abraham's long episode. The declaration of Abram's faith in Genesis 15:6, "Abram believed the Lord, and he credited it to him as righteousness," reflects his faith as a whole. It is not Abram's one-time response to a particular promise of God at a particular time, but his general response to God. To this faith of Abram, God responded through the ritual of confirming his covenant. Abram's faith, as a whole, was neither pure nor consistent in practice to be reckoned by God as righteous. Abram left his pagan culture in obedience, but his journey was continuously characterized by struggles between trust and distrust, as the long episode reveals. What matters in God's approval of his faith is how God reckoned his faith, not how successfully Abram believed. The point of the text "he [God] credited it to him as righteousness" is God's long-suffering grace that considered his faith acceptable, though it was not proved true in reality; and based on that consideration, God determined him as righteous. God does not determine salvation based on the test of sinners' faith; instead, out of his grace, he calls and declares their salvation and then matures their faith. God's grace reminds us of our sinful status that cannot by itself reach up to God. The author of Genesis continuously reminds the readers of the advancing age of the already old couple and her barrenness. It is his tool to highlight God's gracious faithfulness to his promise despite the impossible human condition. It was not Abraham's work of circumcision either that made him righteous, for the circumcision instruction was given after the proclamation of his faith. Circumcision is a sign of his being one of God's people. The episode does not show that Abraham and Sarah pretended to have good faith. It narrates shameful stories of struggles, conflicts, and doubts that included his and Sarah's laughing at God's promise. Their responses to God were transparent. The response that God expects from his people is genuine, voluntary faith, not great or successful faith. For faith is not a human accomplishment, but God's gift to humble, broken-hearted people. This theology of faith will guide the whole history of salvation in the Bible, as revealed by Paul in the New Testament.

As the covenant continued from Abraham to his descendants, they were to maintain the covenantal nature of faith in their living:

> Abraham will surely become a great and powerful nation, and all nations on earth will be blessed through him. For I have chosen him, so that he will direct his children and his household after him to keep the way of the Lord by doing what is right and just, so that the Lord will bring about for Abraham what he has promised him. (Gen. 18:18-19)

Some significant characteristics of the covenant can be gleaned from this passage. First, the covenant functioned in a communal and progressive way. As the covenant came with a promise, the covenantal relationship between God and his people would continue through the generations from Abraham. The scope of Abraham's descendants extends beyond racial backgrounds to include all peoples. With this comprehensive aim of the covenant, Israel was chosen to be the light for all nations. Second, though the covenant was made out of God's sheer grace and was a contract, it required a proper response from the recipients. The proper response was faith, trusting God's promise. Faith means a wholistic faithfulness, not simply religious or spiritual loyalty, and thus it requires conforming actions in life. The extension of the covenant involved Abraham's directing his children to "keep the way of the Lord by doing what is right and just." That God required faithful living of his covenant people from the beginning of salvation history proves that the tension between faith and action is misplaced. Conforming actions are not the mere consequence of salvation, but an integral aspect of faith that saves. Faith expresses itself by an obedient life.

Reflection

We have seen God's use of the covenant for the purpose of establishing his people. The covenant set the stage for salvation, which determined the way God treated his people and the nature of faith God demanded of his people. God's covenant provided humanity with a reality of the world that was totally different from Abraham's and Sarah's early understanding. Assuming faith, that is trusting his covenant promise in the challenging situation, was not automatic. Growing in faith is not like miraculously replacing unbelieving parts in the human heart with genuine heavenly parts. God never forced Abraham and Sarah to have faith against their will; instead, he guided them in personal ways in the covenantal relationship. In return, God required them to have genuine, transparent faith. Maturing faith is like taking a journey with God—learning the way of walking in trust and experiencing gradual fulfillment of his promise that transforms our whole person. What characterized their life before God the most was their faith in God's mystery. They did not know the reason God chose them or treated them as he did. Faith is not based on knowledge, though knowledge supports faith. What made Abraham and Sarah the foundation of God's people is God's faithfulness to his covenant. The faithfulness of God in humanly impossible situations makes us humble before God and gives us comfort for now and hope for the future. As God called him when he was a typical sinner, so God is calling us as who we are. As God worked for Abraham faithfully in his actual life situations, so God works faithfully in our lives.

Discussion Questions:

1. Why do you think God uses a covenant to save his people?
2. Why did God choose a man like Abraham?
3. What does God demand from Abraham?
4. How much time is passing in the story of Abraham? Why is this significant?

CHAPTER 9

Exodus: liberation as the beginning of Israel

The book of Exodus takes a significant place in redemptive history in that it provides a paradigm of the nature of salvation, which will be progressively unfolded. Exodus shows how God, then the God of the Hebrew people, proved his universal lordship in the international setting and consequently delivered Israel out of bondage to the evil lord and shaped them as his people. The main theme of Exodus is repeatedly found in God's claim that both Egyptians and Israelites will know "that I am the Lord." God's lordship directly relates to the liberation of his people. From the time of the exodus, liberation became a significant subject in the Bible as the meaning of salvation. God heard the prayers of the oppressed, isolated, and helpless people and came down to save. In the context of liberating his people, God was known as Yahweh, who relates to his people as he faithfully keeps his covenant. The faithfulness of God is a significant aspect of God's plan for salvation since God uses a covenant, which is a promise, as its means. In such a context of salvation, both parties, namely God and Abraham's descendants, are required to remain faithful to the covenant. However, the life situations of Israel were not favorable for maintaining faithfulness.

The narrative of the exodus itself and the subsequent movement of Israel to the wilderness is to be read from the perspective of covenantal faithfulness in which God fulfilled his promise made to Abraham. Salvation began with liberation and proceeded to shaping Israel as God's people. The liberation left the people with another challenge: they were led away from the short-cut highway and into the wilderness, where there was no support for life. How would they live as God's free people in the wilderness? This question raises issues as to the nature of liberation and the use of the law for Israel.

The context of the Israelites in Egypt at the beginning of Exodus lays the pagan background to underscore how the God of Israel competed with the pagan gods and came to be known to all. Politically and economically, the Israelites were one of the minor slave tribes in the great empire. Culturally and religiously, they maintained a subculture within the prevalent polytheistic culture, and their God was known only within their community, practically a minor deity of the slaves among many prominent gods in the empire. Having lived in the polytheistic culture for generations, many Israelites probably had absorbed the pagan religion. Within this politically and religiously oppressed context of the Israelites, God came to be known to them as the God faithful to his promise and as the true Lord to Egyptians.

The story of Exodus begins with the proliferation of the Hebrews in Egypt. When the Pharaoh, the king of Egypt, who did not know Joseph, came to the throne, he considered the Hebrews a threat and oppressed them. He commanded the midwives to kill any baby boys that were born among the Hebrews by throwing them into the Nile River. The Israelites, named after the patriarch Jacob, whose name was changed to Israel, cried out to the God of their ancestors. God "heard their groaning, and he remembered his covenant with Abraham, with Isaac and with Jacob: "So God looked on the Israelites and was concerned about them" (2:24-25). The names of God revealed in chapter three must have meant God's vindication of his people and comfort to the Israelites, who suffered under a malicious king: "I am the God of your father, the God of Abraham, the God of Isaac and the God of Jacob" (3:6). This name reminded the Israelites, who had probably lost many of their ancestors, of God's covenant faithfulness. God spoke to Moses: "I am who I am. This is what you are to say to the Israelites: 'I am has sent me to you'" (3:14). This name also signifies a dependable God, faithful to his covenant. Another name with which God is known is the famous title *Lord*: "Say to the Israelites, 'The Lord, the God of your fathers—the God of Abraham, the God of Isaac and the God of Jacob—has sent me to you'" (3:15). The "Lord" is derived from the Hebrew word that means "to be." The title Lord also denotes the unchangeable character of God. The title would be known in the unfolding history of salvation as the relational God, signifying that he is reaching out to his people. God claimed numerous times that his people "will know that I am the Lord." Prior to the liberating acts, which would be provocative, God prepared the Israelites by reminding them of who he is. God's lordship and faithfulness to his covenant motivated them to follow his lead through the exodus journey.

God established Moses as Israel's leader. The story of his birth and deliverance from water anticipates a God-given mission for Israelites. For his name Moses means "to draw out." He was saved out of water to lead God's people through water. God gave him a mission as his representative: to bring judgment upon the Egyptian gods, to lead the Israelites out of Egypt, and eventually to declare to all peoples that he is the true Lord. God's intention was clear from the outset: "I have come down to rescue them from the hand of the Egyptians and to bring them up out of that land into a good and spacious land, a land flowing with milk and honey" (3:8). The land motif is noticeable here and continues from the promise that God made to Abraham. The land motif alludes to God's transfer of his people out of the grip of the evil lord to the service of the true Lord, which would define the meaning of living as God's free people.

The Ten Plagues

The Ten Plagues that eventually led to the exodus began with the Israelite God's demand to Pharaoh to let his people go. Pharaoh did not consider it a serious threat and scornfully replied, "Who is the Lord that I should obey him and let Israel go? I do not know the Lord and I will not let Israel go" (5:2). Now the stage was set for the conflict.

The Ten Plagues suggest that God caused significant difficulties for Egyptians. The first nine plagues were natural disasters, and the last one was the death of firstborn sons of Egyptian families. When we look at the structure of the Ten Plagues, however, we find what the natural disasters were intended for. The first nine plagues were a continuous series, set apart from the tenth plague, which culminated all the previous plagues. The nine plagues were arranged into three sets, with three plagues in each set. Each of the three sets was arranged with a common beginning phrase, as you see in each row in the table below.

Structure of the Ten Plagues			organized by unique opening phrases
1. Water turns to blood (7:14-)	4. Land swarms with flies (8:20-)	7. Hail destroys crops (9:13-)	"Go to Pharaoh, in the morning, to the water"
2. Frogs leave water and cover land (8:1-)	5. Livestock in field die of plague (9:1-)	8. Locusts devour all that is left (10:1-)	"Go to Pharaoh"
3. Land is filled with mosquitoes or gnats (8:16-)	6. Boils cover man and beast (9:8-)	9. Thick darkness covers the land (10:21-)	Description of action

The first set is composed of the first, fourth, and seventh plagues, which are described with a common beginning phrase, "go to Pharaoh, in the morning, to the water." The second set, the second, fifth, and eighth plagues, share a common phrase, "go to pharaoh," without mentioning when and where. The third set of plagues are the third, sixth, and ninth plagues. In each case, there is no mention of any of the above, but Moses and Aaron were called to make a gesture to start the plague. For example, in the ninth plague, God commanded Moses to stretch his hand toward the sky to have darkness cover Egypt for three days. While the Egyptians suffered in thick darkness, the text reveals that the Israelites had light in their dwelling places. Many times the plagues did not touch the Israelites because God was protecting his people.

This structure highlights the beginning and the last, the first and the ninth plagues. The first plague changed all waters in Egypt into blood, including the Nile River. The Nile was an indispensable source for Egyptian prosperity, for it provided abundant water for agriculture and an efficient way of transportation. When the water of the Nile turned to blood, it became the source of death. The ninth plague covered the sun for full three days. Since the sun was another significant source for Egyptian prosperity, life without sun light caused tremendous difficulties in Egypt. Both plagues meant tremendous natural and economic disaster to Egyptians and, thus, must have challenged Pharaoh's power. However, in the structure mentioned above, which reflected the Egyptian religious culture, the two plagues were intended to point beyond the natural disasters to the gods that the Nile and the sun represented. Egyptian culture was highly idolatrous, with many gods in the forms of animals and celestial objects. The nine plagues are directed to the diverse gods of Egypt. Of all gods Egyptians worshipped, two major gods were the sun god, Ra, and the Nile god, Happi. From this religious standpoint, each of the natural disasters represented God's challenge to one of the Egyptian gods.

The Ten Plagues were structured in such a way as to reveal God gradually intensifying his blows to the gods of Egypt in his appointed times, to the culmination in the death of Pharaoh's firstborn son. Pharaoh was considered a representative of gods on earth. The firstborn son of Pharaoh would be a god of Egypt. The last plague brought the ultimate blow to the Egyptian gods. The message of the Ten Plagues was that the God of the Israelite slaves had judged the prominent gods of pagan Egypt, and consequently, he had proved himself to be the true lord over all creation. Now the God of Israel revealed himself internationally in the great Egyptian empire. This aim of the Ten Plagues was set when God sent Moses and Aaron to Pharaoh:

> You are to say everything I command you, and your brother Aaron is to tell Pharaoh to let the Israelites go out of his country. But I will harden Pharaoh's heart, and though I multiply my miraculous signs and wonders in Egypt, he will not listen to you. Then I will lay my hand on Egypt and with mighty acts of judgment I will bring out my divisions, my people the Israelites. And the Egyptians will know that I am the Lord when I stretch out my hand against Egypt and bring the Israelites out of it. (7:2-5)

God did all these acts that were foretold in this text and proved his absolute lordship in Egypt. God's mighty acts were characterized by his controlling Pharaoh's heart, by his "acts of judgment" on the Egyptian gods, and by his governing authority over the nature. Each plague demonstrated his lordship over each aspect of creation—from the waters, to the animals, to the weather, and to humans. Many of these natural objects represented deity in Egyptian religion, so God's bringing disasters by using them was meant to be a challenge to the Egyptian gods. The Ten Plagues reflect the creation account in that the God of Israel was the Creator God. God claimed, while sending the plague of hail, "[that] I might show you my power and that my name might be proclaimed in all the earth… so you may know that the earth is the Lord's" (9:16, 29). All God's mighty acts were directed to the culmination that the Creator God had judged the Egyptian gods (12:12), as a lesson to Israelites—"then you will know that I am the Lord your God" (6:7)—and the same lesson to Egyptians—"the Egyptians will know that I am the Lord" (14:4,18).

The God of Israel was once known as the Lord to Egyptians—during the years of Joseph. Genesis chapter 41 describes the episode in which he was summoned by Pharaoh to interpret Pharaoh's dreams. Joseph was then a young Hebrew slave imprisoned in the dungeon. It was very unusual for Pharaoh to summon a young slave to ask question about his dream, for he himself was considered divine, and he had many wise and powerful men around him. Imagine the scene of Pharaoh's palace when a young Hebrew man stood before Pharaoh, surrounded by many wise men. The story implicitly contrasts the lowly young Israelite man to the high, pagan Pharaoh, which anticipates a certain dramatic consequence, as does the conflict between Moses and Pharaoh at the outbreak of the Ten Plagues. Joseph interpreted Pharaoh's dream and suggested storing some of harvested grain during the seven years of abundance—to be used for the seven years of famine that would follow. Pharaoh and his men welcomed his suggestion: "The plan seemed good to Pharaoh and to all his officials. So Pharaoh asked them, 'can we find anyone like this man, one in whom is the spirit of God? [There] is no one so discerning and wise as you'" (41:37-38). And he appointed Joseph to a high position, right below himself, to take care of the harvest of all Egypt. Then came seven years of abundant harvest, followed by seven years of famine, as Joseph had predicted. When famine hit all the lands and people suffered, Egyptians had food. Now, the point of the episode is that Pharaoh and his wise men trusted Joseph's interpretation of the dream and considered his suggestion so wise that they believed he must have "the spirit of God." Does this make sense? Isn't it common sense to save some for the days of trouble?

The common sense according to the Egyptian religion was fatalism. They believed gods rule over humans by determining their fortune and misfortune. When gods willed famine, humans had no other option but to perish. Against the pagan fatalistic wisdom, Joseph presented a different wisdom for life. His wisdom came from his God, who not only knows but also governs all, including Egypt. Joseph's interpretation of

Pharaoh's dreams was nothing but his informing Pharoah of God's message. Joseph served as God's messenger to Pharaoh: "It is just as I said to Pharaoh: God has shown Pharaoh what he is about to do" (41:28). The Pharaoh accepted the way of living that the God of Israel offered; as a result, God saved many thousands of Egyptian lives.

Both Joseph's episode and the Ten Plagues, which worked publicly, ended with the sovereign lordship of the Israelite God, which was contrary to the expectation of the main culture of Egypt. The former left a consequence of saving Egyptians' lives when Pharaoh accepted God's will, and the latter, devastating destruction when he refused. Together, the stories teach us the all-embracing nature of God's lordship. The God of Israel is not a tribal god, but the God and Lord over all, who was first known to Israel and progressively to all. Though in the Bible we find God in conflict with pagan peoples, such as in Egypt, in the Promised Land and in a number of empires during Israel's exile, God was not simply saving Israel from the threats of other nations. Rather, he was progressively revealing himself as the Lord over all nations, either by saving and incorporating some of them into his people or using them as tools to discipline and shape his people for service. God's dealing with the nations proved that God is at work to fulfill his promise of shaping his people, beginning with Abraham and Israel and extending to all nations.

Passover

The tenth plague occasioned the Passover of the Israelites. The term Passover came from the occasion when God destroyed the firstborns of Egypt but passed over Israelite families and saved them. Blood was the sign of the Passover. For the night the tenth plague struck, God called the Israelites to prepare a "Passover sacrifice" to the Lord from sheep or goats, then spread its blood over their door frames so that God's destructive power would pass over them. The Passover points to the ultimate Passover occurrence, Jesus Christ. As the blood of the sacrifice animal served as the sign for Israelites' redemption, all God's people would be redeemed by the blood of Jesus, who is the fulfillment of the sign. Jesus' last meal with his disciples, arrest, trial, and execution on the cross all took place during the Passover feast. Because the Passover set the decisive nature of salvation, God made it a lasting feast so that all Israelites throughout generations would remember how God had saved them out of Egypt. For the same reason, God commanded them to arrange their calendar with the Passover as beginning: "The month is to be for you the first month, the first month of your year" (12:2). And the Exodus deliverance would become a prelude to the law, which stipulated the mode of life for God's people.

Exodus is rich in images that delineate the meaning of salvation. While the blood of the paschal sacrifice discloses God's saving grace, the water image reflects his power in his saving actions. Water signifies a destructive power in many parts of the Bible. In the creation account, God separated waters, and he set their limit and made the dry land. God drew Moses out of water and established him as a leader to lead his people through the Red Sea. God's creational authority reveals itself in his salvific actions. God turned the sea "into dry land. He divided the waters, and the Israelites went through the sea on dry ground" while the Egyptians were destroyed when God brought the waters back together (14:21-22). Paul, in the New Testament, interprets the deliverance in the Red Sea to point to baptism in Christ: "They were all baptized into Moses in the cloud and in the sea" (1 Cor. 10:2). As they submitted to Moses as the leader and were saved from the evil power, all God's people are united in submission to Christ and are saved.

In the wilderness

Liberation is described in Exodus as both a consequence of God's powerful victory against evil lords and his tender care for his people in their most vulnerable situation. In the prelude to giving his law, God said to his people, "You yourselves have seen what I did to Egypt, and how I carried you on eagles' wings and brought you to myself" (19:4). The image of God here as mother eagle, described in an unusual feminine form, reinforces the idea of God's loving care. God's loving care includes his acts to mature Israel in the wilderness, as reflected in Deuteronomy 32:10-11. Like the mother eagle, who stirs the nest and drops her youngsters to teach them to fly, but also gets ready to catch them on her wings when they fail, God guided Israel in the wilderness.

The Israelites were politically and economically free in the wilderness. Would the newly achieved freedom be of any value in the wilderness, where there was no support of life whatsoever? This situation questions the nature of freedom. The ex-slaves were set free from their former bondage. But the freedom they achieved as a whole was defined by God's moving them out of service of the evil lords and into service of the true Lord. Soon in the wilderness, Israel would receive God's law that stipulated their worship of God. As was alluded to above, the transposition of people is a necessary course for salvation. Moving in terms of space, earlier for Abraham and Sarah from Ur to the place God led, and for Israel from Egypt to the wilderness, motivates a change of their hearts and a resetting of their object of worship. This cause of freedom was made manifest in God's command to Pharaoh: "Let my people go, so that they may worship me in the desert" (7:16). They were now free to live in a way that obeyed God for the great deliverance he had brought to them. With this freedom, they not only become God's people but also become truly human. Humans would not be free in an absolute sense. As created beings, their true happiness would lie in the way the Creator set for them.

How would they live as God's free people in the wilderness? This question asks why God led them there. Why did not God, who destroyed the mighty Egyptians, lead the Israelites directly to the Promised Land through the highway? The wilderness was situated between the exodus out of Egypt and the Promised Land. The wilderness experience was a transition for Israel. God chose the wilderness as his "school" to form them into his people by assuring them of his divine faithfulness and protecting them as his people. God provided manna and meat from the air and water from a rock. Throughout the journey in the wilderness, their clothes were not worn out. In the wilderness they were to learn to live by trusting God, by obeying his law. Trusting God, Moses reminded the Israelites of God's objective for their wilderness experience:

> He humbled you… to teach you that man does not live on bread alone but on every word that comes from the mouth of the Lord…. Know then in your heart that as a man disciplines his son, so the Lord your God disciplines you. (Deut. 8:3-5)

The Israelites wandered in the wilderness for forty years, which symbolizes a full period of time. Did they learn the lesson that God intended to teach? The Bible tells the story that many perished in the wilderness because of their grumbling and disobedience, and only two men of that generation survived and entered the Promised Land. Israel's wandering in the wilderness underscores God's long-suffering faithfulness even to unfaithful Israel.

Reflection

This book suggests a recurring paradigm of God's seven acts of deliverance that are found in the Bible: God calls and moves his people, puts them back in the pagan culture where he struggles with evil gods and proves himself as the true Lord, saves his people from the bondage of the evil deity, and shapes them into his people. This paradigm of salvific acts shows we are on the road as pilgrims, the road to find our own identity in God's kingdom. After our first human ancestors committed sin before God, they hid themselves from his presence and were banished from Eden. From that time on, humans are on the road till they reach their true home. The physical journeys in the Old Testament suggest a process of spiritual renewal and maturation. Moving his people through pagan, challenging situations, God demands conversion of their hearts, through which they become assured of his faithfulness, live by trusting his Word, and eventually become part of God's mission in the world. The book of Hebrews in the New Testament teaches the nature of pilgrimage:

> By faith Abraham… obeyed and went, even though he did not know where he was going. By faith he made his home in the promised land like a stranger in a foreign country…. For he was looking forward to

the city with foundations.... And they admitted that they were aliens and strangers on earth. (Heb. 11:8-14)

God saves his people by liberating sinful humans from evil bondage and by placing them in the maturing process. God judged that the wilderness experience was necessary in order for the Hebrew ex-slaves to be shaped as God's people—to be cleansed of the pagan sediment in which they had lived for generations and to learn the godly way of living. The wilderness, where there was nothing to rely on, was the perfect place for the cause.

In humanity's journey to full salvation, the book of Exodus occupies a significant place. We can learn a spiritual lesson from its similarity to the present situation. Believers today have been delivered through the blood of the ultimate paschal lamb, Jesus Christ, and set free from bondage to the evil lord. Believers are God's free people in his kingdom, but they are still in the process between deliverance and entering the ultimate Promised Land, the New Heaven and New Earth. In that sense they are still in the wilderness. As God continued to provide food and water for the Israelites, he is still providing all the necessary things for his people. As the Israelites were to learn to live by trusting God's Word, believers are to learn the same, by trusting God's Word, revealed in the Bible. Believers are in the school of the Holy Spirit to be formed into God's people and to learn to exercise the newly achieved freedom to serve God in a genuine and voluntary spirit. Though believers are in a similar spiritual progress, their present status is significantly different from that of the Israelites in that what the Israelites were unable to keep has been fulfilled by Christ for believers. In Christ, believers are considered faithful people of God, as if they have kept God's Word. However, Christ's obedience, which was transferred to believers, does not waive believers' responsibility to obey God's Word, but rather reinforces it by empowering them to do so. For they are now empowered by the new life. The manna was a sign of the true food that was offered to believers in Christ. Christ is given to believers as the "Bread of life," and his flesh is "real food" and his blood is "real drink," in his own words.

Discussion Questions:

1. God's leading his people to and from pagan cultures suggests his leading them on a spiritual journey. How does God lead your spiritual journey?
2. Exodus shows God's liberating act for his people. How does God set his people free today?
3. What do the names of God found in Exodus mean to you today?

Chapter 10

Covenant and law: the means of salvation

How would the Israelites live in the wilderness as God's free people? By keeping the law! In the wilderness, God proceeded to shape the recently saved Israel as his people. He gave his law to consecrate them and fulfil his covenantal relationship with them, which eventually would be phrased, "I will be your God, and you will be my people." Paul said, in the New Testament, that God added the law to the covenant to make a relationship with his people possible. By making a covenant, God elected his people; by requiring obedience to his law, he shaped them into his people. It is important to see the *missio dei* of God's establishing his people in his world from the covenantal perspective.

The covenant

In the preface to giving the law, Moses reminded Israel that their God was a loving God, who faithfully kept his covenant:

> But it was because the Lord loved you and kept the oath he swore to our forefathers that he brought you out with a mighty hand and redeemed you from the land of slavery, from the power of Pharaoh king of Egypt. Know therefore that the Lord your God is God; he is the faithful God, keeping his covenant love to a thousand generations of those who love him and keep his commands. (Deut. 7:8-9)

When Israel was facing a new challenge in the wilderness, knowing God as faithful to his promise was much needed. They were supposed to live by trusting God's promises and not by what they could see. Their challenge was to adopt a new perspective of seeing reality. How could they adopt the new perspective? By trusting the promise that their God made to them. God's gracious love is first manifested in his making a covenant with unmerited people and continuously enacting it through his faithful acts.

The covenant is the means that God uses to accomplish his plan of salvation. In the ancient Near Eastern culture, a covenant served as a binding contract between two parties. It worked when both parties kept it faithfully. In the Bible, the covenant was formulated in such a way that

God, as the King, announced his solemn oath to his people. The covenant ritual described in Genesis 17 shows the reciprocal nature of the God-initiated covenant: "As for me, this is my covenant with you. You will be the father of many nations... [;] as for you, you must keep my covenant, you and your descendants after you for the generations to come.... Every male among you shall be circumcised" (3-10). Faithfulness of both parties was the required key for the working of the covenant. Faithfulness from God's side was to keep his promise, and from the people's side, obedience to God. God chose his people and made his covenant with them unconditionally, out of his sheer grace, and promised to be faithful to the covenant promises. However, the covenant works neither automatically nor unilaterally, for a covenant demands faithfulness of both parties.

The covenantal relationship that God made with his people reflects the initial grace of the Creator God that is manifest in the creation account. The divine grace is highlighted by its stark contrast to the pagan narratives of creation and covenant. According to some popular pagan creation accounts, gods made only kings in their image and then made ordinary humans to serve kings. Within the creational context, god's covenant relationship with his people was to extract their service and nourishment. In the Christian Bible, God created all humans in his image and commissioned them to rule over his world, signifying that all humans were made as kings. The covenant reveals the Creator's will to reverse the effect of sin and restore humans to their original status.

The covenant established a special relationship. The covenant "I will make you into a great nation" was initially realized by the exodus experience and further throughout the history of salvation. God shaped Israel as "a kingdom of priests and a holy nation" (Ex. 19:5-6) and "his treasured possession" out of many nations (Deut. 7:6). The covenantal relationship became settled in the popular epithet "you will be my people, and I will be your God" (Jer. 30:22). The sense of belonging was a great gift to the people in challenging situations.

However, the mutual faithfulness was not, in fact, realized as it was expected. The twist, caused by human incapability of fulfilling the mutual faithfulness, makes the whole point of the gospel. God's unswerving commitment to covenant faithfulness satisfied the requirement even to the point of satisfying the requirement of the unfaithful disobedient people. The continuous enacting of God's gracious faithfulness had shaped Israel's relationship to God in his covenant love; otherwise, it could have been simply a legal relationship. The covenant love that was kept by God reminded Israel of God's faithfulness when they were wandering in the wilderness, struggling in the Promised Land surrounded by pagan neighbors, exiled in judgment among the empires, and waiting for the Messiah for hundreds of years. Covenant love continuously comforted the people and nourished the hope of restoration to the lost and oppressed people.

In the Old Testament we find generally four covenants:

> The Noahic covenant (Gen. 9): God made a covenant with Noah, his family and descendants, and with all living creatures, not to destroy the world with waters; the whole world is in view.
>
> The Abrahamic covenant (Gen. 15, 17): God made a covenant with Abraham and his descendants to establish his people on his foundation; this covenant came with promises of descendants and land.
>
> The Sinai covenant (Ex. 19-24): God made a covenant of law with Israel to maintain the covenantal relationship; the promise came with the condition of keeping the law; later this covenant of law became renewed as the new covenant because of Israel's disobedient heart (Jer. 31:31-33).
>
> The Davidic covenant (2 Sam. 23:5): God made an "everlasting covenant" with David regarding the kingly reign in Israel.

The diversity of covenants implies not different kinds of covenants used by God, but instead, one plan of salvation applied in different modes in the progressively unfolding history of salvation. The unity of the covenant and one people of God continues in the history of salvation. Each covenant is to be read within the historical context as part of the integrated working of salvation. The Noahic covenant, "Never again will all life be cut off by the waters," God made with Noah, humanity, living creatures, and even the earth. It was made as an "eternal covenant" (Gen. 9:8-16). The Creator God un-created the earth due to human sin and re-created it, analogous to his original creation. God sees the original created world as the prototype of his re-creation. After the flood waters receded, God maintained his original purposes of the creation, while allowing some changes to be made in human relations to the world. The Noahic covenant anticipated the nature and scope of salvation that would come true in later times—cosmic salvation after judgment on sin in the world. While the Noahic covenant set the nature of future salvation in terms of its correlation to creation, the Abrahamic covenant set out to achieve such salvation in concrete history with one person. With the election of one person, God began to establish his people in his world. The Abrahamic covenant extended down through his family and was initially realized by the exodus of Israel. God added the covenant of law as the means of consecrating Israel and shaping them into his people. The Davidic covenant came into being to fulfill the promise of Israel by enforcing the law. What God needed, in order to achieve the promise of his people, was a faithful Israel, the true descendants of Abraham. But Israel proved to be unfaithful. God's commitment to covenant faithfulness provided the answer to the deadlock of the salvation plan.

God's covenant faithfulness eventually directed his people to Jesus Christ. Christ came as the new Israel, coming from the line of king David, and faithfully obeyed the law and thus fulfilled the covenantal relationship. Justification (being declared to be just) is based on righteousness (being right with God). And righteousness is determined by full obedience to the law. Christ did not replace the law requirement with faith for the way of salvation, as if assuming opposition between faith and law. Rather, Christ carried out the Old Testament plan of salvation—satisfying the requirement of the law and fulfilling the covenant promise, eventually to achieve salvation through faith for the new Israel. The new Israel is composed of all believers, who are united with Christ in faith—thus fulfilling the covenant that God would establish with his people, out of all nations, on the foundation of Abraham. When penitent sinners receive Jesus as Christ, their sins are forgiven, and they become considered righteous, as people of the new Israel. They inherit the blessings that God promised to Abraham since they are the true descendants of him.

Christ's new Israel also fulfills the promise made to Noah. Christ reconciles all things of the world to himself and uses his redeemed people as ambassadors to achieve cosmic reconciliation. The new humans, born-again into new life, are committed to the new lifestyle of obedient ruling over the world. The one plan of God's salvation to establish one people of God is achieved by Christ's obedient fulfillment of God's covenant.

Law

Israel's knowing their God motivated their keeping his law:

> You yourselves have seen what I did to Egypt, and how I carried you on eagles' wings and brought you to myself. Now if you obey me fully and keep my covenant, then out of all nations you will be my treasured possession. Although the whole earth is mine, you will be for me a kingdom of priests and a holy nation." (Ex. 19:4-6)

God begins the preface of the law with the reminder that he, as the powerful and gracious God, is the lawgiver, as was proved in their past experiences. The renewed knowledge of God was necessary for the Israelites to obey his law. It is so, in the theological sense that the law reflects God's nature, but more so, in the pastoral situation of Israel in the wilderness. The "covenant" in the text means the covenant law that Israel must obey. As we have discussed above, the law was given in the initial overarching context of the Abrahamic covenant as a means to achieve its goal. Paul summarizes the purpose of the law in terms of covenant achievement:

> The law, introduced 430 years later, does not set aside the covenant previously established by God and thus do away with the promise.

> For if the inheritance depends on the law, then it no longer depends on a promise; but God in his grace gave it to Abraham through a promise. What, then, was the purpose of the law? It was added because of transgressions until the Seed to whom the promise referred had come." (Gal. 3:17-19)

Paul emphasizes that God made the Abrahamic covenant as the foundation of salvation, to which the law was added 430 years later. The point is that Abraham was chosen as the father of God's people without keeping the law. Abraham and his children were commanded to be circumcised—a requirement of the law. However, it was done as a "sign of the covenant" (Gen. 17:11). Grace precedes and inspires the use of the law. The law serves as the regulating principle to maintain and mature the people's covenantal relationship with God. By keeping the law, Israel was to show their loyalty to God, and God would know, by it, that they were his people. Israel responded, "We will do everything the Lord has said" (19:8). With this agreement the covenant of law was sealed.

The law is a legal matter that depends on satisfying the conditions, as is cited from Exodus 19: "If you obey me fully and keep my covenant, then out of all nations you will be my treasured possession." The description of blessings and curses incurred, depending on obedience and disobedience respectively, in Deuteronomy 28, shows that the law requirement was a serious matter to Israel. A comment is needed on the reason for the law's legal nature. God delivered Israel from Egypt out of his sheer grace. After that, is he now demanding legal requirements from Israel to keep them as his people? The pattern of God's shaping his people is that grace precedes obedience. The law requirement does not mean that God's commitment to save Israel depends on their obedience, but that God demands their obedience as response to his covenant love. God is saying to Israel, "Since you are my people, you are to live as my people." The conviction of God's gracious love inspires the grateful response of obedience. Law obedience is not a legalistic obedience, as if the object of obedience is contained in the law. The law serves as a means for obeying the Lord. The preface to the law clarifies that law obedience is a personal matter: "Obey me fully and keep my covenant." In the personal and relational nature of this agreement is captured the very fundamental nature of worshipping God—obedient acts out of a worshipping heart. Later, when Israel continued to disobey, God re-established the law in their minds and hearts:

> The time is coming... when I will make a new covenant... [;] it will not be like the covenant I made with their forefathers... [;] because they broke my covenant... I will put my law in their minds and write it on their hearts. I will be their God, and they will be my people." (Jer. 31:31-33)

The change from the written law on the stone tablets to the engraved law in the heart does not imply changing modes of law, but instead highlights the nature of true obedience.

The law governed all aspects of Israel's life. The law-abiding life was for ordinary daily living, not limited to so-called religious realms. The law of Israel was quite unique in that while the divine laws in pagan religions were restricted to religious laws defining worship, the laws of Israel defined all aspects of life, both the spiritual and the mundane. There were various types of law in Israel: ritual law (regulations on religious worship), moral law (the Ten Commandments, regulating daily moral acts), and civic law (regulations on everyday social life). While the ritual law pertained to administration of spiritual purity and sacrifices, civil and moral laws prescribed Israel's daily living.

Leviticus 19 illustrates various laws that were introduced by God's holiness: "Be holy because I, the Lord your God, am holy" (v. 2). The holy life is ordinary life lived with justice and love. God's law commanded Israel to live ordinary life for the extraordinary worshipping of God. For example, when harvesting, they were to leave edges of their field ungleaned for the poor and foreigners. They were not to hate or seek revenge against their people, but to "love your neighbor as yourself." They were to treat a foreigner as their own countryman and "love him as yourself" and to "use honest scales and honest weights." These are examples of moral and civic laws. Exodus prescribes more examples of civil law: "Do not mistreat an alien or oppress him… [;] do not take advantage of a widow or an orphan [;] if you lend money to one of my people… charge him no interest. If you take your neighbor's cloak as a pledge, return it to him by sunset" (22:21-26).

The law demanded that all people be allowed to live with human dignity; it required God's people to pay special attention to the socially vulnerable people, such as the poor, widows and orphans, and foreigners. Some regulations were made within the androcentric and oppressive social system of the ancient periods. The status of women and slaves are such examples. Even within such an oppressive ancient system, some devices for human dignity were prepared, unlike the pagan legal codes. The law requirement of love and justice was prominent in the Ten Commandments, an example of moral law. While the first four commandments prescribed Israel's worship, the rest prescribed their everyday life.

Several laws imply negative connotations as to the use of the law. Such ideas may be formed because of its use in accusing sinners (Rom. 3:20), in expressing salvation in the form of keeping the law, and in Christ's and Paul's opposition to the legalist attitude of keeping it. The former two uses of the law were enacted "accidentally" to serve an original and primary purpose. Paul talks about the accidental function of the law: "I found that the very commandment that was intended to bring life actually brought death" (Rom. 7:10). The purpose of the law, being "holy, righteous, and good" (Rom. 7:12), reflecting God's own nature, was to shape Israel into his people, to which Paul refers as "to bring life." Law cannot tolerate, but judges, disobedient Israel, which Paul refers to as "death." Pau's juxtaposition of the intended purpose of the law and its actual outcome presupposes the primary positive use of it. The criticism of the legalist observation was directed to a misunderstanding and misuse of it.

Christ himself attests to the law's complementary role for salvation: "I have not come to abolish them (the Law and the Prophets) but to fulfill them" (Matt. 5:17. See also Rom. 3:31). Christ obeyed the law and prepared the way for believers to become righteous. In the sense of accomplishing the requirement of the law, "Christ is the end of the law so that there may be righteousness for everyone who believes" (Rom. 10:4). And Christ, in Matthew 5, reinterpreted the moral requirements and demanded believers to obey them. And he even commanded them to be morally perfect, citing from Leviticus, "Be perfect, therefore, as your heavenly Father is perfect" (Matt. 5:48).

What is law for the Christian life? Calvin understood it from its primary positive use: "I understand by the word 'law' not only the Ten Commandments, which set forth a godly and righteous rule of living, but the *form of religion* handed down by God through Moses."[1] The law established a comprehensive norm of human life for Israel, in which were found provisions for her moral, religious, and social life. Because of its normativity, it served as both the means and the goal for shaping Israel into his people. In this primary use of the law, we can see that the laws are not God's random rules to restrict his people's religious life or make them busy with certain activities. Specific actions and provisions that the law stipulated derived from God's good nature and will to accomplish the covenant promise. Thus, the law incited voluntary obedience directed to the Lawgiver himself, rather than grudging obedience. The issue of keeping the law was not if one acted it out or not, but if one obeyed the Lawgiver or not. It forbade legalistic outward submission out of duty. Psalm 119 shows a comprehensive picture of living with the law. These verbs are used to describe the attitude of obeying the law in the first 16 verses: "seek him, follow his ways… [;] consider all your commands…. I will praise you…. I learn your righteous laws…. I will obey your decrees…. I seek you with all my heart…. I rejoice in following your statutes…. I meditate on your precepts and consider your ways…. I delight in your decrees." It is noteworthy that the author speaks directly to the Lawgiver himself when meditating the laws. Through obeying the law, God's people were seeking him and praising him. Obeying the law meant obeying God: "You are good, and what you do is good; teach me your decrees…. The law from your mouth is more precious to me than thousands of pieces of silver and gold" (vv. 68-72). The pious attitude toward obeying the law pointed to its deepest form: "Oh, how I love your law! I meditate on it all day long" (v. 97).

Christ, who fulfilled the Old Testament law, gave his people the "law of Christ": "Carry each other's burdens, and in this way you will fulfill the law of Christ" (Gal. 6:2). Christ is not commanding a new burden, but a mode of Christian life. Love fulfills the law—love for God and for neighbors.

Reflection

Keeping the law is fundamentally a matter of the heart that works in action. In the books of the Prophets, God did not pour his wrath on Israel because they neglected details of religious laws. Their major sin was religious hypocrisy: while keeping religious laws, they were actually living far away from God in their hearts and committing injustice in life. The heart aspect of keeping the law—the matter of loving God—had long been neglected in the history of Israel. Then religion became a callous ritual and a selfish means to maintain the status quo in society. After judgment was poured out, God restored Israel with the new covenant in their hearts. Unfortunately, present Christians have not learned from Israel. Without proper understanding of how the law works, people see it simply as a burden that accuses consciences, obstructs otherwise happy lives, and shackles otherwise free lives. When you fail to obey it, you suffer feeling guilty. Motivated by guilt, you obey it legalistically. Then, obedience becomes mechanical, heart-detached action. You are trapped by the law for the sake of the law. While you do the action, you do not realize how it relates to worshipping God. This legalistic idea of law has been formed in a spiritual vacuum, which lacks the knowledge and benefit of salvation and gratitude as its consequence. The law is for the people: "The torah [the law] was… a characterization of life-principles reflecting the state or quality of the sacred people, a living thank-offering to the God of their salvation.… Torah is thus not a burden placed on Israel but a gift designed to lead God's people in the way of life."[2] As the law reflects God's beneficent love, all of it is directed toward love: love for God and for neighbors.

The law functions like the manual of an automobile for the Christian. Consider, for example, the Volkswagen Beetle. Its manual requires regular maintenance as to fuel, engine oil, tire pressure, and so on. The manufacturing company has written the manual because they designed and constructed the automobile and know it best. The manufacturer writes the manual. Doing all the chores of maintenance may be hard and burdensome. However, the Beetle needs regular maintenance service because it is made with limitations. The Beetle is made to run on gasoline only. It is made to run on two-wheel drive on a paved road. It needs certain air pressure in the tires. The manual is given in order for the vehicle to properly function, not to busy the owners with chores. The moral law in the Bible is like the manual of the Beetle. It was written and required by the Creator God for the benefit of humans—to properly live as God's people. The law does not consist of arbitrary rules to burden humans or make them suffer as a consequence of sin. The laws are God's gift to reshape and restore humans to their original status.

The mission of Israel for the sake of nations

The exodus experience was profound enough to reshape the Israelites' knowledge of their God—especially that of Moses, who had been raised in the very heart of the Egyptian religion and culture. Their God proved himself as the Lord over the most powerful nation. The God of Israel, formerly known as "the God of Abraham, the God of Isaac and the God of Jacob," is now known as the God over all nations.

Let us go back to the preface of the law and see how the law reshaped Israel's identity in her relationship to other nations: "Now if you obey me fully and keep my covenant, then out of all nations you will be my treasured possession. Although the whole earth is mine, you will be for me a kingdom of priests and a holy nation" (Ex. 19:5-6). With the exodus incident, God was advancing his covenant to the nations. The identity of Israel as "my treasured possession," "a kingdom of priests," and "a holy nation" suggests, first, that she belonged to God among the nations; secondly, that she must be consecrated and distinguished from the pagan nations; and thirdly, that she had been given a mission for the sake of all nations, since a priest serves the people as mediator. Though the context is fairly early in the history of Israel and did not provide specific services that Israel was to offer, it is clear that the people of Israel were becoming the means of advancing God's covenant to the other nations. Later, in the book of Joshua, Israel became the means of extending God's covenant to pagans; and in the Prophets, Israel was made the "light for the gentiles." An early example of such priestly service may be found in Joseph, even long before the law was given. In Egypt, Joseph belonged to God, kept his faith, set himself morally apart in the midst of the pagans, and served the Egyptian people as a middleman with God-given wisdom. He saved many lives; otherwise, they would have died out of hunger.

The law, in conclusion, offered two milestones for the future of Israel. First, the blessed identity of Israel was conditional: it depended on consecration of themselves to the Lord. Beginning with the wilderness experience and going forward, Israel was to live as God's people in obedience to the law. Second, their faith in the universal God and the law-commission provided a stage for public spirituality. Israel was now to live as God's people among the nations.

Discussion Questions:

1. How does the law work with the covenant for salvation?
2. How does the law reflect God's nature?
3. Share the benefits of being God's people, the sense of belonging, in today's broken, isolated life.
4. What is the use of the law for the present Christian life?

Endnotes

1. John Calvin, *Institutes of the Christian Religion*, II.vii.1. Italics added.

2. Charles H. H. Scobie, *The Ways of Our God: An Approach to Biblical Theology*" (Grand Rapids: Eerdmans, 2003), p. 748, including citation from J. M. Myers.

Chapter 11

The Promised Land

After the five books of Moses end, God's covenantal relationship with Israel continues into a new phase. At the beginning of the book of Joshua, Israel was about to enter the Promised Land. This new venture was a historic moment for Israel, for they knew it had been promised to their ancestors, and finally they were leaving the challenging experience in the wilderness behind.

God moving his people
The route through which God led Abraham and Sarah covered the so-called Fertile Crescent, which reaches from Mesopotamia through the Canaanite land to Egypt. On the east side, the great rivers of Tigris and Euphrates provided very fertile soil and productive marshland, with the consequence that Mesopotamia became a source of ancient civilizations. On the west was the Egyptian land, nourished also by abundant sunlight and the freshwater of the Nile. The Canaanite land was nurtured by the Jordan River. Since the Canaanite land, located between the Mediterranean Sea and the desert, served as the narrow bridge for

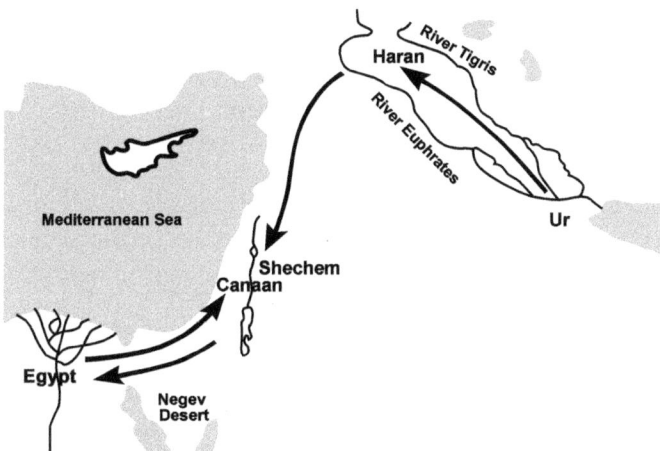

Route of Abraham through the Fertile Crescent

transportation and trade between the two world powers, the two powers wanted to take the land under their controls to expand their powers. The Canaanite land later became the kingdom of Israel, where God would shape his people and eventually send his Messiah. The gospel is born out of these international and cross-cultural contexts, dealing with many peoples. Though Egypt and Mesopotamia represented evil pagan powers that oppressed God's people and from whose grip they longed to escape, God does not act as a tribal God of Israel but as the Lord over all peoples and nations. The book of Joshua shows how God deals with all peoples in his salvation for Israel. It will shape a proper understanding of God as the true lord, correcting ethnocentric views of his people.

God moved his people back and forth along the route of the Fertile Crescent. Israel's moving to the Promised Land was actually a return. It was the fulfillment of God's promise made to Abraham. Abraham's great-grandson Joseph followed the footsteps of his ancestor and moved to Egypt, and there his descendants grew in number to finally became the nation of Israel. Egypt, the prosperous pagan empire, served as the cradle for the birth and growth of Israel as well as the evil power that later oppressed her. God proved his lordship against the Pharaoh and delivered them out of its bondage. God led them through the wilderness (the Arabian Peninsula) for forty years before leading them to the Promised Land.

God's moving his people for such a long period of time (from Abraham to crossing the Jordan) between the great world powers and then to and from the desert must be seen in light of the covenant fulfillment. So, what was God doing with Israel by fulfilling his covenant to Israel? When God delivered them out of Egypt, he had a plan to bring them to the Promised Land of Canaan. In fact, Terah, Abraham's father, also intended that the Promised Land would be his destination when his family left from Ur. The Canaanite land was the only option when one determined to move away either from Mesopotamia or Egypt unless he wanted to move into desert. God himself introduced the Promised Land to Israel as the "land of flowing with milk and honey" (Ex. 3:8, 17). Egyptians at the time knew the place as a prosperous land with good herding and horticulture. The whole progress of deliverance from exodus through the wilderness experience to the Promised Land probably was not intended to show God's purpose to bless Israel with natural, material abundance. In fact, famine and hunger often hit the land, and its residents had to move to neighboring countries to find food and shelter. If natural prosperity had been the goal to pursue, they would have better remained in Egypt. In fact, many grumbling Israelites in the desert longed to return to lush Egypt. Israel had to move away from both pagan empires, and then there was no other way to go but through the bridge land after they came out of the desert. The blessing of the Promised Land signifies what God provides, not what the land provides. The milk and honey of the

Promised Land was the promised reenactment of manna in the desert. Israel's moving throughout the Fertile Crescent, which in fact served as the Temptation Crescent to Israel, shows that God's blessing does not come from natural, material abundance but from God's faithfulness to his promise.

Finally leaving the challenging years of wilderness wandering behind, the Israelites were moving to the God-promised land. God was fulfilling his promise to "give" the land to Israel by way of his own battle, but Israel was called to be active as God's covenant partner. First, they had to engage in wars with its residents, which meant actual fighting and suffering casualties. Second, taking the land was described to include both destroying the residents and incorporating some of them to Israel. These two points were directed toward the goal God had for Israel: Israel was called to be God's holy nation, not in terms of total exclusivity from other nations, but, through being distinguished from them by keeping God's law, to carry on the kingdom mission of being God's priest for the sake of other peoples (Ex. 19:6). The location of the Promised Land in the middle of the Fertile Crescent provided for Israel a strategically significant bridge for connecting to other people, to whom Israel was to serve as the light and priest nation. God chose Israel to be the model people to relay God's salvation to others. The Fertile Crescent, which served as the Temptation Crescent against Israel, now became the Gospel Crescent, in which Israel was to serve others. Isaiah prophesied that both Egyptians and Assyrians would acknowledge the God of Israel as the Lord:

> In that day there will be a highway from Egypt to Assyria. The Assyrians will go to Egypt and the Egyptians to Assyria. The Egyptians and Assyrians will worship together. In that day Israel will be the third, along with Egypt and Assyria, a blessing on the earth. The Lord Almighty will bless them, saying, Blessed be Egypt my people, Assyria my handiwork, and Israel my inheritance. (Isa. 19:23-25)

The mission of Israel as the priest nation provided the background of their entering into the Promised Land, where we understand God's command to drive away and destroy the residents, a passage which if taken out of context would be unacceptable.

Entering the Promised Land

"Be strong and courageous, because you will lead these people to inherit the land I swore to their forefathers to give them": God himself gave the commission to Joshua three times, each time with more intensifying force, which indicates that God would surely accomplish it. The commission was accompanied by the obligation of law obedience: "be careful to obey all the law my servant Moses gave you." On the condition of law obedience, God assured their success in the land: "then you will be prosperous and successful" (Josh. 1:6-9). Law was the new help for Israel; with it they could know more clearly how to trust and obey God. Questions may arise as to the meaning of God's saying "I am giving you the land" when it was already home to its residents; or the meaning of Israel's "taking" or "inheriting" the land, for they actually took the land from its residents by force; and the meaning of God's command that seems like violent genocide of the residents. We will try to read the texts from the standpoint of God's covenant working, as described above.

We need to understand, first, that the God of Israel is the Creator God, and Israel's battle was his battle. When the ark of the covenant, which symbolizes God's presence, moved ahead of the people into the Jordan River, which was "at flood stage," water stopped flowing and made a "heap a great distance away." While the priests and the ark stood on dry ground in the middle of the river, all Israelites crossed on dry ground (Josh. 3:9-17, 4:1-7). This episode, being parallel to the crossing of the Red Sea, was described with the reminding images of the creation account to reveal God's creational sovereignty. Israelite men were circumcised and celebrated the feast of Passover right before going out to battle. That is not a good idea in terms of battle strategy. But God deems consecration prior to work. Though Joshua was the leader, it was "the commander of the army of the Lord," a heavenly figure, who actually led the people to battle. And the only tactic to destroy the city of Jericho was Israel's shouting against it. All these events—popular Sunday school lessons—may not be read as if God simply performed great miracles against the natural order. They signify that Israel's campaign of moving into the land was made possible by God's sovereign acts.

Joshua sent out spies across the river. There they met Rahab, a prostitute in Jericho. From her lips we hear a great affirmation of the God of Israel: "When we heard of it, our hearts melted and everyone's courage failed because of you, for the Lord your God is God in heaven above and on the earth below" (2:11). She had come to know the God of Israel from rumors about how Israel had advanced to the Jordan River. However simple and limited her knowledge of God in her pagan and oppressed situation, she surely acknowledged the God of Israel as the sovereign Lord, who was different from the Canaanite gods. She put her recognition of God into action that might have put her family in great danger.

Rahab takes a significant place in the history of salvation for her faith. James illustrates her as an example of true faith that is practiced in action, along with that of Abraham (2:25; see also Heb. 11:31). More significantly, she is mentioned in Matthew 1 as part of the ancestry line of King David, from which Jesus came. The significance of Rahab is highlighted by the ironic contrast to Israel's attitude to their God. As it was written regarding the first generation who were delivered out of Egypt, "since they had not obeyed the Lord… they would not see the land that he had solemnly promised" (5:6). While Israel disobeyed after being richly nourished by God's covenant and law, the pagan prostitute who had been religiously deserted heard the rumor of God's people and trusted.

The story of Rahab reveals the gospel, a story of God transforming people. Are you ready to learn the gospel from a pagan prostitute? How would the Israelites feel when they heard her story from the spies? Would they praise God for extending salvation even to her, or would they feel offended? God is the God of all. He is also God of Rahab the Canaanite, the Gibeonites, Ruth the Moabite, and the people of Nineveh, all enemies of Israel! The gospel should correct any egotistic, ethnocentric view of others. We should learn—from Rahab's confession on "the God in heaven above and on the earth below"—who God is and what kind of salvation he is working in and around us.

The way God shaped his people should guide our reading of his command to destroy the Canaanite residents. Often a contrast was assumed between the violent God of the Old Testament and the loving God presented in Christ. Indeed, God's command to drive away the residents and destroy them seems very hard to understand for its apparent violence and ethnocentric attitude. However, the contrast is wrongly posited, for the Scriptures reveal the same God working for salvation differently in the historical progress. Let us take a closer look at some related texts and find what God was doing to Israel as well as to other nations. Israel was commanded,

> When the Lord your God brings you into the land you are entering to possess and drives out before you many nations… then you must destroy them totally. Make no treaty with them, and show them no mercy. Do not intermarry with them… for they will turn your sons away from following me to serve other gods, and the Lord's anger will burn against you… This is what you are to do to them: Break down their altars, smash their sacred stones, cut down their Asherah poles and burn their idols in the fire. For you are a people holy to the Lord your God. (Deut. 7:1-6)

If God intended to systematically destroy all the Canaanite residents, then the other commands, such as not to make a treaty with certain nations, not to marry with the Canaanite people, and more than anything else, the command to destroy their religious icons, which was emphasized in a four-fold phrase, did not need to be mentioned. The purpose, as highlighted by "this is what you are to do to them," was to establish Israel's religious integrity.

The Deuteronomy 20:10-18 text provides a detailed order for dealing with the Canaanite residents, and part of it stipulates making the offer of a peace treaty and possibly saving them. Israel was commanded, "When you march up to attack a city, make its people an offer of peace."

If they were to refuse, it was because God had hardened their hearts, and they would be destroyed. If they accepted the peace offer, they would be saved and serve Israel; that possibly meant admitting them to the "assembly of the Lord." However, the peace treaty was not offered universally. God forbade making such a treaty with the "seven nations larger and stronger than you" in the text cited above and with the Ammonites or Moabites (Deut. 23:3-6). Joshua 9 describes such a case of making a peace treaty. Israel made the treaty with the Gibeonites, saved them, and used them as forced laborers (Josh. 11:19). Deuteronomy 20 provides the fundamental reason for such a way of dealing with the pagan residents: "otherwise, they will teach you to follow all the detestable things they do in worshipping their gods, and you will sin against the Lord your God" (20:18). Again, this approach was to maintain Israel's religious purity.

The command of destruction, indeed hard to understand from a moral standpoint no matter how it is explained, shows neither dehumanizing mass-slaughter of any people that we have witnessed in modern history nor ethnocentric hatred toward any people. The God of Israel is not a tribal god who favors Israel only in exclusivity of others, but the Lord of all, who shapes Israel out of all, as is demonstrated in his admitting Rahab and the Gibeonites. Destroying and admitting remain God's mysterious acts of election, but admitting pagans into his people continues in the progressive unfolding of salvation, beautifully described in the story of Ruth.

Reflections

Applying the message of the Bible to life is commendable for Christian living. Is God's command to Israel to drive out the pagans and destroy their idols applicable today? Would God command us to practice it? God has been pursuing the goal of salvation differently in different times. During the early stage of salvation history, God formed Israel out of descendants of Abraham and shaped them into his people by direct rule. He ruled by the law that stipulated how they were to maintain their identity as a holy nation: by practicing the marks of consecration. The marks of spiritual consecration were defined to be recognized by physical distinction. Israel's sins were to be forgiven by way of then making animal sacrifices. Some days such as the Sabbath and festivals were distinguished as holy days, the tabernacle and temple were holy places, and certain human body conditions were considered clean before God. Israel entered the Promised Land with this law effective for them.

The goal of the Old Testament marks of consecration has been achieved by Christ's death and resurrection, by which sinners are justified to be holy people. Now, as Christ reconciles to himself all things of the world, the consecration is no longer limited to marks of physical distinction (Read the story of Cornelius and Peter in Acts 10). Israel is now composed of all believers of Jesus Christ; and all redeemed reality, including all days, places, and bodily conditions, is considered to be holy. The progress from the earlier limited mode of God's shaping his people by law, to its full realization in Christ, provides a way to see the matter. The goal of the command was not to demolish icons, but to maintain loyalty to God by denying idols. With the goal of consecration achieved in Christ and empowered by the Holy Spirit, denying icons physically is still commendable; however, Christians are now called to a more noble mission—to live out the already-fulfilled consecration in every aspect of life.

Could not God have led Israel to the Promised Land in an easier and safer way? He guided Israel not only through a long wandering detour but also to a fully occupied land. The whole first generation out of Egypt were judged and perished in the wilderness, and the second generation, who were born there, were allowed to enter the land only by engaging in war with its residents. And the land was different, at least physically, from the promised land "flowing with milk and honey," for it was in fact full of idol worshippers. What was God doing to Israel? Apparently, his goal was not simply to transfer them to a new land. The Scriptures describe God's acts of salvation as a process of shaping unruly sinners into his people. God was transforming people in concrete historical situations. Though Israel might have complained of God's lead as an inefficient detour that demanded unnecessary sacrifices, God chose the best way of training that fits the sinful characters of Israel. God's grace is shown in the way he led Israel.

We are living in a culture where efficiency is considered more valuable than integrity, and result than process. Modern expectations of reaching the Promised Land in an efficient way are shattered before God's way of handling the matter. God was transforming the whole person and establishing his nation out of such people. That process demanded a long period of struggle to know and trust him. It took twenty-five long struggling years for Abraham and Sarah to have the covenant baby, Isaac, and forty years for Israel to enter the land. The blessing of "the land flowing with milk and honey" did not lie in the natural provision, but was a gift that God's people experienced in their faithful lives. Israel pre-tasted such a gift in the wilderness, where there was no support at all for life. Now they were called to live out the blessing in the God-given land.

Discussion Questions:

1. Why do you think God chose the Canaanite land as the Promised Land for Israel?
2. What, do you think, is Rahab's significance in the history of salvation?
3. What images of God do you find in the book of Joshua?

CHAPTER 12

Ruth: the salvation of nations

Does the book deliver a love story between the Jewish gentleman Boaz and the young foreign widow Ruth? Or is it a religious story that shows how God restores his people from suffering to blessing? Or is it a religious story that shows God's all-embracing love even for foreigners?

The book of Ruth tells us a compact story composed with vivid and dramatic Jewish literary devices, such as the familiar chiastic structure, unexplained but powerful messages hidden in the Hebrew names, and repetition of the key term. From the beginning to the end, the story unfolds a Jewish family's experience in the context of their own culture. In the genuinely Jewish narrative is revealed the message of salvation: that God loves, incorporates, and uses Ruth, a pagan woman, in and for Israel, eventually to direct readers' attention to the unfolding of the gospel that God shapes Israel out of all people. In the story, God does not directly appear to take action, but by effecting his law for Israel, he unmistakably directs the history of salvation. In the grand action of God's salvation is disclosed a genuinely human story that makes readers' hearts warm. It begins with trouble—leaving home and finding shelter in a foreign land, death of family members, and helplessness and loneliness—and then changes to a different set of experiences—going back home, finding help, and restoring the family. At the very center of this transition is the confession, by Moabitess Ruth, of faith in the God of Israel and her following marriage to the Jewish man Boaz. The underlying providence of God leads the whole story in such a way that gives joy to the redeemed family at the present time and anticipates greater hope for the future.

"When the judges ruled…"

It is the story of a family in Bethlehem in the Promised Land "When the judges ruled." Israel, previously dedicated people of God, had become complacent and loose in their faith and morality in the Promised Land. The tribes of Israel suffered from continuous battles with the neighboring countries. Israel at the time was a loose confederation of the twelve tribes gathered around the common faith and did not yet have centralized leadership. That political situation worked negatively for Israel in their military endeavors against the hostile settlers of the land. Judges ruled them. Though sent by God, the judges were only temporary and local leaders. Israel was in need of a new stable leadership, the kings. Then famine hit the land, which aggravated the already unsettled situation of Israel.

The introduction describes the tragic story of a family who lived in the town of Bethlehem. Bethlehem in the Hebrew means "house of bread." The father's name was Elimelech, meaning "my God is king," and his wife's name was Naomi, meaning "pleasant." They had two sons, Mahlon and Kilion, whose meanings are not certain. The message of the introduction gets intensified with what is hinted in the background: in the "house of bread," a family of God, Mr. "my God is king" and his wife, "pleasant," happily lived with their two sons. Suddenly a famine hit the "house of bread," and the family of God had to leave their hometown to find food in the enemy land. Do you see the great irony the author tries to relay? The suffering gets more aggravated. Mr. "my God is king" died in the pagan land, and his two sons had to marry to manage their lives there. Then both sons also died. Now an old Jewish widow and her two young Moabite daughters-in-law were left without help. In the ancient Near Eastern society, the surviving female members were in a most hopeless situation. It all happened "when the judges ruled," which suggests that a ruler, king, was needed. Later Naomi, "pleasant," returned home and asked for the name "Mara," meaning bitter.

In the transition from the family's tragedy to the widow's return home is Ruth's faith. When Naomi demanded that she return home, Ruth replied, "Don't urge me to leave you or to turn back from you. Where you go I will go, and where you stay I will stay. Your people will be my people and your God my God. Where you die I will die, and there I will be buried. May the Lord deal with me, be it ever so severely, if anything but death separates you and me" (vv. 16-17). Her faithfulness to Naomi on the personal level was highly commendable, considering Naomi's helpless situation. Her decision is contrasted to her sister-in-law's decision. While Orpah left Naomi and went back "to her people and her gods," Ruth "clung to Naomi" (vv. 14-15). The statement that she would be buried with Naomi suggests a significant commitment, for burial with family or community was very common during this time. Here Ruth's decision is described as a religious commitment as well as personal faithfulness. Though expressed in the form of speaking to Naomi, Ruth's confession is in fact dedicated to the God of Israel. Ruth's faith in the God of Israel was sincere enough to make her turn away from her family's religion and culture and adopt the new faith. Ruth's faith implies her dedication to God, while Orpha's return might have led her to offer her child in worshipping the pagan gods. Ruth's confession in saying "your people will be my people and your God my God" was made in the context of God's covenantal relationship with Israel. Ruth in her faith is grounded in the working of the covenantal God, who is shaping Israel as his people.

Back in Bethlehem

Naomi returned to Bethlehem with "Ruth the Moabitess" when "the barley harvest was beginning" (1:22). The author provides a double hint that anticipates what will take place for them in Bethlehem. The first hint is the barley harvest season, which implies the renewal of the hunger-trodden family. The other one is what the name "Ruth the Moabitess" suggested to the Jews. The Jewish attitude toward the Moabites was settled while they were on the way to the Canaan. After the Moabites tried to impede and curse the Israelites, the Israelites' enmity toward the Moabites resulted in a law in Israel: that none of their descendants "may enter the assembly of the Lord" (Deut. 23:3). From that time on, the Jewish epithet "Ruth the Moabitess" embodied their discriminating and despising attitude. God initiated and worked out the gospel of salvation in racial and cross-cultural contexts. God moved his people through diverse cultural settings that were composed of great empires such as Egypt and Babylon and a good number of insignificant tribes and subcultures that were managed under the influences of the empires. Among the tribes and cultures were found struggling, discriminating, and despising attitudes toward one another. In such complicated and painful racial and cross-cultural contexts, seeing how God treated diverse peoples in his unfolding of salvation of Israel is very important to the full meaning of salvation. Salvation, which would be enacted as redemption and reconciliation, inevitably includes renewed relationships with others.

Boaz radically changed the Jewish despising attitude toward Ruth. Ruth went to the field, which later came to be known as belonging to Boaz, a sign of God's providential guidance. There she faced the harvesting crews' discriminatory remark "She is the Moabitess who came back from Moab with Naomi." But Boaz, the landlord, welcomed her to glean in his field and offered her drink. He also promised to protect her from the possible harvesting crew. During harvest season, the morality of crews was loose, and they could be a danger to women. Boaz treated her as if she were a family member, which is signified by her staggering remark, "Why have I found such favor in your eyes that you notice me—a foreigner?" Then Boaz praised her sacrificial family loyalty toward her mother-in-law and leaving behind her own father and mother and coming to a new land. On Ruth's coming to Bethlehem "to live with a people you did not know before" (2:11), a commentator finds an implied correlation to Abraham and Sarah, who left behind their fathers and mothers in Ur in obedience to God and became the foundation of Israel. With that connection in mind, Ruth is viewed as a religious matriarch who became a foundation of Israel in the line of Abraham and Sarah,[1] which is implied in the genealogy at the end of the book. An underlying message is that God not only incorporated pagan foreigners into his people but also used them as foundations of it.

Boaz said to Ruth, "May the Lord repay you for what you have done. May you be richly rewarded by the Lord, the God of Israel under whose wings you have come to take refuge" (2:12). Boaz invoked God's blessing on her that she took refuge under God's wings. The blessing is being realized in 3:9: "spread the corner of your garment over me, since you are a kinsman redeemer." The typical Hebrew wordplay that is found between "Ruth took refuge under God's *wings*" and her request to "place your *garment corner* over me" highlights the main theme of the book: that only God can confer the blessing of redemption and that God accomplishes it by using a mediator, the kinsman-redeemer.

Fulfilling the duty of kinsman-redeemer

Ruth's request for Boaz to cover her with his garment corner means asking for marriage. It probably sounds too provocative for a decent woman to do, but in fact she reminded Boaz of his responsibility to fulfill the law. The law of kinsman-redeemer regulated how a poor family would be restored to the family land through the redemptive act of kinsman-redeemer: "his nearest relative is to come and redeem what his countryman has sold" (Lev. 25:25). Ruth was asking Boaz to fulfill the duty of kinsman-redeemer for the family of Elimelech. Another law was to be involved, for the Elimelech family came back home not only in poverty but also without offspring to continue the family line. Family lineage played a significant role in the working out of salvation, for salvation works with the covenant promise of God from one generation to another.

The other law required for the redemption of the Elimelech family was the levirate marriage. It stipulated how family lineage continued when a man died without a son: "His widow must not marry outside the family. Her husband's brother shall take her and marry her and fulfill the duty of a brother-in-law to her. The first son she bears shall carry on the name of the dead brother so that his name will not be blotted out from Israel" (Deut. 25:5-6). By lying near Boaz, Ruth was asking him to carry out the law requirement. Two seemingly little twists in regard to who carried out the double duty of levirate marriage and kinsman-redemption settled the unique message of the whole story. First, Naomi was the natural choice to fulfill the duty; however, being too old for childbearing age, she ascribed the duty to Ruth. Natural offers to redeem might have come from Elimelech's family, like from one of his brothers, but there is no mention about them in the story. Second, Naomi's closest kinsman-redeemer, whose name is not revealed, agreed to buy back the land; however, he did not want to marry Ruth: "…I cannot redeem it because

I might endanger my own estate" (4:6). Probably he was afraid of jeopardizing his own estate for Ruth's son. Against the complex situation that highlights the hopelessness of the family, the point that changed the direction of the story and thus captured its theme is that Boaz took up the duties of kinsman-redeemer and levirate-marriage out of his voluntary generosity, while he was not in the line of responsibility. And Ruth took up the Jewish responsibility by her self-sacrificing dedication to Naomi and faithful commitment to God.

Boaz finalized the transaction of the double duty before the witnesses, and they blessed Boaz and Ruth: "May the Lord make the woman who is coming into your home like Rachel and Leah, who together built up the house of Israel. May you have standing in Ephrathah and be famous in Bethlehem" (4:11). The images of house and home in this blessing remind and reinforce the idea of redemption—the lost family members are restored into the family by the service of kinsman-redeemer. In marriage with Boaz, Ruth was blessed with the calling of building God's people, on the same level as Rachel and Leah, who were called "the two pillars of Israel." She had now not only incorporated herself into God's people but also raised herself up to matriarchal status in Israel. Obed was born from Ruth and Boaz. Naomi's friends said to her, "Praise be to the Lord, who this day has not left you without a kinsman-redeemer.... He will renew your life and sustain you in your old age" (4:14-15). After it began with descending to despair and suffering, the story reaches its ascending climax of restoration and joy, with meeting Boaz as the kinsman-redeemer as the middle point. It began with hunger and death but ends with blessing and new life.

Ending with a genealogy

The story ends in a unique way by giving a genealogy of Obed. Genealogy was used to indicate connectedness and identity in Israel. Naomi had lost her family in the pagan land, and now she was restored to her family in Israel. This restoration reflects the spiritual reality of redeeming a lost family member into the family of God. Ruth had lost her Moabite family origin, but she was now adopted into the family of God.

At the same time, the genealogy points to a certain direction in the future. The genealogy begins with Perez: "May your family be like that of Perez, whom Tamar bore to Judah" (4:12). The author lists the genealogy from Perez, through Boaz and Obed, to David (4:18-22). It is an interesting plot that the author composed: Obed's family connection from Perez. For Perez was also born from the levirate-marriage of his parents, Judah and Tamar, who were the direct ancestors of king David. Probably the blessing "may your family be like that of Perez" is reiterated in the detailed genealogy that leads to David and later becomes fulfilled by the birth of Jesus, who came from the line of "Judah the father of

Perez" (Matt. 1:3). Ending the story with Obed in the family line that leads to David, the author directs the readers to anticipate an extended fulfillment of the present blessing in the future. In the descending introduction, the author describes the suffering of a family of God when there was no king, moves ascendingly to fulfillment of kinsman-redeemer duty, and guides the readers to anticipate a further fulfillment in the future—the coming of the King.

Message

Is Ruth a love story? We find Ruth's faithful love for Naomi, Boaz's kind favor for Ruth, and prevalent throughout the story though hidden, God's providential love for Israel. Love is realized by the overarching theme of redemption, which is found more than twenty times in various forms in the book. Redemption basically means to purchase or buy back troubled people for a price. In the book of Ruth, redemption is described in an agricultural context: that the troubled family of Elimelech was purchased back from their trouble to their original family status by the service of his kinsman-redeemer. The kinsman-redeemer is the close brother to the lost family. By ending with the genealogy of king David, the author alludes to the future fulfillment of God's act of redemption in Christ. Christ, who came as a full human, is our brother and kinsman-redeemer, who redeems us from our trouble, sin, to restore us into the family of God.

Reflection

Faith is essential for the working of redemption for all the related parties. Naomi, throughout suffering and despair, did not lose her faith, which led her back to Bethlehem. With the newly acquired but sincere faith, Ruth dedicated herself to the new possibility of life. And by faith, Boaz sacrificed himself for the redemption of his brother's family. Though the story describes mainly human experiences and actions, God the King is definitely at work among his people with the law of kinsman-redemption. The story is presented in the Jewish lawful and cultural backgrounds, using its beautiful literary devices, but its message is powerfully inclusive and inviting. The covenantal God is shaping Israel, not by blood or race but by faith—a central Christian gospel that will be more clearly unfolded in the history of salvation.

Ruth must have learned about God from Naomi's life during the years of suffering. From Ruth's own religious standpoint (Moabites worshipped their own gods), all that happened to Naomi's family could have proved that Naomi's god was incapable of protecting his people, and trusting that god was not conceivable. However, her confession does not reflect any hint of doubt, struggle, or hesitation with the God of Israel. For Ruth, faith meant trusting the new God and his promise in the unfavorable situation. Against the real challenges of repudiating her old faith and suffering in reality, her new faith meant determined living according to God's promise, not by sight. Faith is a gift of God, implanted in the hearts of afflicted men and women, and working in a mysterious way against the common understanding. Faith forms a new person, raising up the beaten and strengthening the helpless, equipping them to go through challenging situations. By equipping his people with faith, God does not grant shallow promises for immediate saving from danger and prosperity. David, in Psalm 23, sings for God, who helped him "walk through the valley of the shadow of death," fearing no evil and experiencing God's comforting rod. Though God saves his people from danger, the purpose of God's providence is not simply to transfer them from danger to a happier life but to form them as his people.

Faith is the means that God uses to redeem and shape his people. Ruth's faith serves as the momentum that transfers the story of suffering to that of restoration and hope. Trusting God, Ruth left behind her homeland and culture and followed Naomi to a new land, went to the field to glean grain, and met Boaz. Throughout the story, Ruth is suggested as the model of a faithful life among the Israelites. Boaz praised her faithful actions: "May the Lord repay you for what you have done. May you be richly rewarded by the Lord, the God of Israel, under whose wings you have come to take refuge" (2:12). Here, God's reward is not to be understood as God's compensation, as if he is obliged to pay in return for Ruth's meritorious work. The reward is related to Ruth's faith in God. Trusting God, she took refuge under God's wings, and the refuge was granted. The reward was granted as God's fulfilling her faith, and her faith is God's gift, in taking her under his wings. As the story unfolds, Ruth's reward extends beyond her personally taking refuge under God's wings to her becoming a matriarch for shaping God's people. Every other form of reward, whether material or spiritual, is also found in the story.

Discussion Questions:

1. Why does Ruth have a significant place in the history of salvation? Her name is found in the genealogy of Jesus in Matthew 1.
2. The story describes everyday people's story. Reflect how faith forms and grows in life situations.
3. Ruth was an outsider to Israel. Discuss Christian attitudes toward outsiders.

Endnote
1. Robert L. Hubbard, Jr., *The Book of Ruth* (Grand Rapids: Eerdmans, 1988), 2:11.

Chapter 13

Prophets: the judgment and promise of restoration

By making a covenant with Israel, God created a unique relationship with them: "I will take you as my own people, and I will be your God" (Ex. 6:7). The covenantal relationship depended on the keeping of the law. With Israel's consent to obey his law, "We will do everything the Lord has said" (Ex. 19:8), the Sinai covenant had been solemnly established, and the covenantal nature of Israel's future had been set. The covenant implied progress of time till its fulfillment, which turned out to be long to Israel; therefore, it needed to be periodically renewed to new generations. When Israel was about to end the wilderness experience, old Moses offered the renewed covenant to the generation who were born in the wilderness. He laid the renewed covenant on the renewed memory of God's faithfulness:

> You are standing here in order to enter into a covenant with the Lord your God, a covenant the Lord is making with you this day and sealing with an oath, to confirm you this day as his people, that he may be your God as he promised you and as he swore to your fathers, Abraham, Isaac and Jacob. (Deut. 29:12-13)

When God made a covenant with each generation, they were actually participating in the one covenant, which was made with their forefathers. The renewed covenant was applicable to the present generation as well as their not-yet-born generations (vv. 14-15). Renewed periodically, the covenant now became an ongoing relationship between God and his people.

God sent various types of servants to Israel to establish and mature the covenantal relationship with her. The first group were the patriarchs, Abraham being the first one. They were the founding fathers of God's people in that God established the covenant people with them. The covenant that established God's people extended from Abraham to the nation Israel. After God shaped Israel as his people by the covenant of law, God sent three types of servants to Israel to maintain and mature the covenantal relationship: priests, kings, and prophets. They served God's covenant community for a long period of time until the birth of Jesus.

Priests and kings

The priests were middlemen between God and his people, and their work was carried out in the tabernacle and later in the temple. The tabernacle was basically meant to be the meeting place where God met his people. Since they were not able to meet God as sinful people, God prepared a way for them to meet their God. God's provision became the duty of the priests: to administer what the law prescribed on matters of holiness, purity, and instruction to the people (Lev. 10:10-11). The law prescribed spiritual holiness and spiritual cleanness and uncleanness in terms of concrete places, times, and human-body conditions. Through priests' law administration and teaching, the people came to know the way of worshipping God and maintaining their covenant relationship with him. Another significant duty of the priests was to offer sacrifices to God for forgiveness of Israel's sin (See Leviticus for various types of offerings). This is why the holy tabernacle and temple became the gracious but dreadful places where innocent victims, the animals, became sacrificed for the sake of sinful Israel. The law prescription for forgiveness of human sin was directly connected, through the long history of law administration, to the cross of Jesus Christ for our salvation. Administering these duties, priests served as the people's representatives before God.

As the Israelites divided the new land among themselves and tried to settle down, they were struggling with neighboring countries. They were just recent settlers, while the residents had long-established cities. More than that, the Israelites were a loosely gathered confederation without organized rulership, while the residents were unified under efficient central governments and military powers. God sent judges occasionally to save Israelites from neighboring oppressors. But they were temporary local leaders. Within this historical context, the Israelites asked for a king, the tangible leadership that their neighboring countries had. God's reluctant response reflects their little mindfulness of their covenant relationship with God: "It is not you [Samuel] they have rejected, but they have rejected me as their king" (1 Sam. 8:7). Underlying their request for a king was a religious reservation on who they believed ruled over them. In the ancient Near Eastern culture, politics and religion were inter-related, to the extent that what people believed to be gods led them in battles. To the Israelites' eyes, the residents were prosperous and powerful, and the Israelites became enticed by their gods, who appeared to be both powerful and tangible. Being tempted, Israel was confused as to who their Lord was.

God allowed kings and initiated the process by appointing Saul as the first king. Moses specified the work of the kings. There were three don'ts and one do, in regard to the way of their rule. Three don'ts were: do not acquire great numbers of horses; do not take many wives; and do not accumulate large amounts of silver and gold (Deut. 17:15-17). This instruction forbade kings from ruling with military power, human power, and money power. Imagine how kings at the time ruled over people. Are they not essential sources of power for any political rule? God banned the conventional human ruling power for the Israelite kings. When a king was enthroned in Israel, God said, "he is to write for himself on a scroll a copy of this law.... It is to be with him, and he is to read it all the days of his life so that he may learn to revere the Lord his God and follow carefully all the words of this law and these decrees and not consider himself better than his brothers and turn from the law to the right or to the left" (vv. 18-20). Kings of Israel were to rule by God's law.

Kings were sent to enforce God's law so that he could fulfill his covenant promise made with Israel. The kingship made a significant transition in the history of Israel, from theocracy to indirect ruling—God now ruled through human kings. The kings' authority in Israel was different in nature from that of the surrounding peoples in that it was a delegated authority. Kings would rule only by God's law. Thus, though the political structure of Israel had changed, the nature of God's rule remained—only God ruled over Israel. It is interesting to see how many Israelite kings turned out to be morally and spiritually corrupt, affirming God's reluctance to allow kings.

Prophets

The third human agents were prophets. There were "earlier prophets" such as Samuel, Elijah, and Elisha, who fearlessly proclaimed the word of God and performed miracles. Several prophets in that period showed certain ecstatic behaviors caused by the work of the Spirit. The "writing prophets" were the next-generation prophets who occupied the prophetic genre of the Old Testament. They are classified as four major prophets (because their books are longer in length than those of the minor)—Isaiah, Jeremiah, Ezekiel, and Daniel—and twelve minor prophets, from Hosea to Malachi. The prophetic collection of the sixteen books occupies the largest genre in the Bible and thus covers the very long history of Israel.

What did prophets do for Israel compared to the works of priests and kings? Though there were some ecstatic and frenzied elements among the earlier prophets, the main task of delivering God's word remained and became intensified among the writing prophets. Repeated phrases in prophetic literature such as "thus said the Lord" and "the word of the Lord came to…" reflect the nature of prophetic messages. God sent prophets to deliver his messages to their contemporary Israel. They were messengers and mouths of the Lord.

What message of God did they deliver? A note on the term "prophecy" is needed, because the role of prophecy in the Old Testament is different from its modern meaning. The popular meaning of prophecy today is to predict future incidents. It is true that some prophets in the Bible predicted future incidents. Isaiah predicted that a son would be born of a virgin and would be called Immanuel (7:14), and he described the image of the suffering servant (52:13-53:12). These are called Messianic prophecies that anticipate the work of the Messiah. Though it is true that the promise-fulfillment scheme of the history of salvation demands that readers find Jesus Christ foretold in the Old Testament, a wholesale Christocentric interpretation misses significant messages of the Old Testament, in that prophets had unique messages for their contemporary Israel. Consider the benefits their contemporary Israel would have missed if the prophets had only predicted the distant future. Let us see what the prophetic texts themselves show: "Less than 2 percent of Old Testament prophecy is messianic. Less than 5 percent specifically describes the new-covenant age. Less than 1 percent concerns events yet to come in our time."[1] Most of the prophetic messages were directed to Israel pertinent to their current situations. In that prophetic setting, many predicting messages pointed to their near future, such as warnings of the impending destruction by Assyrians and Babylonians. Prophets delivered God's message to their contemporary Israel, like today's sermons, reinterpreting the law for their situations, judging their disobedient lives, and guiding them to hope of restoration. Prophets did not add new doctrines or a plan of salvation, but reinterpreted and presented the law to accomplish the original covenant.

Prophets delivered unique messages, depending on the different historical and geographical settings, before, during, and after the exiles. The Assyrian army came from the north, the same route that Abraham and Sarah traveled from Ur, and destroyed Israel in 722 BC. The rising Babylon replaced Assyria and seized Judah in 586 BC.

The fall of Israel, northern kingdom 722 BC	Amos, contemporary of Isaiah and Hosea, prophesied in Israel 760-750 BC.
The fall of Judah, southern kingdom 586 BC	Habakkuk prophesied in Judah 620-610 BC. Jeremiah prophesied in Judah 627-560 BC. Ezekiel prophesied in Babylon 593-570 BC.
The early return from captivity 538 BC	Ezra led the second major return to Jerusalem 458 BC.
	The last prophet prophesied in 400 BC.

The prophets' messages are characterized by their covenantal perspective, in which God sovereignly used the then world powers to judge and reshape Israel. Many Israelites were killed, and the rich and gifted were taken into exile in Assyria and Babylon. The ten tribes of the northern kingdom were totally lost among the pagans, whose ruthless policy deported conquered peoples. Some remnants of Judah and Benjamin returned from Babylon only to find the ruins of Jerusalem.

A couple of lessons should be mentioned before we move into the prophetic books. First, God's judgment on Israel's disobedience to the law is a critical matter, for they could not be simply forgiven by God's love. When we face God's harsh judgment of his people, we should be mindful of his higher way of shaping his people. We should humble ourselves before his decree and try not to judge his plan with our wisdom. The prophet Isaiah delivered God's message on this matter: "As the heavens are higher than the earth, so are my ways higher than your ways and my thoughts than your thoughts" (55:9). Second, God is gracious right in the middle of judgment. In the messages of judgment is found the promise of God sending his Messiah. Thus, when God's people face challenging situations, they should not consider it a means of destruction but a means of maturing them. Third, God's covenantal perspective includes all nations and is broader than the perspective of human enemy. As God proved himself the Lord among Egyptians as well as Israelites, and incorporated Rahab, Ruth, and Gibeonites into Israel, God punished Israel by means of Assyria and Babylon.

Amos, prophet of judgment

Amos was a shepherd in the town of Tekoa in the southern kingdom when he was called to prophesy against the northern kingdom of Israel. He was neither raised in a prestigious family nor served as a professional prophet or priest but lived by rough work at a little-known place. His credentials as prophet are interesting when one considers that he delivered God's message of judgment to a neighboring country. Would they receive his prophecy? Amos' ordinary background discloses the very nature of prophecy.

Amos' prophecy began with God's judgments on the neighboring countries around Israel. The judgments were written in a pattern: "This is what the Lord says: For three sins of Damascus, and even for four, I will not turn back my wrath" (1:3). Three sins are enough, but four sins are more than enough sin before God. The same pattern of judgment on pagan countries applies to Judah and Israel. God's people were not different from the pagan people in their sinful lives. This must have hurt their religious pride. Judah's sin was that "they have rejected the law of the Lord and have not kept his decrees" (2:4), and Israel's sin was injustice and immorality (2:6-9). Disobeying God's law is the same as doing injustice. By practicing injustice, they had disobeyed the law.

God responded to Israel's lawlessness by raising up the cruel army of Assyria:

> An enemy will overrun the land; he will pull down your strongholds and plunder your fortresses.... This is what the Lord says: "As a shepherd saves from the lion's mouth only two leg bones or a piece of an ear, so will the Israelites be saved.... On the day I punish Israel for her sins, I will destroy the altars of Bethel; the horns of the altar will be cut off and fall to the ground." (3:11-14)

This prophecy was delivered in the form of a prediction for the near future. The Assyrian army invaded Israel in the next generation. Their disobedient acts were deeply related to their spiritual status:

> "Go to Bethel and sin; go to Gilgal and sin yet more.
> Bring your sacrifices every morning, your tithes every three years.
> Burn leavened bread as a thank offering and brag about your freewill offerings—
> Boast about them, you Israelites, for this is what you love to do," declares the Sovereign Lord. (4:4-5)

A great sarcasm we read in God's Word of judgment. Bethel was Israel's religious center for worshipping God, and Gilgal another place for the same purpose. In what sense have they sinned in their worship centers? In verse 5, the Israelites were proud of their religious heritage and busied themselves with religious practices. However, their religious busy-ness did not square with the worship of God, for their hearts were filled with pride. When the object of love is mislaid, religious practices are distorted. They were not mindful of God. We can peek into their mind in the next verse:

> When will the New Moon be over that we may sell grain,
> and the Sabbath be ended that we may market wheat?
> —skimping the measure,
> boosting the price and cheating with dishonest scales,
> buying the poor with silver and the needy for a pair of sandals,
> selling even the sweepings with the wheat. (8:5-6)

Worship had been reduced to practicing religious rituals. When worship became ritual, the people's hearts were not empty, but filled with something other than God. That something other that takes the place of God is an idol. Their idol was money. They were mindful of their idol, and religion was only an external gesture. That was what they did in their great temples. The sarcasm of God's judgment fits their spiritual status.

Their sin was religious hypocrisy. Such sin was known by their doing injustice in daily life:

> You who turn justice into bitterness and cast righteousness to the ground....

> You hate the one who reproves in court and despise him who tells the truth.
> You trample on the poor and force him to give you grain.
> Therefore, though you have built stone mansions, you will not live in them….
> You oppress the righteous and take bribes and you deprive the poor of justice in the courts.
> Therefore, the prudent man keeps quiet in such times, for the times are evil. (5:7-13)

Is it possible for God's people to be religiously faithful and at the same time morally unjust? What was going on among the Israelites at that time? Both the northern and southern kingdoms were doing well economically and politically. Israel had expanded its territory, which led them to national pride. International trade made merchants rich, which led them to greed. They believed that God favored them because they were the chosen people, and their prosperity seemed to prove it. Religious pride and material prosperity do not prove each other. Rather, religious pride works like a cancer in that though seemingly unnoticed, it seeps into all parts and corrupts the whole body. Religious pride led to religious hypocrisy in living. The Israelites probably worshipped God in their religious activities but not in their hearts. Not worshipping God in their hearts proved itself in their careless life—doing injustice.

God hates religious hypocrisy:

> I hate, I despise your religious feasts; I cannot stand your assemblies. Even though you bring me burnt offerings and grain offerings, I will not accept them…. But let justice roll on like a river, righteousness like a never-failing stream! (5:21-24)

The central message of Amos is found in verse 24: "let justice roll on like a river." The law-abiding life is the life of practicing justice in daily life. True faithfulness is born from the worshipping heart and proves itself in doing justice.

Did the Israelites receive Amos' message of God's judgment? Unfortunately, they did not. Amaziah, the national leader of Israel's religion, rejected him, saying "Go back to the land of Judah. Earn your bread there and do your prophesying there" (7:12). Amos' credential as prophet did not depend on who he was but on who had sent him. Amos replied, "but the Lord took me from tending the flock and said to me, 'Go, prophesy to my people Israel.' Now then, hear the word of the Lord" (7:15). To the disobedient Israel, Amos delivered God's judging message: "Your land will be measured and divided up, and you yourself will die in a pagan country. And Israel will certainly go into exile, away from their native land" (7:17).

At the end of Amos' prophecy, God added his promise of salvation. The promise of salvation does not mean withdrawing the judgment or the immediate saving of Israel out of danger, but restoration of the remnants after the judgment done:

> In that day I will restore David's fallen tent.
> I will repair its broken places, restore its ruins, and build it as it used to be....
> I will bring back my exiled people Israel; they will rebuild the ruined cities and live in them. (9:11-14)

Amos' prophecy of an impending Assyrian invasion came true at around 722 BC. Many from the ten tribes of Israel were killed, and most of the gifted were taken to various parts of the Assyrian Empire. Assyrians implemented cruel policies of relocating the conquered people and forcing inter-racial marriages so that the conquered people lost their national heritage. The ten tribes of Israel never returned but were dispersed into the pagan culture. Amos' prophecy included prediction of Israel's near future, but the prediction had a role in the major message: God was disciplining and reshaping disobedient Israel by way of raising up the Assyrians.

Habakkuk, prophet of the pastoral heart

What Amos prophesied to Israel, Habakkuk prophesied to Judah. Babylonians came from the north via the same route that Assyrians had invaded Israel and seized Jerusalem in 586 BC, about one hundred and fifty years after the fall of the northern kingdom. Habakkuk predicted and probably saw the fall of Jerusalem. Habakkuk's prophecy was unique in that it was composed of his dialogues with God but did not have God's direct messages. Even the words of judgment on disobedient Judah were coming from the prophet himself, not from God. Hearing the perplexing decision of God's raising Babylonians to chastise Israel, Habakkuk raised his voice to God to reveal his deep care for his people, his struggle to comprehend God's way of treating Israel, and his profound faith in God. Habakkuk's pastoral heart for his people—a great model of pastoral leadership—is found throughout the message. With God's harsh judgment determined for the near future, Judah was instructed to live by faith, faith that proved itself by trusting God in the challenging times. This trusting faith is what Paul cited in the New Testament to explain its nature.

Habakkuk's three short chapters are composed of two sets of Habakkuk's complaint to God, God's reply, and Habakkuk's trusting confession at the end. It begins with Habakkuk's raising his voice to God: "the law is paralyzed, and justice never prevails" (1:4). He complained against God regarding Judah's lawless life. When he asked God why he was tolerating his people's disobedience, God responded, "I am raising up the Babylonians, that ruthless and impetuous people" (1:6). God was raising up the ruthless Babylonian army to judge and reshape his people. The text then describes the Babylonian cavalry with terrifying images of leopards, wolves, and vultures. Compared to their cruel power, Israel was just a small, insignificant piece of land far beyond the rivers and desert.

Hearing God's reply, Habakkuk raised his second complaint with a perplexed heart. He reasoned that God was just in punishing his disobedient people, but using the wicked empire to correct them was way too much and missing the point: "Why then do you tolerate the treacherous? Why are you silent while the wicked swallow up those more righteous than themselves?" (1:13). Habakkuk argued that though disobedient and thus deserving punishment, Judah was comparatively more righteous than the pagan Babylonians because they were God's chosen people and had the law. Habakkuk was beseeching God for his people. His perplexity was caused by his honest doubt and agonized heart for the destiny of his people: "I will stand at my watch and station myself on the ramparts; I will look to see what he will say to me and what answer I am to give to this complaint" (2:1). God's reply has two parts. The first part is for Judah: "the righteous will live by his faith" (2:4). This reply is expanded in the last chapter in the form of Habakkuk's prayer. The second part is God's condemnation of Babylon. Because the Babylonians, though used as hands of God's judgment, had ruthlessly plundered many nations, they would be plundered by the plundered.

God did not plainly reveal to Habakkuk why he was raising up the Babylonians and judging his people. In the concluding chapter, Habakkuk responded by grounding his hope in God's mighty lordship over all creation: "He rules over all his creation and no one stands before him." With conviction, Habakkuk pours out his heartful prayer: "in wrath remember mercy" (3:2). Pleading for God's mercy comes from trusting faith. Here we see faith as trusting God's providence regardless of the situation he has determined. Trusting faith is not based on human comprehension. Oftentimes faith does not know what God is doing or why. Faith, rather, is a trusting response to God's fatherly providence. Abraham and Sarah did not understand what God had been trying to achieve with them and why. However, in his time God graciously fulfilled the promise they received. Until the time of fulfillment, they were required to have faith, trusting faith in God's providence for them. Habakkuk poured out his perplexing complaints to God, and he received God's reply, but he still did not understand the way of God. Faith is the way of living with the unfathomable way of God. In the end we find Habakkuk's confession of faith, realistic to the dooming situation but audacious enough in trusting God's faithfulness:

> I heard and my heart pounded, my lips quivered at the sound;
> decay crept into my bones, and my legs trembled.

Yet I will wait patiently for the day of calamity to come on the nation invading us.
Though the fig tree does not bud and there are no grapes on the vines,
though the olive crop fails and the fields produce no food,
though there are no sheep in the pen and no cattle in the stalls,
yet I will rejoice in the Lord.
I will be joyful in God my Savior.
The sovereign Lord is my strength; he makes my feet like the feet of a deer, he enables me to go on the heights. (3:16-19)

The new covenant and hope for restoration

While judging, God was still faithful to his covenant: "The time is coming, declares the Lord, when I will make a new covenant with the house of Israel and with the house of Judah" (Jer. 31:31). The new covenant means the renewed covenant of law. Israel and Judah broke the law because they did not obey the law in their heart, though they looked faithful externally. With the law broken, their covenantal relationship with God had to be terminated. Instead of terminating it, God was now renewing the law with a new condition—a sign of his grace: "I will put my law in their minds and write it on their hearts. I will be their God, and they will be my people" (31:33). With the law implanted in their mind and heart rather than engraved on the stone tablets, they would not need to teach or force others to obey it. God was renewing his original plan of salvation so that his people would be better shaped. God's law implanted in mind and heart may signify the broken, repentant heart, for people would not take God's law in their heart until they realized their sinfulness. To the judged and humbled people, the gracious God was renewing his covenant. As a result, God's judgment did not destroy his people, but restored them.

Ezekiel's vision of the dead bones powerfully reenacts God's grace of renewing his people. The valley full of dry bones symbolizes the lifeless people of God in Babylonian exile. Ezekiel was called to prophesy to the bones: "Dry bones, hear the word of the Lord.... I will make breath enter you, and you will come to life…[;] and breath entered them; they came to life and stood up on their feet—a vast army" (Eze. 37:4-10). God explains the vision: "I am going to open your graves and bring you up from them; I will bring you back to the land of Israel" (37:12). This hope of restoration is called the "covenant of peace" (34:25). The vision of Israel's destiny from death to life is parallel to God's creating human life in the creation account. As God gave his breath to the lifeless body of dust to make it a living being, God gave his breath to the dead bones and made them living people. God was re-creating his judged people.

Righteousness and justice

In both Amos and Habakkuk, and in all the prophetic books, we notice an important theme of upholding justice. Justice embodies the highest value of right relationship with God and others. In modern culture, righteousness and justice may sound like two different concepts—the former belonging to the religious or private realm, and the latter to the public or social. However, in God's act of shaping his people, the two were integrated with each other so that one essentially implied the other.

Abraham was called to be righteous: "Abraham believed the Lord, and he credited it to him as righteousness" (Gen. 15:6). Here righteousness, *tsadeq* in Hebrew, is the intrinsic nature of the triune God. God is righteous and just. Declaring that Abraham is righteous means he is in right relationship with the righteous God. Righteousness is a relationship term. The relationship, when used in its verb form, demands conforming to a standard. The Hebrew term "comprises both active and stative meanings: one 'acts rightly,' one can 'be righteous.'"[2] Thus, in his acts of shaping his people, God demanded that they prove the relationship by keeping his law. To be righteous and to practice justice are integrated in the term so that one implies the other. Oftentimes, *tsadeq* appears along with *mishpat*, which means justice. Such a juxtaposition of terms is found in Amos. There, God reminded his people to live by the law: "let justice [*mishpat*] roll on like a river, righteousness [*tsadeq*] like a never-failing stream" (5:24). Written in a unique Hebrew style of repetition, the second line reinforces the idea of the first. Right relationship with God demands practicing justice.

Habakkuk's renowned teaching, "but the righteous will live by his faith" (2:4), shows the relationship between righteousness and life as well as the relationship between righteousness and faith. Faith encourages the righteous to live with justice. In sum, God himself is the measure of righteousness. Being righteous means being in right relationship with God. The right relationship with God demands living up to the law that he established for the covenantal relationship, in both worship and interpersonal relationships. The integration of righteousness and justice continues into the New Testament and forms the essential meaning of a redeemed life.

Missio dei

From Exodus on, God engaged with pagan world powers and delivered his people as a consequence of proving himself the Lord against their gods. While delivering Israel, God incorporated pagan peoples. Rahab, Ruth, and the Gibeonites are examples. God's way of shaping Israel as his people is much broader than their shaping by their national heritage. Right before their engaging in battle with Jericho, the Angel of the Lord said he was for neither Israel nor her enemy, but came as the "commander of the army of the Lord" (Josh. 5:14). In Amos, God judged the sins of Israel and Judah in the same way he judged the sins of all the nations. Isaiah similarly delivered God's messages to all nations. God raised Assyria and Babylon as his instruments for chastising his people, but he also judged them for their ruthlessness. God judged Moab, Damascus, Cush, and Egypt; his judgment was not to destroy them, but to transform them, along with Israel. A highway would be built from Egypt and Babylon to bring Israel back, drying up the Egyptian sea and Euphrates River (Isa. 11:15-16). The "Way of Holiness" would be built for the return (Isa. 35:8). God's people are not limited to Israel. In God's plan, all are blessed with Israel: "In that day Israel will be the third, along with Egypt and Assyria, a blessing on the earth. The Lord Almighty will bless them, saying, 'Blessed be Egypt my people, Assyria my handiwork, and Israel my inheritance'" (Isa. 19:24-25). The highway between Egypt and Assyria, once the Crescent of temptation, was prophesied to be the Crescent of God's worship. God is the Lord of all, forming his people out of all, with Israel as a model people. The nature and scope of God's salvation clearly appear in these books of the prophets. This overarching *missio dei* should shape the Christian view of history and God's mission that shuns ethnocentrism.

Discussion Questions:

1. How does religious hypocrisy appear in modern culture? How do we get rid of it and worship God in a more faithful way?
2. Habakkuk's argument with God shows his honest doubt. Share your experiences of such questions or doubts against God.
3. Practicing justice is an integral aspect of life in the Old Testament. Does the requirement continue in the church of the New Testament?

Endnotes

1. Gordon D. Fee and Douglas Stuart, *How to Read the Bible for All Its Worth*, Fourth edition (Grand Rapids: Zondervan, 2014), p. 188.
2. David J. Reimer, "*tsadeq*," in *New International Dictionary of Old Testament Theology and Exegesis*, vol. 3 (Grand Rapids: Zondervan, 1997).

Chapter 14

The Messianic expectation

Historical background

The exile left a tremendous impact on the destiny of God's people. God scattered the northern kingdom of Israel, ten tribes of his people, into the pagan empire, and they never made it back home. In 538 BC, Cyrus, king of the Persian Empire, issued an edict allowing the first group of the two tribes of the southern kingdom to return to their homeland. Twenty years later they rebuilt the Jerusalem temple. At around 450-400 BC, Ezra and Nehemiah led a reformation of the Jewish religion. Malachi, probably a contemporary of Nehemiah, served as the last prophet. There are about four-hundred and fifty years between Malachi and the first figure of the New Testament. That long period of time, called the inter-testament period, was a "dark age" to Israel, for there was no Word of the Lord while Israel was continuously under foreign oppression.

Prophets described the cruel acts of Assyrian and Babylonian armies committed against God's people. All these descriptions, so hard to swallow, they saw as God's sovereign acts. We cannot help trembling, along with Habakkuk, when we read the lofty way of God's salvation. However, another awesome act of God—promising restoration—is found right in the midst of the harsh judgment. The hope of restoration of God's people was given in the form of God's promising the Messiah. When all hopes were gone, when Israel seemed like lifeless bones and stumps of cutdown trees and when the crushed remnants cried out to God for mercy, he answered their prayers with the promise of the Messiah. The expectation of the coming Messiah developed at around 500 BC and steadily grew. The promises of the Messiah bridge the two testaments in the unique structure of a silenced dark age between the two.

The term "Messiah" came from the Hebrew word *masiah*, which means "to anoint." Anointing was the ritual act of pouring oil to separate persons or objects for God-given service. The anointing defined the holy identity, character, and acts of the anointed one since it was understood as God's act. Significant for understanding the nature of anointing was the fact that God chose and sent the anointed to accomplish special tasks. The authority and power of the anointed were not their own, and thus they were to be used according to God's will. The term *masiah* was used as a general term to refer to diverse cases of anointing. Priests, kings, and prophets were anointed for their special tasks. In an extended sense, the term was even used to refer to Cyrus, the pagan Persian emperor. Cyrus was not anointed in Israel, but he was said to have been anointed by God for the task that God gave him (Isa. 45:1).[1]

During the inter-testament period, Israel's hope for restoration grew in conjunction with the notion of a messiah, and the Israelites developed the idea of "the Messiah." They were waiting for the Anointed One. In the Old Testament Prophets, there are a few direct mentions of the One Messiah. The Hebrew Old Testament was translated into Greek at around the third century BC. In that translation, called the Septuagint, *masiah* was translated to *christos* and was used in the New Testament. It is translated as Christ in English. The Messiah is Christ. As early as in John 1, we find the notion and mention of the established Messiah. Andrew said to his brothers regarding Jesus, "we have found the Messiah" (1:41), and Nathanael called him "the King of Israel" (1:49). They meant the One Messiah, whom Jews had been waiting for. Thus, when we read the Old Testament Prophets retrospectively from the perspective of the Jesus event, many passages are found to refer to the promised Messiah.

Let us take a close look at several significant prophecies and see what images were used to describe the promised Messiah. Then we will compare them with the history of Jesus in the Gospels to see who Jesus is.

Messiah, the king

As God sent kings to enforce his law in Israel, they were one of the major human agents God used to accomplish her salvation. The king image of the Messiah begins with God's promise to raise kings from the line of David to rule over his eternal kingdom, in 2 Samuel 7. The vision of the Davidic kingship anticipates fulfillment of the kingly rule described in Deuteronomy 17. Kings of Israel were supposed to rule by God's law, not by conventional means of human resource, material wealth, or military power. Psalm 89 sings God's faithfulness for establishing and keeping the Davidic kingship for Israel: "I have found David my servant; with my sacred oil I have anointed him.... I will establish his line forever, his throne as long as the heavens endure" (vv. 20-29). God's faithfulness to the Davidic kingship persists, the Psalm continues, even with kings' breaking his law: "I will punish their sin with the rod," but "I will not violate my covenant" (vv. 32 and 34).

The long-suffering faithfulness of God to the eternal kingship of the Davidic line is reflected in the king image of the Messiah. When we read in the history of Israel that many kings of Israel actually failed to live up to the ideal kingship and that the Davidic kingship was defeated by the pagan empires, the images used to describe the promised Messiah are seen to refer to the renewed ideal king.

Chapter 9 of Isaiah begins with the situation of the northern kingdom, when "the people [were] walking in darkness." During such a crisis, God promised light. The image of light expands to a child:

> For to us a child is born, to us a son is given,
> and the government will be on his shoulders.
> And he will be called Wonderful Counselor, Mighty God,
> Everlasting Father, Prince of Peace.
> Of the increase of his government and peace there will be no end.
> He will reign on David's throne and over his kingdom,
> establishing and upholding it with justice and righteousness
> from that time on and forever. (vv. 6-7)

The son is a royal son coming from the line of king David. The images of child and son symbolized a new beginning and hope, with the status of his being born from a father or being sent from a king. The image of a servant was used for a similar purpose. The son is described with various images of king. Among them, the four titles of the king—"wonderful counselor, mighty God, everlasting father, and prince of peace"—are prominent, especially to the contemporary people of Isaiah. Israel needed a mighty king who would bring peace. No new doctrine or plan for salvation was added here, only God's faithfulness and zeal to send the true king to Israel. The promised royal son would reign as a great king and mighty general, with justice and righteousness, unlike the failed kings. Here justice and righteousness are an epithet of the law.

Against the immediate situation of the fall of the northern kingdom, as described in verses 1-5, the vision of the ideal king might have referred to the son of the king at that time. In an extended sense, indeed, the promised ideal king anticipates the coming of the Messiah. Israel at the time of Jesus' birth was under Roman rule, and they were still waiting for the mighty king who would bring peace. Thus, the Christian church sings this Messianic prophecy during the season of nativity. In application, if you are longing for peace for your life and the world, you are part of Israel, who are waiting for full restoration of God's kingdom through the Messiah.

Isaiah chapter 11 also describes the Messianic reign with the image of a king. Against the background of Assyrian captivity, Isaiah envisions the "day the Root of Jesse will stand as a banner for the peoples" (v. 10). God will create the Messianic kingdom, where remnants of Israel return home and God will be praised among all nations as the Lord, and all will live in peace. Again and again in the Bible, God's vision of salvation works with the restoration of Israel and extends to the world. In that day, Israel will be restored, the remnants will return from all nations (vv. 11-16), and "the nations will rally to him [the Root of Jesse, the promised

Messiah]" (v. 10). In chapter 60, Isaiah illustrates more fully his vision of the Messianic kingdom:

> Nations will come to your light, and kings to the brightness of your dawn....
> Then you will look and be radiant, your heart will throb and swell with joy;
> the wealth on the seas will be brought to you, to you the riches of the nations will come... to the honor of the Lord your God, the Holy One of Israel,
> for he has endowed you with splendor.
> Foreigners will rebuild your walls, and their kings will serve you.
> Though in anger I struck you, in favor I will show you compassion....
> You will drink the milk of nations and be nursed at royal breasts.
> Then you will know that I, the Lord, am your Savior (vv. 3-16).

This passage may be understood to refer to the contributions made by the pagan kings, such as Darius and Artaxerxes, when they decreed to assist Israel's return out of their royal treasury. At the same time, along with the wider vision of the transformed situation of humans and the animal kingdom (11:6-9) and the ultimate vision of the new heavens and new earth (66:22), we may view this verse as anticipating the time when the Messiah will establish his kingdom.

The visions that this prophecy anticipates depend on who the Root is. He will come as a shoot out of a cut-down tree, of the Davidic line, and on him the Spirit will rest. The Spirit coming down symbolizes the power and wisdom of the king. He will judge with righteousness and justice (vv. 2-4), unlike the corrupt kings in those days in Israel. And he will strike the earth "with the rod of his mouth," which signifies the Lord using Assyria as his means of chastising his people. The Messiah will come from the line of king David in Israel and will restore the whole world.

Messiah, the shepherd king

The image of a shepherd is used to augment the status of the Messianic king. The use of shepherd-sheep metaphors to describe God and his people's relationship is found throughout the Old Testament. The custom of shepherding has been lost in much of the modern culture, and we need to visit the biblical times to see what it meant. When King David realized God was the shepherd and he was a sheep in his pasture, he knew God by personal intimacy. For he knew what shepherds were doing for their flock. Shepherds stay with their sheep day and night, for sheep are helpless without their constant care. Shepherds know their habits and preferences of food and habitats. They know how to lead, feed, and protect sheep from danger. Without a shepherd, sheep are lost in the dangerous wild. In that context God is called the shepherd to Israel.

God had shepherded his people out of Egypt and exile: "He brought his people out like a flock; he led them like sheep through the wilderness" (Psa. 78:52); "He tends his flock like a shepherd; he gathers the lambs in his arms" (Isa. 40:11);"It is he who made us, and we are his; we are his people, the sheep of his pasture" (Psa. 100:3).

God anointed human shepherds, the kings, to tend and take care of his people. However, they turned out to be unfaithful, taking care of themselves and scattering people in the wild. Ezekiel 34 reveals God's wrath on the bad shepherds and his promise to provide the right shepherd: "I will place over them one shepherd, my servant David, and he will tend them; he will tend them and be their shepherd" (v. 23). With the Davidic messiah ruling finished, God is making "a covenant of peace" with Israel (v. 25). Peace came to Israel in the immediate context of their return to Jerusalem and would be fully achieved with the coming of the Messiah. With the tasks of human shepherds fulfilled, God says, "You my sheep, the sheep of my pasture, are people, and I am your God" (v. 31). God, the true shepherd, is sending the shepherding Messiah.

Messiah, the suffering servant

Matthew, in chapter 12, cites Isaiah 42:1-4, the servant song, as a reference to Christ. The servant in the text is the Messiah. The image of a servant does not imply an ordinary servant, but instead shows the status of being sent as a representative to accomplish the will of the sender. Being sent from God, he comes with his law, and he rules over the earth with justice. The servant is given the task of king:

> Here is my servant, whom I uphold, my chosen one in whom I delight....
> I, the Lord, have called you in righteousness; I will take hold of your hand.
> I will keep you and will make you to be a covenant for the people and a light for the Gentiles,
> to open eyes that are blind, to free captives from prison
> and to release from the dungeon those who sit in darkness" (vv. 6-7).

The servant in Isaiah signifies the new Israel: "You are my servant, Israel, in whom I will display my splendor" (49:3). By completing the duty of the ideal kingship of the Davidic covenant, the servant will fulfill the task of Israel. Then, Israel will be model people of God to the Gentiles. Being a light for the Gentiles, Israel will bring the good news "to the ends of the earth" (49:6). The servant's faithfulness in pursuing righteousness and justice will free people from bondage of all kinds.

The servant is further described as a suffering servant in Isaiah 52 and 53. The servant comes from dry ground with an unbeautiful appearance, is despised and rejected by people, and suffers death for others

(53:2-5). The servant dies for others: "Surely he took up our infirmities and carried our sorrows, yet we considered him stricken by God, smitten by him, and afflicted. But he was pierced for our transgressions, he was crushed for our iniquities; the punishment that brought us peace was upon him" (53:4-5). Isaiah clarifies why he died for others:

> Yet it was the Lord's will to crush him and cause him to suffer,
>   and though the Lord makes his life a guilt offering,
> he will see his offspring and prolong his days, and the will of the
>   Lord will prosper in his hand.
> After the suffering of his soul, he will see the light of life and be
>   satisfied;
> by his knowledge my righteous servant will justify many and he will
>   bear their iniquities. (53:10-11)

The servant is sent to be offered as guilt offering. The guilt offering was required when an Israelite committed sin in regard to holy things of the Lord. Animal sacrifice was offered as "restitution for what he has failed to do" (Lev. 5:16). An animal's life was sacrificed in place of the sinner's life. The servant is the restitution. Verse 11 compactly summarizes God's plan of salvation, namely to justify sinful Israel as righteous. God justifies sinful Israel by means of substitutionary death, first by the animal's life (the type), then by the life of Christ (the anti-type). This text envisions the substitutionary death and atonement that Jesus has accomplished as the Messiah. The innocent servant died the death of judgment, bearing condemnation of sinners, and earned the credit of righteousness. Sinners will be given that righteousness and become the "offspring" of God in the servant. This plan of God's salvation was faithfully carried out by the servant. And God vindicated the servant's faithful obedience by raising him up from death, his resurrection. The text "the will of the Lord will prosper in his hand" was fully achieved by Christ, the suffering servant.

Images used to describe the character of the promised Messiah anticipate God's future working for salvation. The first-century Jews, living under foreign oppression for a long period of time, tried to see the man Jesus in light of the Messianic prophecies to see whether he was the Messiah. The kingly images that Jesus seemed to prove by his miracle-performing authority and heavenly teaching fitted perfectly their expectation. However, much of his external form seemed to betray their expectation. They found several conflicts among Jesus' acts. His criticism of the priests and law teachers, his interpretation and application of the law, his manner of coming into Jerusalem, and more than anything else, his mention of his death instead of political restoration of Israel, were hard for the Jews to fit with their images of the Messiah. Consequently, they were confused between what they saw Jesus do and who he said he was. While the images of king and shepherd were popularly received, the notion of the suffering servant did not fit their political and religious expectation. Hence, the question from the Jewish situation, as we close the Old Testament and move to the New, is how God is working salvation through the promised Messiah.

God's plan of saving Israel did not change but has continued since the time he sent human agents with anointed tasks. Sadly, it turned out that those human agents proved unfaithful and earned God's judgment:

> The priests did not ask, 'Where is the Lord?'
> Those who deal with the law did not know me; the leaders rebelled
>   against me.
> The prophets prophesied by Baal, following worthless idols. (Jer. 2:8)

The human agents in this text were priests, kings, and prophets. It was not in serving their tasks that they were corrupt and unfaithful but that they themselves did not worship God. This religious situation continued, and the first-century Jews did not recognize Jesus. Jesus came and picked up where the fallen human agents had dropped off.

Discussion Questions:

1. Share your ideas of how the king image and suffering servant image work together in the person of the Messiah.
2. Share what images of God you have for your life?
3. In what ways did the Messiah become the New Israel?

Endnote

1. John N. Oswalt, "*masiah*," in *New International Dictionary of Old Testament Theology and Exegesis*, vol. 2 (Grand Rapids: Zondervan, 1997).

Chapter 15

The gospel: who Jesus is and what he accomplished

The New Testament begins with the gospels. The gospels are the first four books, which record the primary witnesses of Jesus' events. Gospel means *good news*. The good news is that Jesus is the Messiah. Peter delivered the good news to the Jewish religious leaders and the confused public: "it is by the name of Jesus Christ of Nazareth, whom you crucified but whom God raised from the dead, that this man stands before you healed" (Acts 4:10). The name "Jesus Christ of Nazareth" delivered the most succinct but beautiful confession of Christian faith. The man Jesus, who lived in Nazareth and "whom you crucified," was the God-promised Messiah.

The question regarding Jesus' identity is the most important inquiry for humanity, for your answer to the question determines who you are and how you live. That was so to the first-century Jews and is still so today. The disciples knew Jesus as the Christ, the Messiah. Their way of knowing Jesus, namely against the historical background of Israel from the inception of the Messianic expectation through the inter-testament period, is still the best way for us. For Jesus did not appear out of nowhere to claim he was the Messiah. The disciples' view of knowing him is also practically helpful because it provides us with their undisguised experience of Jesus in faith and doubt. Their stories of growing faith through confusion and doubt comfort and challenge modern readers, who share a similar experience.

Between the testaments

Jesus came after the inter-testament period of about four-hundred years. Those were silent times for Israel. The status of Israel "without king or prince, without sacrifice," as Hosea prophesied for the period of exile, continued after the return from the exile. The Jewish religion had been significantly altered since the exile of Israel and the successive changes of the world powers around the Mediterranean region. It is necessary for us to review the historical and religious changes made in the Jewish community during the inter-testament period in order for us to see how God's plan of salvation worked out through the Messiah.

Though there was no Word of the Lord to Israel, Paul viewed these years as a period of preparation: "But when the fullness of the time was come, God sent forth his Son, made of a woman, made under the law" (Gal. 4:4). During the inter-testament period, God rearranged the scenes of history, much as stage crew rearrange the stage sets after the curtain has fallen; for when the curtain rises, there is an entirely new scene, the coming of the Messiah. After Joel, Jonah, and Malachi had ceased their prophesying at about 430 BC, God allowed a period of time for his Word to spread throughout the world. That was done by the exiled Israel. What a tragedy it was, from Israel's point of view, that God's Word was spread by the punished people of God!

Nations became familiar with Israel's religion through the presence of the Israelites among them. Kings of Persia encountered their religion and even praised their God. The book of Ezra describes the Persian kings' decrees in favor of the Israelites, even commissioning Ezra to teach God's law to the Israelites who would return from exile. After Alexander the Great brought an end to Persian rule, the Jews came under the heavy influence of the Greek culture in 334-63 BC. As its language was popularly used in the Mediterranean world, the Jews translated the Hebrew Bible into Greek. The translation, now called the Septuagint, made in the mid third century BC, was accepted in the Jewish community as the authoritative text of their religion and was used by the New Testament authors. The geographical distance between the diaspora Jews in Egypt and Babylon and the Judean Jews created theological variations. The diaspora Jews, who no longer had access to the temple at Jerusalem, developed loose ideas of the law, such as temple worship and animal sacrifice. In place of the temple, the synagogue was developed as the place of prayer and worship as well as social gathering of the diaspora Jews. Synagogues had also been built in Palestine and even in Jerusalem by the time of Jesus. As Jesus himself regularly visited the synagogues to read and teach the Bible, it had become a significant platform for his public ministry.

When Jesus was born, the Palestinian Jews were under Roman rule. Herod the Great was the king of Judea from 37 to 4 BC, a puppet regime under Rome. Roman officer Pontius Pilate ruled as the governor. Religiously, the Jews generally maintained the monotheistic faith of their ancestors, along with their identity as God's covenant people, based on the Torah—the five books of Moses—and other books of the Hebrew Bible. However, the mainline political and religious culture, which was characterized by polytheism, emperor worship, and pagan philosophy, instilled conflicting diversity in the Jewish community in regard to details of interpreting and applying the law and dealing with the political situation as God's chosen people. Acts 4 provides a Jerusalem scene where Jesus' disciples were challenging religious leaders about Jesus' identity. The religious leaders failed to recognize Jesus as the Messiah. Popular among the Jewish religious leaders were priests, Pharisees, and Sadducees.

Since the time when the Jerusalem temple was rebuilt in 516 BC, priests had held prominent leadership in association with the temple and the area around it. High priests began to form the leading elite of Sadducees. Sadducees were the upper-class leading group of the Jewish community, fulfilling many political and religious offices and managing the Jerusalem temple, the center of religious and political activities. They maintained the authority of the Torah only, and they rejected the authority of other parts of the Hebrew Bible, such as prophets and the oral tradition. They believed that the Torah validated the ruling power of priests. Influenced by Hellenism, they did not believe in resurrection or life after death. That is why they were disturbed by Peter and John's testimony of Jesus' resurrection (Acts 4:2). They maintained only the value of moral actions in this life.

Pharisees emerged as a group of law interpreters and teachers when the Hellenistic influence shifted the religious leadership from the temple. Unlike the Sadducees, the Pharisees resisted the Hellenistic influence. Pharisees maintained the high authority of the oral tradition along with the written Torah. While Sadducees focused on the temple services and rituals, Pharisees emphasized the importance of the law and applied it in the present life. They believed in bodily resurrection and life after death. Paul came from the Pharisaic tradition. The Pharisees received popular support from the common Jews, while many of the Sadducee leaders were stigmatized by corruption. It is noteworthy to see that Jesus was very critical of both Sadducees and Pharisees in light of the failed leaders in the Old Testament.

Historians have excavated scrolls of the Essenes and studied their characteristics. They opposed both Sadducees and Pharisees for their impure practices of supposedly achieving true righteousness. Fewer in number and smaller in public influence, the Essenes separated themselves from the public, lived in their isolated community, and maintained strict rules on prayer, Sabbath observance, denial of personal property, dietary law, and an ascetic moral life.

Another group that presented the first-century Jews were the Zealots. They led an aggressive political movement, with an aim to overthrow Roman rule and reestablish Israel. Theologically, they faithfully held to the traditional confession that God is the only Lord. Jesus chose Simon the Zealot as one of his disciples.

The racial and cultural conflicts between returned Jews and Samaritan Jews made another significant setting for the ministry of the Messiah. When Assyria seized the northern kingdom, they deported its inhabitants and brought foreigners to its place (2 Kings 17). The remaining Jews in Israel intermarried with the foreign settlers. The new settlers brought in their religions and did not worship the Lord of Israel (Ezra 9 and Neh. 13). Though descendants of the inter-racial marriage identified themselves as Jews, they were called Samaritans. The conflict between the two groups continued to be aggravated when the returned Judeans found that the Samaritans were not cooperating in rebuilding the temple. The Jews of the southern kingdom did not agree or associate with them. The conflict reached its peak when the Maccabees of Judea destroyed the Samaritan temple at Mt. Gerizim at around 113 BC. The distrusting relationship between the Judean Jews and Samaritan Jews developed during most of the inter-testament period.

Jesus' teaching was often situated in racial conflict. In Matthew 11, Jesus judged unbelieving Jews in Chorazin, Bethsaida, and Capernaum by comparing them to the most wicked cities of the Old Testament—Tyre, Sidon, and Sodom (vv. 20-24). The three Jewish towns, located at northern shore of Lake Galilee, were the center of Jesus' ministry, and Jesus called Capernaum his own town. Even the people of those wicked cities—Tyre, Sidon, and Sodom—would have believed if he had performed the same miracles there, Jesus said. This is the same method of rebuking Jews as in his parable of the Good Samaritan. Jesus found good faith in a Canaanite woman in the region of Tyre and Sidon. Though Jesus refused her by saying that he was sent for "the lost sheep of Israel," the woman demanded mercy of Jesus (Matt. 15:21-28). The dynamic inter-cultural context of the first-century Jews provided a significant platform on which the gospel of Jesus Christ was shaped.

It was during the politically unstable and interculturally dynamic situation that significant preparations for the Messiah's coming were made. The Old Testament had been translated into vernacular Greek so that Israelites would have access to God's Word in the common language, and synagogues had been set up as a platform for religious gatherings. Synagogues would become the center of Jesus' ministry. The Israelites continuously suffered under foreign rule, and their religion was broken into diverse groups. As in the previous ages, they needed the true priest, king, and prophet. Their hope for the coming Messiah was becoming ever fresh in their situation.

Who is Jesus?

Imagine how the first-century Jews saw Jesus in such a fluctuating situation. Jesus was born a baby boy from an unmarried couple, Mary and Joseph, and was raised in Nazareth. Jesus' birth was witnessed by shepherds and later by a group of magi who came from the east. Neither group was a reliable witness in the Jewish community. Jesus was an ordinary man from a mediocre family background, with nothing to give him recognition. John the Baptist's introduction of him regarding his divine origin did not penetrate to the public's ordinary mind (John 3). When Jesus claimed he was the promised Messiah, the Jews of his hometown Nazareth disowned him. They asked, "Isn't this Joseph's son?" (Luke 4:22). Matthew provides a fuller reaction of the Jews: they knew his mother, Mary, and his brothers and sisters in the village. Eventually they "took offense at him" (Matt. 13:57). Someone even asked, "Can anything good come out of Nazareth?" The disciples also wondered at Jesus' authority of controlling nature. When Jesus calmed the storm in the lake, they were amazed and asked, "What kind of man is this? Even the winds and the waves obey him!" (Matt. 8:27). If there had been a newspaper like *the Jerusalem Daily*, the last part of Jesus' life might have been reviewed like this: Jesus, a man from Nazareth, who claimed to be Israel's king and Messiah, and was accused of blasphemy by the Jewish ruling parties, was executed on the cross by Roman soldiers.

The gospels reveal mainly two things: who Jesus is and what he has done. Though the gospels provide the history of Jesus, they reveal more than historical information about Jesus, for they invite readers to make a personal decision about the identity and work of Jesus. The gospels are good news for people.

Jesus' noted claim—"I am the way and the truth and the life"—shaped the biblical method of knowing him. He said to anxious but seeking Thomas, "Anyone who has seen me has seen the Father.... Rather, it is the Father, living in me, who is doing his work. Believe me when I say that I am in the Father and the Father is in me, or at least believe on the evidence of the works themselves" (John 14:9-11). This must have sounded puzzling to Thomas. Jesus made it clear that he was sent by God to accomplish God's plan of salvation. What he did is the very act of God's salvation. The trinitarian structure of Jesus' identity and work is the common method that the New Testament authors employed. In that sense, he is the way, the truth, and the life.

Let us follow this trinitarian structure of revelation and see how Jesus is known in Mark's gospel. The gospel begins with the "good news about Jesus the Messiah, the Son of God" (1:1). The good news is that Jesus, the human person, is the Messiah. And the Messiah is also the Son of God. In the first half, Mark focuses on the identity of Jesus as the Messiah, and in the rest of Mark's gospel, on Jesus' work. The author describes Jesus as the mighty Son of God, who has the authority to drive out demons, heal the sick, feed the hungry (chs. 1, 5, 6, 7, 8), forgive sinners (ch. 2), interpret and teach the law (chs. 2, 3, 6, 7, 8), and subdue nature (chs. 4, 6). These descriptions present Jesus' authority as king and prophet. Right in the middle of the book is placed Peter's confession of Jesus as the Messiah. Next, Jesus illustrates the nature of his Messiahship; for there, Jesus identifies himself as the Son of Man, signifying his suffering as the divine Messiah, his favorite title for himself. The Son of Man, he says, must suffer, be rejected by the Jewish religious leaders, be killed, and rise from dead in three days (8:31). Jesus mentions the way of the cross three times in chapters 8-10. In all three cases, he mentions death as well as resurrection. He had to go through death as suffering servant: "For even the Son of Man did not come to be served, but to serve, and to give his life as a ransom for many" (10:45). Jesus not only announces the radical way of the Messiah for himself but also commands the same for his disciples (8:34-38), destroying their human expectation.

In chapter 11, Mark describes Jesus' kingly march into Jerusalem. Citizens welcomed Jesus as king, shouting "Hosanna" (meaning "save us!"), citing from the Psalm on the Davidic king. But Jesus looked radically different from their conventional image of a king. Jesus' identity and work remained a mystery to the people. When Jesus disclosed himself as the suffering servant, his disciples argued about who was greatest among themselves. Jesus warned the disciples not to tell others about his Messiahship (ch. 8), his driving out demons (ch. 1), his healing power (chs. 5, 7, 8), and the disciples' experience of Jesus' transfiguration (ch. 9). It was not to keep Jesus a mysterious Messiah, but to teach the public the right identity of Jesus as the suffering Messiah. Jesus was to be known by his actions.

In Jerusalem, Jesus rebuked the religious leaders by reforming the temple from its misuse (ch. 11) and, through the parable of the tenants (ch. 12), pointing out their mismanagement of religion. As a consequence, the religious leaders looked for occasions to accuse and get rid of Jesus. In chapter 14, an unnamed woman poured out expensive perfume on Jesus, signifying his forthcoming death and burial. Jesus prepared himself for the final phase of his servant work with agonizing prayer. After that prayer, he was arrested and sent to stand before the Sanhedrin, the Jewish ruling party. They questioned and beat Jesus but did not find anything to indict (14:55). Then Jesus was sent before the Roman authority. While Mark indicated Pilate's assumption of Jesus' innocence, Luke, in chapter 23, recorded that Pilate and Herod found no basis for Jesus' death penalty four times. Being afraid of a Jewish riot, Pilate gave in to the Jews' demand to "Crucify him!" Jesus, the innocent, was accused by his own people, especially by the religious leaders, and was executed as a criminal on the cross by the hands of Roman soldiers.

Jesus' death on the cross remarkably conformed to the Old Testament prophecies of the suffering servant. See below some examples that show promise-fulfillment connection from Psalms 41 and 22:

Mark 14:18, "… one of you will betray me—one who is eating with me"—from Psalm 41:9, "… he who shared my bread, has lifted up his heel against me"

Mark 15:34, "My God, my Gold, why have you forsaken me?"—from Psalm 22:1, "My God, my God, why have you forsaken me?"

Mark 15:24, "and they crucified him"—from Psalm 22:16, "… they have pierced my hands and my feet."

While the citations above prophesied Jesus' death, the citation from Isaiah below fore-tells what Jesus' death would achieve:

> "Yet it was the Lord's will to crush him and cause him to suffer, and though the Lord makes his life an offering for sin, he will see his offspring and prolong his days…[;] by his knowledge my righteous servant will justify many, and he will bear their iniquities." (53:10-11)

Jesus the Messiah died as a suffering servant to atone for the sins of his people. A radical twist of the usual priest-sacrifice relationship was that Jesus the high priest offered his body as a sacrifice. Jesus was both high priest and sacrifice (Heb. 9:11-14).

Jesus is God among us.

Those first-century Jews who actually believed that Jesus was the promised Messiah knew him as more than a man. John's gospel begins with Jesus' divine nature:

> In the beginning was the Word, and the Word was with God, and the Word was God. He was with God in the beginning.… The Word became flesh and made his dwelling among us. We have seen his glory, the glory of the One and Only, who came from the Father, full of grace and truth (John 1:1, 14).

This text reveals Jesus in the trinitarian form, which is the most beautiful mystery to believers. The Son pre-existed with God, he was God, and he became "flesh" to dwell among men. God became a man in Jesus! If you read this Johannine text, along with the nativity story of Matthew and Luke, you see with wonder how God reached out to humanity in their concrete, limited reality to save them. Now, see what Jesus said of himself: "I and the Father are one" (John 10:30). Next, see what his disciples said of him: "Thomas said to him, 'My Lord and my God!'" (John 20:28).

Jesus' dual nature, divine and human, is God's means of vicarious salvation, which was anticipated from the law of atonement through animal sacrifice. As a full human being, Jesus could be the substitute for all humans; and as a full deity, he could overcome the power of death. Being Immanuel, God among us in a human body, he lived his life for us, experiencing the full human life that you and I are living. With a body, Jesus could experience and suffer human miseries. The weary and thirsty Jesus talked with a betrodden woman over a cup of water. In that occasion, he told her he was the Messiah. In bodily form, he knew human suffering, healed the sick, fed the hungry, and preached the gospel to the poor. With a body, Jesus could die the human death. With a body, he could be raised back to life. With a body, Jesus could fulfill the work of the high priest: "For we do not have a high priest who is unable to sympathize with our weaknesses, but we have one who has been tempted in every way, just as we are—yet without sin. Let us then approach the throne of grace with confidence" (Heb. 4:15-16).

However, Jesus' own claim of a divine nature and his disciples' worshipping him as God posed a radical challenge to the Jewish monotheistic faith. This theological issue was so fundamentally significant that the New Testament authors had to find ways of settling it, and the church had to formulate it in its confession. The issue was how to describe, in human language, the mystery of the relationship between Jesus and the God of the Old Testament, while satisfying two requirements: that Jesus and God are distinctively revealed but are one and the same in the godhead. The New Testament writings agree that Jesus the Messiah is the God of the Old Testament. This theological issue started a doctrine, which is later called *the doctrine of the triune God*.

The New Testament authors arranged a couple of ways to settle the issue. One way was by referring to Jesus as *Lord*, which was applied to God the Father in the Old Testament. When Jesus said "I praise you, Father, Lord of heaven and earth" (Matt. 11:25), he was applying the Old Testament form of speech. The same authority that the title Lord carried in the Old Testament applied to Jesus in the New. Confessing "Jesus is Lord" was essential for salvation in Romans 10:9: "If you declare with your mouth, 'Jesus is Lord,' and believe in your heart that God raised him from the dead, you will be saved." God vindicated Jesus' faithful work, raised him from death, and exalted him to the universal lordship. Matthew 8:23–27 describes the moment when Jesus calmed the stormy sea: the disciples were frightened by the threatening waves and cried to Jesus, "Lord, save us," and he calmed the storm. This Jesus event corresponds to Psalm 107, in which God's people cried out to God as "Lord": "Then they cried out to the Lord in their trouble, and he brought them out of their distress. He stilled the storm to a whisper; the waves of the sea were hushed" (vv. 28–29). Thomas recognized Jesus, saying "my Lord and my God!" (John 20:28). Confessing Jesus as Lord indicates that he indeed is the same Lord as the Lord of the Old Testament, God himself. The title "Lord," then, is used for both Jesus and God the Father, "until the appearing of our Lord Jesus Christ.... God, the blessed and only Ruler, the King of kings and Lord of lords" (1 Tim. 6:14-15). Other passages show an arrangement that keeps the title Father for God while keeping the title Lord for Jesus: "Now may our God and Father himself and our Lord Jesus clear the way for us to come to you" (1 Thess. 3:11).[1]

The New Testament authors would sometimes title the Son as the power and wisdom of God: "But to those whom God has called, both Jews and Greeks, Christ the *power of God* and the *wisdom of God*.... It is because of him that you are in Christ Jesus, who has become for us *wisdom from God*—that is, our righteousness, holiness and redemption" (1 Cor. 1:24, 30). Jesus, the power and wisdom of God, is with the Father: "Through him all things were made; without him nothing was made that has been made" (John 1:3). Referring to God's power and wisdom does not indicate Jesus' subordination to God as if he is only God's visible character; instead, it reveals the distinction and unity of the godhead at the same time. For he himself is disclosed as the Creator in John 1 and Colossians 1.

The most popular way to distinguish Jesus and God as one deity was by describing Jesus' and God's relationship as one between a father and son. Within the gospel books, Jesus frequently refers to God as his Father: "All things have been committed to me by my Father. No one knows the Son except the Father, and no one knows the Father except the Son and those to whom the Son choose to reveal him" (Matt. 11:27). These arrangements in the Bible were made from analogies of human relationship to describe the intimate relationship between God and Jesus, and Jesus' salvific acts as commissioned by God.

Jesus in confession

The issue of the person of Jesus was the biggest challenge to the early church when the New Testament was not yet fully collected as the Canon. The fundamental issue of Jesus' identity was settled in the Nicene Creed (AD 325), decided at the first ecumenical council of the church. This creed was structured in a trinitarian formula, similar to the Apostle's Creed. Since the immediate interest of the creed was Jesus' divinity, its writers paid special attention to the second part:

> We believe in one Lord, Jesus Christ,
> the only Son of God,
> eternally begotten of the Father,
> God from God, Light from Light,
> true God from true God,
> begotten, not made,
> of one being with the Father....

The authors tried to emphasize the biblical teaching that Jesus is as divine as God and that Jesus is God himself. While mostly using biblical terms, the authors used a philosophical term to illustrate the truth to the contemporary church. It is the Greek term "*homo-ousios*," meaning "of the same nature." Jesus is of the same divine nature as God of the Old Testament. The Nicene Creed is still in use as a common confession on the identity of Jesus.

What did Jesus do?
The New Testament considers the historical event of Jesus' death and resurrection as the foundation of Christian theology. At the earliest stage of the church, when the Jews were amazed by the outpouring of the Holy Spirit, Peter witnessed to nothing but Jesus' death and resurrection: "You killed the author of life, but God raised him from the dead. We are witnesses of this" (Acts 3:15). Paul gives his personal witness of meeting the resurrected Jesus while he was persecuting the church. His encounter with the resurrected Jesus changed his life and transformed him to a disciple of his gospel. In 1 Corinthians 15, he extends the historicity of Jesus' event from the prophecies that foretold it to the history of those whom the resurrected Jesus met: "After that, he appeared to more than five hundred of the brothers and sisters at the same time, most of whom are still living" (15:6). Without Jesus' death, there is no salvation; without his resurrection, Christian faith is futile. Jesus' crucifixion climaxes, and his resurrection accomplishes, God's plan of salvation.

Jesus' resurrection is a physical phenomenon: Jesus was crucified, died, was buried, and then on the third day rose to life in bodily form. What Paul says in 15:44—"it is sown a natural body, it is raised a spiritual body"—indicates the radical transformation of bodily condition from sinful to glorified, and it does not make a distinction between the physical and spiritual. The sinful body dies in its perishable, dishonorable, and weak condition, but the new body is raised to life in an imperishable, glorious, and powerful condition. The resurrected body is not a kind of ethereal or disembodied form; but being cleansed of sinful influence, humans receive the God-originally-intended and salvation-achieved human body. Jesus' resurrection is such a profound basis for salvation that without its truthfulness, the Christian faith would be futile and the witness false. If Jesus remains in death, believers also remain judged in death. Christ's resurrection is the archetype, which will apply to all believers: "but Christ has indeed been raised from the dead, the first-fruits of those who have fallen asleep" (v. 20). The first-fruits were dedicated to the Lord at the beginning of harvest season to signify that all who follow also belong to the Lord. Thus, they are like a pledge of what follows. All who belong to Christ will be raised to eternal life in a transformed bodily form.

Christ's earthly ministry moves to a new phase with his ascension and sending the Holy Spirit. God approved Christ's atoning work and vindicated him by raising from the dead. The resurrected Jesus ascended to heaven. Heaven is where God is, not an ethereal space beyond our reality. Christ's sitting at the right hand of the Father started a new era of his ruling over the world, and thus vindicated his people before the Father. Now Christ is the supreme Lord, "to bring all things in heaven and on earth together under one head, even Christ" (Eph. 1:10). Ruling from heaven, Christ has brought his kingdom into the world. Consequently, the new creation has arrived in the world, and all who have faith in him may enjoy the blessings of his kingdom.

The disciples did not understand God's way of working salvation. When Jesus said that he would leave, they were discouraged, for they had just gathered around him with rekindled hope. His leaving was for their benefit. Jesus said to them, "… it is for your good that I am going away. Unless I go away, the Counselor will not come to you; but if I go, I will send him to you. When he comes, he will prove the world to be in the wrong about sin and righteousness and judgment" (John 16:7-8). The Holy Spirit is the Spirit of Christ, who works as the "advocate" and "helper" for his people. The basic meaning of the Greek term for the Holy Spirit is "alongside." The Holy Spirit's presence alongside the church was what Christ promised, and it gives rest and comfort to the church. The Holy Spirit continues Christ's work by instilling faith in individual believers so that they may believe and be united with him. In that sense, he is the "life-giving Spirit." With the Holy Spirit's empowering presence, the disciples were transformed to witness Jesus' resurrection, and the church was established in the world.

Discussion Questions:

1. The question regarding the identity of Jesus was the biggest query in the early church. Who is Jesus to you?
2. Why does Jesus have to be both God and man?
3. Share what Jesus has achieved by his death and resurrection for you.

Endnotes

1. Hans Bietenhard, "Lord" in *The International Dictionary of New Testament Theology*, Vol. 2 (Grand Rapids: Zondervan, 1979).

CHAPTER 16

The way of righteousness

The New Testament authors read the history of Jesus from the covenantal standpoint. Since they viewed the person and work of Christ as the fulfillment of the covenant promise that had been progressively unfolded in the Old Testament, a typological understanding of the two Testaments is central for reading their writings. In this chapter, we will see the holistic view of salvation that Christ brings in the world, holistic in the sense that personal salvation by faith pertains to the whole-person transformation, with a vision of participating in Christ's mission of reconciling all things to his will. Holistic salvation indicates the meaning and place of personal salvation in God's grand drama, which moves from creation to re-creation. Holistic salvation shapes Christian spirituality and worldview for the kingdom life here and now. Holistic salvation determines the identity and calling of believers in the world, which will be discussed in the following chapters. Now we will see how Christ's death and resurrection works for the way of righteousness.

Atonement

The apostle Paul sees Jesus Christ as achieving God's object of leading Israel to righteousness:

> Now the righteousness of God, apart from the law, has been manifested, being witnessed by the law and prophets. This righteousness of God comes through faith of Jesus Christ for all those who believe, for there is no distinction. (Rom. 3:21-22)

How does God make sinners righteous? That means, how does God make sinners justified so that they can stand before God acquitted? Paul explains the way of transforming them to righteousness by pointing to the covenant law: the ones who actually obey the law are declared righteous (Rom. 2:13). Becoming righteous by keeping the covenant law has been God's plan of salvation from the beginning, and it has never been changed. The problem is with sinners, for no human being is able to obey God's law, neither Jews nor Gentiles (3:9-20). God's way of salvation seemed stuck in a deadlock, with humans remaining under condemnation for sin. The central message of the gospel, and new in the New Testament, is that God's righteousness is available by faith in Jesus Christ. In the Old Testament we heard that "the righteous will live by his faith" (Hab. 2:4). What is new in the New Testament is that one receives life only by faith. The righteous, then, are those who are justified by faith.[1]

The way of making sinners righteous through their obeying the law has not been changed or abolished but comes from Jesus Christ. Christ lived obediently to the requirement of the law and thus fulfilled God's covenant of salvation. Christ's work may be summarized as atonement. Atonement means reparation, amendment, or restoration for an offense or injury. As the atonement for sin, Jesus Christ saves us; his atoning work is the central message of the Christian religion. Since the punishment of sin is death, sinners must be punished by death. However, God graciously prepared a way of atonement so that sinful humans may be forgiven of their sins and restored before God. God could neither simply cancel human sin nor forgive sinners because of his justice. Atonement must satisfy both aspects of his nature—love and justice. His love found a way to satisfy his justice. Sacrifice was the chosen way of atonement in the Old Testament. When, according to the law, a sinner's life was "transferred" to the sacrificed animal and its blood was presented to God, the offerer was "covered," and he was atoned for. Atonement had two parts: removal of sin and restoration before God. The ritual system was arranged by God's gracious promise to accept the sacrificial blood as ransom. Blood represented life. The Christian way of salvation is vicarious atonement from the beginning, for it is based on the sacrifice of ransom.

How is that ritual system of animal sacrifice related to Christ's atoning work? It is through the typologically progressive revelation from the Old to the New Testament. Jesus Christ accomplished the Old Testament plan of salvation by offering himself as the sacrifice. The ritual of animal sacrifice was not meant to teach Israelites to believe that animal's blood

Typological reading of Christ's atoning work

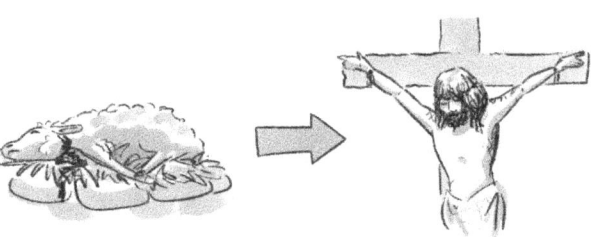

animal sacrifice	Isaiah 53:3-7	Jesus Christ
"type"	Messiah prophesied	"anti-type"
in the OT law	as suffering servant	in the gospel
		of the NT

per se was powerful enough for God's forgiveness of their sins. Animal sacrifice was offered to God as a "type" of ransom, which pointed to its "anti-type," the fulfillment of its ritual goal. The type was offered in the form of promise in the ritual law, and its goal was reached by the ultimate sacrifice, Jesus. The typological structure of Christ's atonement shows that the way of God's salvation is found in the covenant-law relationship.

Jesus offered his life "as a sacrifice of atonement" (Rom. 3:25). As the high priest, he offered his body as ransom for sinners:

> He did not enter by means of the blood of goats and calves; but he entered the Most Holy Place once for all by his own blood.... For this reason, Christ is the mediator of a new covenant, that those who are called may receive the promised eternal inheritance—now that he has died as a ransom to set them free from the sins committed under the first covenant. (Heb. 9:12-15)

God's wrath becomes appeased because his justice is satisfied, and the sinners are forgiven and restored before God.

Vicarious atonement and penal substitution capture the main feature of Christ's atonement in judicial terms. The Bible employs judicial terms to describe the nature of atonement. Mark describes Jesus' death as a ransom: "the Son of Man did not come to be served, but to serve, and to give his life as a ransom for many" (10:45). A ransom is a price paid to release someone from suffering and sin. Jesus gave his life as ransom to free many lives from the penalty of their sins. Redemption is another significant judicial term. Paul says, "In him we have redemption through his blood, the forgiveness of sins" (Eph. 1:7). Redemption means an act of salvation done by making proper payment. Jesus redeemed humanity; that is, he paid the required price by his death, and as consequence believers' sins are forgiven.

To whom is the ransom dedicated in the judicial understandings of Christ's atoning death? Whose justice and wrath are to be honored? Is it God the Lawgiver or Satan who is afflicting sinners? It is God's justice that must be satisfied and his just wrath to be appeased. Retribution belongs only to him (Rom. 12:19). For he is the one who preordained the way of the world. God uses guilt, suffering, and death to punish sinful humans, and God uses Satan's scheme as the means of punishment. Satan serves God's government, and for that purpose only he is given power, even the power of death. Satan did not own the world, nor did God give up the world to him. When we trust that Christ's atoning death satisfies God's justice, we are set free from Satan's grips, and his ultimate tyranny of death dies.

Forgiveness of sin is declared in terms of justification. Believers are pronounced to be just before God: "We have now been justified by his blood.... For..., while we were God's enemies, we were reconciled to him through the death of his Son" (Rom. 5:9). Justification is a proclaimed state of being right with God even while believers do not realize it in life. Reconciliation is another way of describing God's salvation. Sinners, who were enemies to God, are now reconciled to God through Christ's death (2 Cor. 5:18-20; Col. 1:20-22), and the world also becomes reconciled to God through believers' lives.

Diverse judicial images and concepts have been employed to yield a full understanding of Christ's atonement. A rich combination of images, such as sacrifice, blood, and ransom, reveals the tremendous price that Christ has paid to make vicarious atonement for us. Another combination—of forgiveness of sin, justification, redemption, and reconciliation—gives a rich meaning of the effect that atonement brings to us. Surely, its effect is wholistic, encompassing the legal, spiritual, moral, and physical aspects of human life.[2]

It is important not to reduce atonement to a legal matter. The Bible provides evidence of other aspects of atonement. Liberation is a powerful image used in the history of salvation. Israelites remembered their ancestors' experience of the exodus throughout their long history of oppression. Prophets used the images of a just king, a shepherd king, and a liberator-king to describe the Messianic work. Jesus used such images when he revealed himself to the confused and oppressed Jews (Luke 7:22). The idea of salvation associated with the image of liberation is still relevant to modern believers. As Jesus set us free from the bondage of sin, such as shame, guilt, and feelings of loneliness, alienation, incompetence, and failure, we can have hope in his new life. Christ's liberation does not stop at religious liberation but also promotes justice. As the Old Testament law centered on worshipping God and practicing justice among people, the law of Christ requires the redeemed to love God and people.

The Liberator Christ is the Victor Christ. While the satisfaction theory sees the human problem of sin as violation of God's justice, the Christ-the-Victor theory sees it as a conflict and victory against the evil power. Christ is the Victor! This theory captures well the goal of the history of salvation—God's sovereignty over all creation. Beginning with Exodus, God continuously competed with the evil power and proved his lordship over all creation. Only Christ the Victor can send his Spirit and continue his salvation work in the sinful world. The image of Christ-the-Victor may be even more relevant for believers who think they are waging spiritual warfare with the evil power. It provides them assurance of God's mighty power and victory for them. That is a tremendous comfort to suffering believers.

Finally, "justification by faith" summarizes the biblical way of receiving righteousness. How shall we receive Christ's righteousness and become justified? It is by faith, which is the work of the Holy Spirit in sinner's heart. By faith, we accept the reality of Christ's transfer of his righteousness to us. This way of becoming righteous applies to all who have faith in Christ's atoning work (Rom. 3:22-23). Faith is born out of a generally judicial framework of atonement. But faith is more than a legal matter. As sin, according to the Bible, is a totality that infects the whole person to the point of dedicating all human faculties in revolt against God, so in the reverse order, faith must involve the whole person's loyalty to God's way of restoring. Faith has been defined as a combination of certain knowledge and wholehearted trust. The knowledge aspect of faith is essential, as it provides what to believe. Trusting is another essential aspect of faith, as it accepts God's offer of salvation and puts the salvation into practice.

Faith and good works

In salvation, God aims at a whole-person transformation. Now we will continue the discussion of the essential connection between righteousness and justice, which we started in the Old Testament. The Hebrew term *tsadeq*, meaning "righteousness," was translated into Greek in the New Testament as *dikaiosyne*. The Greek term signifies both righteousness and justice. Paul uses the term three times in Romans 3:26: "He did it to demonstrate his *justice* at the present time, so as to be *just* and the one who *justifies* those who have faith in Jesus." The first two may be translated to "righteousness" and "righteous," as found in some English Bibles. The double meaning of the term should not confuse readers, but provide them with a rich concept of justification. In the New Testament, to justify means to make someone right with God. To be righteous and to be justified are integrated in the word so that to be righteous implies being justified, and vice versa. The two are not separated in God's intent of salvation. It is true that righteousness has a legal connotation, signifying that God declares repentant sinners righteous in his court. However, the legal connotation is included in its principal relationship, meaning that it signifies restoration of sinners to the right relationship with God.

Justification, as it pertains to a right relationship with God, always requires the appropriation of it. John the apostle joins spiritual righteousness and the practice of justice into the concept of salvation: "He who does what is right is righteous, just as he is righteous" (1 John 3:7). The divine object of justification is to proclaim and mature the righteous as righteous in their I-thou relationship to himself: "Righteousness, then, is not merely found in the beginning; it sustains the whole course. The believer is drawn by it into the movement of the rule of God. Hence, the statements concerning justification should not be separated from the life-giving dominion of Christ."[3] Finally, righteousness is teleological, looking forward to a future of living in fellowship with God.

Paul directs the church to live a righteous life by obeying the law of Christ: "Carry each other's burdens, and in this way you will fulfill the law of Christ" (Gal. 6:2). The law of Christ is not a new doctrine or a set of regulations added to salvation, but a Christian moral principle. The law of Christ may be found in his teaching on the great commandments. Jesus answered the question "What is the most important commandment?" this way: "The most important one… is this. 'Hear, O Israel: the Lord our God, the Lord is one. Love the Lord your God with all your heart and with all your soul and with all your mind and with all your strength.' The second is this: 'Love your neighbor as yourself'" (Mark 12:29-31). Love completes all the moral commandments.

One may recall the text in which Paul seems to teach that one is saved by believing with the heart and making confession with the mouth. Let us compare the text with the other that seems to teach differently:

Romans 10:9, 13	Matthew 7:21
"That if you confess with your mouth, 'Jesus is Lord,' and believe in your heart that God raised him from the dead, you will be saved…." "Everyone who calls on the name of the Lord will be saved."	"Not everyone who says to me, 'Lord, Lord,' will enter the kingdom of heaven, but only he who does the will of my Father who is in heaven."

Paul's argument is based on the truth that Christ is "the end of the law" (10:4). He made the righteousness (that he earned by satisfying the law) available to believers through their faith. Sinners become righteous by faith in Christ and not any longer by the working of the law. This is true to all, both Jews and Gentiles. Paul is dealing with the way of salvation in its progress from the working of the law to putting faith in Christ. In Matthew 7, Jesus raises a different issue that pertains to living with faith. Jesus' point is that living faith bears good deeds. The criterion of the good deeds is doing "the will of my Father."

Righteousness and justice are integrated in salvation; that is, as the declaration of righteousness and acting with justice are not separable, and as one implies the other, then faith is complete in a godly life. Paul teaches that "the only thing that counts is faith expressing itself through love" (Gal. 5:6). James echoes Paul by saying, "faith by itself, if it is not accompanied by action, is dead" (2:17). James uses Abraham as an example of such faith: "You see that his faith and his actions were working together, and his faith was made complete by what he did" (2:22). Paul and James do not set faith and actions in conflict but put them together so that one does not work without the other. Faith lives in good moral acts, and good acts make faith complete. Faith is not a stand-alone religious status that we cherish in our hearts; its power overflows from there to be lived out in everyday lives.

Such an integral idea of faith is dramatically illustrated through the episode of Zacchaeus and Christ. The story describes a significant lesson of salvation in that Zacchaeus' change of economic life is followed by Christ's announcement of salvation: "Today, salvation has come to this house, because this man, too, is a son of Abraham" (Luke 19:9). "A son of Abraham," a true Jew, is a designation that Jews would cherish. The story was set against the first-century Jewish socio-religious background. Tax collectors were regarded as traitors and sinners. Zacchaeus was a high-ranking tax collector and was rich. Jesus pronounced the man saved. This episode reflects a typical way of Jesus' teaching—converting the broken-hearted and humbling the proud. The episode does not record any of Zacchaeus' religious conversion but assumes a coherent connection from an internal change to an external transformation of life. How would he attempt the most-likely dangerous shift of life without internal conviction? The promised change alludes to an obvious risk that he will face when he loses his money and power in the socio-political culture. Behind his action is highlighted, silently but strongly, the internal change that meeting with Jesus has caused. Jesus emphasizes through the story that the internal change causes an external change of life. The episode leads to readers' immediate recognition of the holistic connection between faith and acts.

When you hear that faith and good acts are inseparable, and that you are to obey the law of Christ, do you feel an obligation? Indeed, the gospel compels us to live out our salvation. Hear what Paul has to say to you: "continue to work out your salvation with fear and trembling, for it is God who works in you to will and to act in order to fulfill his good purpose" (Phil. 2:12-13). The command to work "with fear and trembling" sounds as if the Christian life is a great burden. Paul's teaching is just opposite; he means assurance and comfort. He encourages believers to "work out your salvation," which God has already achieved for you, not to work for your salvation. God is continuously working in us until our salvation is made complete in a good life. God knows the challenging situation and does not leave the Christian life to human ability only. Our Christian life actually manifests what God is working in us. How comforting and humbling it is to know that every attempt of our works is the result of God's labor in us.

Personal and cosmic aspects of salvation

Salvation in the Christian religion is more than a personal way of avoiding human predicaments. It is structured in the archetype of creation. The Bible reveals the overarching drama of salvation this way: the sovereign God created the world, and he created humanity as rulers over it; humans fell into sin and consequently corrupted all of creation; God did not leave the world and humans under the grip of condemnation but sent Christ to redeem the created world. Salvation is God's act of reversing the effect of sin in his world. Just as through humanity, sin came into the world and corrupted it, so through restoring humans, God transforms the world. This process of salvation is uniquely embedded in the structure of the world; the world is God's kingdom, as he dwells in it; and humans are delegated rulers, as they were created in God's image. The object of God's salvation is his entire kingdom, his full domain, in which all creatures dwell in their intricate relationships under the rule of the King. Transformation of humans is realized by way of personal salvation, which is by faith. The cosmic salvation envisions the restored kingdom of God, which began when Christ came and will be completed in the new heaven and the new earth. From Christ's death and resurrection till his return to complete the new heaven and new earth, Christ is recreating humans and sending them into the world to participate in his reconciling mission. Salvation is structured in the Bible with two aspects: personal and cosmic. The structure of salvation does not mean two different salvations, but one salvation with double aspects.

As the goal of salvation is to shape the whole person in the all-embracing kingdom of God, it is only natural that God's salvation works in all of creation. When the Bible teaches that we become justified by faith, faith means personal faith. The personal nature of faith does not imply individualistic salvation, for faith is born and nourished among covenant people. Personal faith indicates that the offer of salvation must be personally appropriated. Nobody can believe for you or make you believe. You have to meet Jesus and have a personal relationship with him—just as disheartened Zacchaeus, as well as a lonely Samaritan woman who had been mistreated her whole life, and doubting Thomas met Jesus. Some have overwhelming experiences with Jesus, but that is not the only sign of meeting Jesus. Jesus healed and performed miracles in front of many, but he also talked softly to isolated people's hearts. The Holy Spirit chooses the best way of a person's meeting Jesus, according to the situation and personal characteristics.

In the early stage of establishing a Christian community, Colossian Christians were struggling with pagan influences. One of the problems was gnostic dualism, which contended that salvation was made possible by receiving knowledge of spiritual secrets. Gnostics denied the goodness of the physical creation, the physical reality of Christ's body, and the Christian freedom to use the body for living a godly life. As a consequence of this non-Christian teaching, believers there were tempted to either rationalize the pursuit of immortality or accept mystic asceticism. They were afraid of supernatural powers. The problem of a wrongly postulated relationship between spirit and body lingers still in modern culture in diverse forms of spiritism and the New Age Movement.

In Colossians 1:15-20, Paul offered a theological answer to their struggle:

> He [Christ] is the image of the invisible God, the firstborn over all creation. For by him all things were created: things in heaven and on earth, visible and invisible, whether thrones or powers or rulers or authorities; all things were created by him and for him.
>
> He is before all things, and in him all things hold together.
>
> And he is the head of the body, the church; he is the beginning and the firstborn from among the dead, so that in everything he might have the supremacy.
>
> For God was pleased to have all his fullness dwell in him, and through him to reconcile to himself all things, whether things on earth or things in heaven, by making peace through his blood, shed on the cross.

As "the firstborn over all creation," Christ is the Creator. Though the term "firstborn" seems to imply creatureliness, in fact the Greek idiom is clarified at the end of verse 16: "all things were created by him and for him." There is nothing in the world that was not created by Christ, even the spiritual powers such as "thrones or powers or rulers or authorities." After establishing Christ as the Creator, Paul moves on to the churchly primacy of Christ. As the firstborn from among the dead (in v. 18, written parallel to v. 15), that is the first-fruit of the resurrection, Christ is the Redeemer of the church:

> As the firstborn of creation, Christ is the *Creator* of creation.
> As the firstborn among the dead, Christ is the *Redeemer* of the church.

Christ is the Creator *and* Redeemer. The one who created the world came down to save it. Here Paul emphasizes the primacy of Christ in both creation and redemption. In the God-created world, there is no distinction of value between the visible and invisible. Rather, the creation as a whole, highlighted by "all things," is under the primacy of Christ. This view of the world rejects any gnostic or dualistic view of creation. Why should Christ love the world (John 3:16) and lay down his life for it? It is because he created it all. In the Bible, redemption is structured in creation.

With the background of Christ's supremacy as Creator and Redeemer, Paul moves to his concluding remark on salvation: God is reconciling all things in Christ. It is significant that salvation is characterized as reconciliation. As the term reconciliation implies past broken relationships, it illustrates the overview of salvation history—which started with the creational good relationship and continued through the sinful broken relationship, to the reconciled relationship in Christ. What is God reconciling? All things that God created, but that became corrupt by sin. A commentator explains the text:

> The "reconciliation of all things" ought to be understood… to mean that the "universe has been reconciled in that heaven and earth have been brought back into their divinely created and determined order…, the universe again under its head and… cosmic peace has returned"…[;] this universal reconciliation has been brought about, not in some other-worldly drama, but through something done in history, the death of Jesus Christ upon the cross.[4]

Christ's crucifixion has achieved the goal of God's creation. Salvation is structured to pursue and complete the archetypal goal of creation. God's one plan for salvation—that he laid out in his making Noahic and Abrahamic covenants, through his giving the law, and through his sending priests, kings, and prophets to shape his people—has been achieved in Christ's cosmic reconciliation of all things to God. The place of human personal reconciliation is found within the broad object of reconciliation, as Paul explains in verses 21-22.

The cosmic reconciliation does not mean universal salvation. Through the texts that show sinful humans as enemies of God who need Christ's reconciliation (as in v. 21), and other innumerable evidences in the Bible regarding sin, we should conclude with the church that reconciliation is available only through faith in Jesus Christ.

Bavinck's well-known summary of the cosmic reconciliation is that "grace restores nature and takes it to its highest pinnacle, but it does not add to it any new and heterogeneous constituents." God does not create a new world but renews the sin-damaged world with its originally intended goal. Bavinck continues to describe the reality of the reconciled world with these words: "by his cross he restored the organism of creation, both in heaven and earth, and these two also again in conjunction."[5] All created reality, both spiritual and physical, is again unified, and the dwellings of God and humans are merged in Christ's lordship. As a result, Christ may rule over the world from heaven, and believers may pray to him so that his will is carried out on earth as it is in heaven. God in his Spirit remakes each creature, animate and inanimate, and rededicates them in the renewed world. Since the renewed and rededicated lives are analogous to the original creation, we can find the place and mission of the reconciled humanity from our study of the creation and its accomplished form in the new heaven and new earth. This perspective of seeing the present Christian life is significant for both moral and scientific mandates.

Discussion Questions:

1. Share what it means that Jesus saves you.
2. Discuss how the integrated faith-and-acts life may be lived out to extend your personal salvation to the cosmic reconciliation in your learning or work.
3. Share how sin still hinders your redeemed life in both personal and public areas.

Endnotes

1. Gottlob Schrenk, "dikei, dikaios," in *Theological Dictionary of the New Testament*, ed. Gerhard Kittel, vol. II (Grand Rapids: Eerdmans, 1964).
2. Herman Bavinck, in his *Reformed Dogmatics*, vol. 3 (Grand Rapids: Baker, 2006), pp. 447-452, provides a fuller list of biblical description of Christ's atonement.
3. Gottlob Schrenk, "dikei, dikaios," in *Theological Dictionary of the New Testament*.
4. Peter T. O'Brien, *Colossians: Word Biblical Commentary* (Waco, Texas: Word Books, 1982), on Colossians 1:20.
5. Bavinck, *Reformed Dogmatics*, vol. 3, pp. 577, 473.

CHAPTER 17

The kingdom of God we live in

As we discussed the atoning work of Jesus Christ in the previous chapter, we now move to its consequence—the kingdom of God. The way of becoming righteous is through faith in Jesus Christ, who accomplished the requirement of the law for us. Righteousness means transformed spiritual status before God, combined with its appropriation in life. The Christian life is essentially extended to the public realm, with a vision of participating in Christ's reconciliation of the world to God's will. The kingdom of God is the stage where believers live out righteousness. Some queries arise regarding the nature of the kingdom life. Without Jesus' presence in the world—for he ascended to heaven, leaving behind a promise to return—and while we are struggling with the effects of sin, is the kingdom present and does it work here and now? Or is the kingdom a future reality? What did Jesus mean when he claimed, "the kingdom is among you"? The biblical teaching of the kingdom provides us with the unique nature of the kingdom presence, which shapes the identity of believers and their life in the world. Thus, the subjects regarding the kingdom are significantly practical as well as theological.

The kingdom of God is the present reality of the world that Jesus the Messiah brought in among his people. It is the central message of Jesus' ministry that the New Testament is structured around. At the beginning of his ministry, Jesus preached, "Repent, for the kingdom of heaven has come near" (Matt. 4:17), which John the Baptist also preached prior to Christ's coming. Matthew generally used the terms "kingdom of heaven" or "kingdom of the Father," while Mark and Luke referred to the "kingdom of God." They used different terms to refer to the same entity, depending on their given situations. "The kingdom" indicates God's reign. The biblical teaching of the kingdom of God hinges on the absolute kingship of Jesus Christ. Since such absolute kingship is not operative in the modern mind, we need to adjust our thinking to the mindset of the biblical times to appreciate the kingdom reality among us. Kingdom citizens start their kingdom life by forming their relationship with the king. Repentance, which signifies "changing mind" and "turning around," brings people to the king. By turning around from serving an evil master to serving the true king, kingdom citizens show their loyalty to the king and become part of the kingdom. Repentance is made possible because the king has already come and is ruling. Believers' repentance is a consequence of the kingdom, not a cause that brings the kingdom in.

How does God's kingdom work in our lives where sin still abounds? Since the kingdom is an achievement of the Messiah, its character may be recognized by seeing the way Jesus had achieved the messianic mission. The first-century Israelites believed that when the Messiah came, he would lead them into a new age. The change they expected was a simple dynamic change from an old age to a new one. The future change would bring restoration of not only Israel but also the world. Jesus did not accomplish his messianic mission as Israelites had expected. Jesus enacted the kingship in the form of a suffering servant. His earthly ministry through his suffering, death, resurrection, and ascension commenced his kingly rule in the world but did not accomplish it. The completed kingdom will come with his return. He created a two-stage kingdom. A great dismay to his waiting, oppressed people, he extended the kingdom realization to two ages: it began with his presence and will be accomplished at his return. The kingdom has already come among believers, and Christ reigns in the kingdom through his Spirit, but it waits to be fully achieved in the future.

Jesus proclaimed the presence of the kingdom. He replied to the Pharisees, "if I drive out demons by the Spirit of God, then the kingdom of God has come upon you" (Matt. 12:28). When the Pharisees asked about the time of the kingdom, Jesus answered, "the coming of the kingdom of God is not something that can be observed, nor will people say, 'Here it is,' or 'There it is,' because the kingdom of God is in your midst" (Luke 17:20). Jesus' words on the presence of the kingdom may sound puzzling because he said the kingdom is not provable by certain observable signs. In fact, the observable signs were exactly what many Jews expected Jesus to perform. What does Jesus mean by saying the kingdom exists and works "in your midst"? Jesus does not make a distinction between spiritual signs and physical signs, as if the kingdom works only in the spirit or heart. Rather, Jesus affirms his unique way of realizing the kingdom in the world.

Characteristics of the kingdom life

Jesus often presented the kingdom life by means of parables. Parables are simple stories that people would readily know. They were not used to deliver new information, but to evoke listeners' immediate response to Jesus' kingdom message. Jesus used earthly images drawn from the cultural setting to deliver the characteristics of the kingdom life.

The points of reference were not readily understood by the people. Though people heard the stories, such as sowing seed and fishing, they did not recognize the message that Jesus was making. The parables communicated the points of reference only indirectly in their context, where people were confused about Jesus. If Jesus wanted to reveal his Messianic kingdom, his disciples argued, he should have exposed it in a straightforward way. Jesus answered their challenge by saying, "the knowledge of the secrets of the kingdom of heaven has been given to you, but not to them" (Matt. 13:11).

The message of the parable of the sowers is found here: "But the one who received the seed that fell on good soil is the man who hears the word and understands it. He produces a crop, yielding a hundred, sixty or thirty times what was sown" (Matt. 13:23). Here the seed stands for "the message about the kingdom" (v. 19). Jesus preached the kingdom message openly so that people would hear and understand it. But the message does not work in a uniform way for everybody: some people hear it but don't understand it; others receive it but lose it; but still others receive it, understand it, and produce an abundant harvest. This parable reveals the mysterious working of the kingdom: it has come and is working, producing its evidence, but not everybody recognizes it. Though the message is preached to all, not all receive it. Jesus is challenging his listeners to consider how they will respond to his message of the kingdom. The parable is an open invitation to the kingdom, but it works as a judgment on the people who will not receive the invitation.

With the parable of the weeds, Jesus describes the kingdom as a seed, an insignificant but a "good seed" sown in the field. As it grows, weeds are also found in the field. The weeds were not expected, for "an enemy" sowed them. The landlord allows the good wheat to grow side by side with the weeds until the harvest so that the weeds will get bundled and burned, and the wheat will be carried to the barn. The story is a common one to the farmers. Jesus' point is the growing kingdom of God at the present time when effects of sin still impede believers' lives. The kingdom citizens live in the sinful world, but the world will not last and will face judgment. Jesus is saying to us, "If farming makes sense to you, then the working of my kingdom should also make sense to you."

Along with the messages of the presence, growth, and judgment of the kingdom, the parables reveal messages of immeasurable blessings and urgency of the gospel. The blessings of the kingdom life are presented in the parables of hidden treasure and a pearl as well as in the parables of the sower, weeds, and net. The invitation to the blessed kingdom life will not last forever, and judgment is impending. The warning of judgment exposes the urgency to receive the invitation while it is available.

We are to translate the parables in our current terms. The kingdom messages highlight the presence and working of the kingdom. The kingdom works in a unique way by God's mysterious ruling. "The secrets of the kingdom" are given to those who receive them. "Whoever has [the secrets of the kingdom] will be given more.... Whoever does not have them, even what he has will be taken from him" (Matt. 13:12). Jesus emphasized kingdom citizens' heartful dedication with understanding and perceiving the message in their hearts (vv. 13-15). God is equipping his people in their challenging life. The field and net in the parables represent the kingdom setting, our life situation such as families, churches, workplaces, and society. There, God's kingdom may not seem existent or significant to the people. If you see the kingdom existent, working, and growing, you are a kingdom citizen and are responding to God's call to a faithful life.

The kingdom is present and yet to come

The unique characteristics of the kingdom life, its presence and growth in the sinful world, are arranged in the two-stage kingdom existence. Luke 18 and 19 present how the two ages of the kingdom are related. When Jesus announced his impending death and resurrection, his disciples did not understand his plan (18:34). Then Jesus healed a blind man, saying, "Receive your sight; your faith has healed you" (18:42). This healing symbolically indicated Jesus' healing the disciples' spiritual blindness of not seeing his Messianic mission. After that and prior to moving to Jerusalem, Jesus spoke the parable of the ten *minas*. While the Jews anticipated that Jesus' kingly march would bring the kingdom "at once," Jesus had a different outline of the future: "A man of noble birth went to a distant country to have himself appointed king and then to return" (19:12). He assumed a long period of time would pass before his return as an appointed king. While the people expected Jesus to miraculously bring his kingdom right away, he required them to live a faithful life until he returns.

The reality of the kingdom is summarized in this way. Frist, the kingdom does not come by way of a political or military king, but by way of the suffering-servant manner of a king. Second, the kingdom of God works in a two-phase movement, present and future. The first stage of the kingdom has come with the Messiah by way of his suffering, and its second stage will begin when the Messiah returns with the authority to judge. All will rise in a resurrected body, believers for eternal blessing in the new heaven and new earth, and the wicked for eternal punishment separated from God. And third, the kingdom in the present age is characterized by a life faithful to the gospel in the challenging situation. Christ's Spirit empowers believers to keep their faith so that they may see and live out the kingdom life. The kingdom life does not mean the kingdom is hidden in spiritual secrecy, as though it works only in the spiritual realm or within the heart. Rather, it means that Christ's kingly rule, wrought in all aspects of reality, makes sense only by faith.

Kingdom life in two stages

The two-stage kingdom raises some issues regarding the Christian life. One of them relates the doctrines of justification (to be justified) and sanctification (to live a godly life). Believers are proclaimed to be justified, even while they are not realizing it in life over the extended kingdom period. The issue pertains to believers' identity and life. Are they saints or sinners, or both? Paul's unique description of the state of salvation with three tenses—past, present, and future—is noteworthy:

> Since we *have now been justified* by his blood, how much more *shall we be saved* from God's wrath through him! For if, when we were God's enemies, we *were reconciled* to him through the death of his Son, how much more, *having been reconciled, shall we be saved* through his life! (Rom. 5:9-10)

Believers have been justified, and the effect of justification continues at the present time, and their salvation will be confirmed at the final judgment. Verses 9 and 10 are structured in a parallel way:

verse 9	verse 10
We have been justified:	We were reconciled:
by his blood	through the death of his Son
shall we be saved	shall we be saved.

Paul's point is the assurance of salvation throughout the extended kingdom period: if God had decreed to save his people by making his Son a sacrificial ransom, we may have confidence that he is working on it and will finally complete it at the final judgment. The combination of three tenses emphatically indicates God's persistently faithful purpose for salvation.

Believers are called to comfort and joy in assurance of salvation. However, the assurance is often disturbed in actual Christian life. In such a context, a question may arise: Am I still saved? A double identity of the believer has been popularly used for comforting struggling believers. It suggests that believers are both saints and sinners. If one reads the conflict in Romans 7—"what a wretched man I am"—as believers' experiential struggle, the double identity may work in this sense: since believers are both righteous and sinful, a wavering Christian life is probable though not ideal. However, the double Christian identity may cause significant theological and practical problems. The Bible does not posit any third identity between sinner and saint or allow any compromise between the two. Rather, the Bible emphasizes a radical conversion from sinner to saint, either being dead or alive. The idea of double identity causes theologically a schizophrenic view of Christian identity and conflicting images of God. Still, it may serve as an easy explanation for a wavering life.

The Christian's experiential struggle is wrongly posited as the problem of identity. Identity of believers and their progress from justification to sanctification are to be seen within the two-stage structure of the kingdom. God places believers in the maturing process in the integrated progress of justification and sanctification. Believers are called to live the life of justification. God's salvation does not begin and stop at justification, as though as soon as believers are justified, they are transferred to heaven. Rather, they are placed in the extended-kingdom stage. This is God's way of shaping his people. In the Old Testament, God graciously chose his people and then shaped them into his people by law. Now God justifies sinners in Christ and matures them to reach completion by the law of Christ. The present working out of salvation, seen through the three tenses of working salvation, is integral to reaching its completion. It is not like a test for believers to prove their faithful obedience to become justified. It is not like a blind struggle. Instead, it is a reverse order of the ordinary test. It is God's invitation to a grateful living, as a consequence of the already-determined justification, with the Holy Spirit as its pledge. During the present period of the kingdom, all believers are given their "minas" so that they can live the life of justification. Christ even promised to reward them for their faithful work. In that way, justification and sanctification are integral to one process of salvation.

The assurance of salvation and doubt are aspects of a justified life in the present context. Assurance of salvation is rooted in God's pledge that his Holy Spirit works in believers. Doubt bred in the maturing process does not destroy believers. Often, doubt grows faith. Doubt may be a sign of fighting faith, and struggle in life may be a sign of maturing faith.

The new creation has come.

While the kingdom language is popular in the gospels, how do the epistles describe the redeemed life? In the text below, Paul describes the new creation that Christ has brought to the world:

> Therefore, if anyone is in Christ, the *new creation* has come: The old has gone, the new is here! All this is from God, who reconciled us to himself through Christ and gave us the ministry of reconciliation; that God was reconciling the world to himself in Christ, not counting people's sins against them. And he has committed to us the message of reconciliation. We are therefore Christ's ambassadors, as though God were making his appeal through us. We implore you on Christ's behalf: Be reconciled to God. (2 Cor. 5:17-20)

Christ has brought a radical change to the world in the form of a new creation. Older translations of verse 17, such as "he is a new creation" or "he is a new creature," highlight radical personal conversion, which is supported by personal forgiveness of sin in verse 19. However, the translation above shows that the radical change is taking place in the world as well as in the personal realm. This newer translation works better within the given context where "God was reconciling the world to himself." The broader scope of salvation aligns well with the overarching theme of biblical salvation: that salvation is re-creation. In the new creation are found the place and meaning of personal salvation.

The new creation is described in terms of the reconciliation of all things, which is mentioned in Colossians 1. Reconciliation indicates repairing an existing relationship with a goal of serving its original purpose. Such an idea of reconciliation reviews the whole history of salvation in relational terms; from the creational blessed relationship, through the sin-damaged relationship, to the restored relationship in Christ. Though the transformation is made radically, as the emphatic "the old has gone" signifies, the nature of the new creation is renewal of the creation analogous to God's original intent. The New Testament uses the adjective "new" in support of God's act of repairing. Two common Greek words used in the New Testament for "new" are *neos* and *kainos*. The term *neos* implies that something is "new, young, and previously non-existent," while *kainos* implies "new in the qualitative sense of something previously unknown, unprecedented, marvelous."[1] While the former signifies a totally new state, the latter signifies a new state by way of a repairing activity. The qualitative sense of *kainos* is used in the following passages:

> "His purpose was to create in himself one *new* man out of the two, thus making peace." (Eph. 2:15)
>
> "This cup is the *new* covenant in my blood." (Luke 22:20)
>
> "We too may live a *new* life." (Rom. 6:4)
>
> "And I saw a *new* heaven and a *new* earth." (Rev. 21:1)

The meaning of renewal is widely used in the Bible to describe the way of salvation, consequence of salvation, and final state of salvation. All these texts are found in line with the relational idea of reconciliation. God does not remove sinners to create a new person; God removes sins from them. God does not destroy the world; God cleanses it of sin and renews it. God's grace is revealed in his forgiving, reconciling, and restoring acts of salvation. This nature of salvation makes us thankful and humble before God.

The reconciled believers are given the mandate of reconciling life to its original intent. The mandate is analogous to God's creation. Take note below of the implied parallel between the proper mode of human life in the original creation and in the re-creation. Each passage attains the mode of human life based on creation of humanity: created in the image of God to rule over the creation and reconciled to serve as ambassadors.

Human life in creation	Human life in reconciliation
Created in the image of God	New person in Christ
Called to rule over creatures: "Let us make man in our image, in our likeness, and let them rule over the fish of the sea...."	Called to serve as Christ's ambassadors to reconcile the world: "... who reconciled us to himself through Christ and gave us the ministry of reconciliation" (v. 18), "not counting people's sins against them. And he has committed to us the message of reconciliation" (v. 19).

The implied parallel indicates that God continues his original intent of human existence through his act of reconciling the world. Humanity's delegated authority for ruling is renewed in terms of ambassadors.

Another parallel is found between verses 18 and 19: Christ gave the ministry of reconciliation to the reconciled and the message of reconciliation to those whose sins are forgiven. Between the parallel passages is found God's cosmic reconciliation, "that God was reconciling the world to himself in Christ" (v. 19). This parallel emphasizes the calling given to the new humanity to live for reconciliation of the world as God reconciled them. God extends personal salvation to public mandate, that is, living out the gospel in the world. God is sending his people to the world by saying, "go out and live the life of reconciliation as you are reconciled." Salvation does not stop at the reconciliation of believing humans to Christ; instead, it extends from there to the so-called "worldly" realm by using believing humans as agents of reconciliation. Reconciliation is the normal mode of human life. And it is to be lived out in the world.

The kingdom life as new creation may be illustrated with the *butterfly effect*. The butterfly effect has been used to explain how a small initial change may end up with unexpectedly bigger consequences. A tiny movement like a butterfly flapping its wings cannot by itself cause a typhoon. However, in certain conditions it could alter the trajectory of a developing weather situation and make a great consequence. The analogy of the butterfly effect may provide an insightful perspective for living the all-embracing work of salvation in the world. Personal salvation is indeed a personal matter, born from a personal change of spiritual status. It does not seem, by itself, like a significant matter that can change the world. And sin affects the Christian life. However, we must consider what kind of salvation God is working in and around us. Consider that the world-damaging effect began with Adam and Eve's personal sin and that God uses humans' personal salvation to establish them as agents of reversing the all-encompassing effect of sin. Think what would happen if the condition of individual believers' lives was the kingdom of God, where God ruled them in all parts of their life. Believers' individual lives are essentially related to the wellbeing of the world. Seen through the *missio dei* of restoring God's kingdom, individual faith-life is essentially public and cosmic.

Kingdom and church

Christ is now ruling as the king wherever he is believed supreme, and believers are the people of the kingdom. Christ has established his church, and believers form the body of Christ. How is the kingdom related to the church? The church's identity and mission are found in the eschatological perspective of completing the kingdom. The church is not the purpose, as though it is going to exist forever. The church is established as a missional body to participate in Christ's mission of reconciling the world to himself.

In order for the church to serve as the missional body of the kingdom, it has to maintain its identity in the world, for existence precedes ministry. First of all, the church is the body of Christ in the sense that believers are united to Christ in common faith in Christ's death and resurrection. Luke, in Acts 2, records that the church was established to be a witness to Christ's work of salvation. The immediate sign of the outpouring of the Holy Spirit, signifying the primary mark of the church, is the preaching of the gospel of Jesus Christ. The Holy Spirit transformed the disheartened disciples into bold witnesses of Christ.

The church should reflect the gospel of reconciliation in the world. The church is a community composed of reconciled people from all cultures and nations. They are reconciled not only to God but also to one another. The reconciled body should reflect the spiritual reconciliation in its moral and cultural settings. The history of salvation in the Bible provides numerous stories of how the messages of salvation were formed within inter-cultural dynamics. God shaped Israel as a holy nation, in distinction from the gentiles, and used her to serve as the light for the gentiles. God employed diverse means of electing and incorporating the gentiles into the people of Israel. The incorporating process included diverse acts of reconciling those pain-afflicted pagans to God in the settings of envy, hatred, and conflict. God treated foreigners and Israelites alike, by the same law (Ex. 12:49). It is intriguing to read that the first sign of the outpouring of the Holy Spirit was the preaching of the gospel in diverse languages. People heard the gospel in their own languages. Preaching the gospel in various languages is a reversal of the curse in language confusion. And listening to the gospel in their languages is the sign of God's grace to all people.

What deep truth about God's kingdom can such mundane stories as planting seeds and harvesting crops, fishing with nets, and finding pearls in a field deliver? They are too simple and worldly, some people may think, to bear the great message of salvation. Also, simple and mundane was Jesus' way of carrying out his messianic mission. His way of mission was not magnificent enough to convince Jerusalem leaders. The King did not satisfy the conventional wisdom of the people. The clash—between the King's mysterious way of realizing his kingdom and people's worldly expectations of the kingdom—continues from the first-century Jews to the people of today. While unrecognized by bystanders, the kingdom is present and grows in the world. Those who see it will act like the farmer who finds pearls in the rented field. Christ's kingdom message is an invitation for the believing heart but judgment to the calloused heart.

Discussion Questions:

1. Share how the kingdom works in and around you.
2. In what way is Christ's reign both present experience and future hope?
3. Share your joy of experiencing salvation as reconciliation and renewal.

Endnote

1. Hermann Haarbeck, Hans-Georg Link, and Colin Brown, "*kainos*," *The New International Dictionary of New Testament Theology*, Vol. 2. Though the two Greek terms are sometimes interchangeably used, the New Testament used *kainos* to "give expression to the fundamentally new character of the advent of Christ."

CHAPTER 18

Christian spirituality and worldview

We have discussed the holistic salvation that Christ offered and the consequent kingdom he brought into the world. We experience the kingdom in two stages; it is already present and working among believers, but the kingdom will be completed with Christ's return in the future. This two-stage kingdom structure calls believers—while being comforted with the assurance of salvation and its future completion—to live the responsibility of conforming to their redeemed status. Living the redeemed life in the sinful and challenging world causes conflicts for believers, between their redeemed status and their actual experience in the world. Believers are called to keep faith in the increasingly secularizing culture. In this chapter, we will discuss whether the Christian faith makes sense in a modern context, i.e., whether it is relevant in a modern rational and scientific culture, and whether the redeemed life can work in the public sphere.

Spirituality and worldview play a significant role in Christian living, for they provide a platform for perceiving the reality of the world. Spirituality refers to the spiritual disposition that faith offers believers, allowing them to accept the reality that the triune God works in the world. Christian worldview offers believers a biblical way to think about and interpret human life in the world. Spirituality and worldview help believers discern their identity and mode of life in the world. Since our lives are formed within a given culture, cultural context affects individual spirituality and worldview. While we remain sympathetic to an individual context, we should maintain a firm grounding for shaping spirituality and worldview; that grounding is the history of salvation in the Bible. Our individual stories are to be continuously criticized and reshaped within God's story of holistic salvation.

Christian worldview

"I believe in Christianity as I believe that the Sun has risen, not only because I see it, but because by it I see everything else": With these famous words, C. S. Lewis concluded his apologetic essay on the truthfulness of the Christian faith.[1] Lewis dealt with the perspectival issue, that is, how Christians come to know the reality. The Christian worldview, the perspective with which Christians view and interpret their lives in the world, is not a byproduct of faith, like the intellectual reflection of what Christians believe. Rather, the Christian worldview is an integral aspect of their confession, and the confession is shaped within the power and scope of their worldview. Just as we know that what is seen and known is made possible with the working of the sun, so analogously, Christ, who is referred to as the sun in John 1:5, is the foundation of our confession. Paul says, "the reality, however, is found in Christ" (Col. 2:17). There Paul contrasts the shadowy presentation of the reality that was ordered by the law to the reality that Christ presented through progressive revelation. The law that provided a transitory viewpoint, thus "a shadow of the things," is now replaced by the "body" itself that casts the shadow. And the body, the true reality, is known through the working of Christ. "In Christ" is the key to forming the Christian worldview. Who Christ is and what he has accomplished, as we discussed in the chapter on the gospels, is integral to forming the true view of reality. Though in the Colossian text Paul refers to the eschatological progress from the law to its fulfillment in Christ, we can extend that progress to the whole trinitarian work for redeeming the world. The trinitarian work of God—from creation, through redemption, to the present ruling—shapes the reality that we are living now.

Let us begin with the need of religion. Religion is commonly motivated by fear. Religion is perceived as a hopeful way of shunning human predicaments and, as a consequence of such escape, reaching a haven of happiness. The universal need of salvation is seen also in the Christian religion, more intensely conceived because of its deep awareness of sin. Christianity, however, provides a different view of religion because of its uniquely fundamental and comprehensive view of the reality. Human suffering per se is not the determining factor for shaping religion, though it may induce humans to be aware of their need for religion. The Christian religion is founded on God's acts—God restores humanity in his world, after they have fallen into sin, to achieve his intended humanity, analogous to the archetype of his creation. The obvious but easily forgetful fact that the Bible begins with creation implies the significant foundation for the Christian religion—that the Creator is the sovereign God and the Lawgiver. Religion begins with God, not with problem of the world. The Creator's will for creation establishes the law that stipulates how the world ought to exist and run. Since all exist and act under the Creator God, all are properly called to be of religious. The creation is God's kingdom.

Humans were established to live their human life while using and caring for the world with the delegated authority of God. This was to be the normal mode of human life and, consequently, the normal mode of the world. When the creational normality became impeded, the Creator God determined to restore it to the archetype of his creation. God is achieving this mission by restoring humans to the originally intended status so that they can resume the normal life mode. God's redemption achieves re-creation. Within the overarching history of redemption, believers are not religiously eccentric humans, but the full humans that God intended.

The most significant quest for the Christian worldview, then, is to see how the personal benefit of salvation (forgiveness of sins and justification before God) correlates with and instigates the cosmic scope of salvation (reconciliation of the world). The correlation between the two aspects of salvation lies less in how believers apply personal piety to their lives in the world, and more in how they live out their double-natured salvation. For as long as the Christian life is deemed as an application of personal salvation, it may be reduced to an optional consequence of spiritual piety. As long as it is deemed a consequence, it is not an essential and a necessary component of the Christian life.

Faith

We proceed to the way believers adopt the Christian view of reality: by faith. Faith is the spiritual disposition that the Holy Spirit creates in humans, concerning God's act in Jesus Christ. Faith shapes the intellect so that it can see and interpret reality. The author of the Hebrews defines faith with these words: "Now faith is being sure of what we hope for and certain of what we do not see" (Heb. 11:1). Faith converts the believers' perspective to God's way of seeing the world. Note the action verbs that describe the acts of faith: "By faith Abraham… obeyed and went, even though he did not know where he was going… [and] made his home in the promised land… [and] lived in tents… [and] offered Isaac as a sacrifice" (Heb. 11:8-17). Faith restructures the view of reality and motivates the believer to live it out.

As the motivating power of the believer's life, faith is neither a blind drive nor an anti-reasoning imagination. Faith is not anti-worldly, nor does it restrict life to spiritual matters in interpreting and living in reality. Rather, faith provides a comprehensive view of reality, governing reason to produce true knowledge of reality. Regarding the mystery of Jesus' being the flesh and drink for eternal life, Peter said, "You have the words of eternal life. We believe and know that you are the Holy One of God" (John 6:69). In another place, Jesus put the verbs "know" and "believe" side by side regarding his divine nature: "Now they know that everything you have given me comes from you…. They knew with certainty that I came from you, and they believed that you sent me" (John 17:7-8). Though these texts were written for a religious purpose in the ancient age, not for a modern rigorous epistemological scrutiny, the use of "knowing" and "believing" interchangeably indicates how religious faith works in the reality of human life. John, in the sixth chapter, used the two terms in the perfect tense to emphasize the character of faith: it matures and includes knowledge. He is saying that when we have come to the state of faith and continue in it, we have certain knowledge of what we believe. John wrote the texts from a religious standpoint to proclaim that Jesus is God incarnate, and he knew that knowing and believing are different processes of handling data of the world. However, by using the two terms side by side, he demonstrates how knowing takes place in the condition of faith. Faith is the proper mode, or condition, of human existence.

Calvin commented on the former text of John—"faith itself is truly the eye of the understanding"—and on the latter—"thus he shows that nothing which relates to God can be known aright but by faith, but that in faith there is such certainty that it is justly called knowledge."[2] Let us take a closer look at Calvin's understanding of faith and knowledge. To establish the Christian case of knowing, he does not passively attempt to provide reasonableness of faith that scientific critics demand. Rather, he restructures the human epistemological setting on the basis of faith, rejecting the reductionistic scientific view of the mind. He claims that humans are created with a certain condition (gift?) that allows them to think and live with certain *a priori* basics about reality. The *a priori* basics of the world include the "seed of religion," a sense or awareness of God in the human mind: "There is within the human mind, and indeed by natural instinct, an awareness of divinity."[3] The basic sense of God is given to all humans as a consequence of being God's image. It works in the human mind, implicitly or explicitly, either in the form of true religion, or in the form of distorted superstition, or in forms of diverse cravings. The basic sense of God works as a guiding perspective of seeing the world, as discussed with the analogy of the sun. When the mind is cradled within faith, its perception is not restricted to things that pertain to sense perception but includes all human activities—the spiritual and the mundane. Calvin goes on to explain how the sanctified mind works:

> When we call faith knowledge we do not mean comprehension of the sort that is commonly concerned with those things which fall under human sense perception. For faith is so far above sense that man's mind has to go beyond and rise above itself in order to attain it. Even where the mind has attained, it does not comprehend what it feels. But while it is persuaded of what it does not grasp, by the very certainty of its persuasion it understands more than if it perceived anything human by its own capacity.... He [Paul] means that what our mind embraces by faith is in every way infinite, and that this kind of knowledge is far more lofty than all understanding.... For very good reason, then, faith is frequently called recognition... but by John, knowledge.[4]

When the mind is "raised up" by faith, it becomes equipped with God's perspective, so as to see and handle reality, both mundane and spiritual. Here faith is the proper mode of human existence and thus generates knowledge. In faith we understand. Calvin neither reduces the role of the mind to save faith, nor puts faith in conflict with the mind and makes faith a fideistic mystery. Rather, he maintains the role of the mind by restoring its function to its proper human epistemological condition.[5]

Does faith make sense in the modern context?

Let us see how faith may work in modern culture. The discussion that follows does not attempt to prove faith. Rather, it is designed, first, to help readers appreciate their faith against the modern context and, second, to present faith in such a way that one is not irrational to accept it. Since the Enlightenment, philosophers have argued for credibility of proof. In the 19th century, William Clifford proposed a classic form of *evidentialism,* which argued that faith must be grounded on sufficient evidence. He proposed a stringent evidentialism: "It is wrong always, everywhere, and for anyone, to believe anything upon insufficient evidence." He meant evidence in terms of logical, rational, and scientific credibility. If anyone believes anything without such evidence, he argued, the person is not only wrong in the act of believing, but also morally wrong, for the person betrays the human responsibility of inquiry: "The life of that man is one long sin against mankind."[6] Clifford's principle is problematic, first, in that it is impractically strict, for no one can satisfy the infinite regress of evidences. Secondly, his principle is based on his insufficient belief in human capability. At the bottom of his argument lies his "belief" that humans are capable of searching out all evidences pertinent to the matter and of concluding whether the evidences are enough or not.

Clifford's strict thesis initiated a long thread of discussion on the reasonableness of faith. The history of such discussion has shown that presenting faith on certain ground is more constructive for an apologetic purpose and for encouraging faith-life than is arguing for non-evidentialist, dogmatic faith. Then, the question is this: What ground or reason shall we present for faith? Put in another way, is faith meaningful? Believers may try to provide a rational scientific ground that evidentialists demand. They may try some "external" evidence as a basis for Christian faith, such as the antiquity of the Bible, its structure showing that the promises came true at later times, or diverse forms of divine acts that suggest the existence of God and faith in him. Though such attempts may be used to foster faith in a Christian community, appealing to external evidence would inevitably fail because it works within the reductionistic scientific condition.

An alternative to presenting faith in a meaningful way is to tackle the epistemological condition itself. Let us look at Alvin Plantinga's defense of faith. Since strict forms of evidentialism, like the one Clifford proposed, were not realistic and practical, philosophers have long accepted certain beliefs as reasonable even when they are not proved by evidence or grounded in other propositions. Such beliefs were called "properly basic beliefs," basic beliefs properly accepted under certain conditions. There had been three conditions accepted to allow properly basic belief: evident to the senses, incorrigible, and self-evident. Any belief that belongs to one of these categories was called properly basic, and thus reasonable to believe. Simple arithmetic, like 2+1=3, or the statement "Man is an animal" are not provable, but they satisfy the self-evident category and thus may be called reasonable. Being incorrigible means to be persistently inevitable, as in the statement "It seems to me that I see a tree." The statement "There is a tree before me" belongs to the category of evident to the senses.

Plantinga agrees on how the traditionally accepted categories are used to admit properly basic belief. However, he challenges the ground of why only those three categories are allowed. There are other beliefs that we deem reasonable but that do not belong to the three categories. According to the traditionally accepted condition, many of our beliefs have proved irrational. Even though propositions about material existence may be properly basic, "the same cannot be said either for propositions about the past or for propositions entailing the existence of persons distinct from myself." An example of propositions about the past, "I had lunch this noon," does not belong to either evident-to-senses, incorrigible, or self-evident, and the belief is not based on other propositions. It is absurd not to accept such a belief as a reasonable belief. Thus, the traditional category of properly basic faith is not coherent with the reality.[7]

Plantinga moves on to argue that belief in God may be admitted as a properly basic belief. We normally accept the existence of self and the world as a properly basic belief without need of rational argument or proof. Belief in God may be accepted in a similar way:

> First, arguments or proofs are not, in general, the source of the believer's confidence in God. Typically the believer does not believe in God on the basis of arguments; nor does he believe such truths as that God has created the world on the basis of arguments. Second, argument is not needed for *rational justification*; the believer is entirely within his *epistemic right in believing*, for example, that God has created the world, even if he has no argument at all for that conclusion… [;] belief in God relevantly resembles belief in the existence of the self and of the external world…. In none of these areas do we typically *have* proof or arguments, or *need* proofs or arguments.[8]

As belief in existence of self and world is neither grounded on evidence nor based on other propositions, but is admitted as a reasonable belief, so in a similar way the Christian belief in God and his world may be admitted as a reasonable belief. The key of the resemblance between the two kinds of belief is "the epistemic right in believing." Plantinga appeals to the epistemic condition in which humans are born and live, which allows certain proper belief. The epistemic condition is a human right, says Plantinga.

However, it is absurd to admit any belief as properly basic. Plantinga delimits the justifying condition for belief in God: "if (a) he [believer] is violating no epistemic duties and is within his epistemic rights in accepting it and (b) his noetic structure is not defective by virtue of his then accepting it."[9] In other words, the believer must reason coherently within the Christian faith structure, and he must be sound in his mind in accepting the faith structure. For the proper epistemic condition that forms Christian faith, Plantinga appeals to Calvin, as is mentioned above. The universal awareness of God serves as the human epistemic condition. In another place of his *Institutes*, Calvin elaborates on his reflection of God externally as well as internally. Since the creation exhibits "as in mirrors, those immense riches of his [the Creator's] wisdom, justice, goodness, and power," men cannot see the world without finding the Creator God there.[10] Thus, awareness of God is doubly convincing to the human mind and serves as the epistemic condition for belief in God.

Plantinga moves to another level of acknowledging God. Assured by the internal and external awareness of God, believers recognize God's working in their ordinary life through such experiences as "guilt, gratitude, danger, a sense of God's presence, a sense that he speaks, [and] perception of various parts of the universe."[11] While these reflections of God are mediated, God's revelation in the Bible is a direct voice of the living God. When it is properly received in the heart, it serves as the "corrective lens" for believers so that they can clearly look into their conscience, otherwise covered with dust of sin, and clearly see the world, otherwise distorted by a sinful perspective. When their Christian epistemic condition is vitalized, the internal, external, and experiential elements complement one another so as to strengthen their faith.

Plantinga attempted to present Christian faith as a meaningful human experience, at least in justifying the way Christians know God. What is significant in his presentation is that he considered the Christian faith engageable in human reality, meaningful, and relevant to human life. He pursued the goal from an uncompromising Christian standpoint in conversation with philosophy. Does this effort matter? Is "faith alone" not enough? Isn't such an endeavor digressing to philosophical speculation and eventually losing the power of faith? Answering the question by choosing a narrowly defined pietistic spirituality or an engaging-the-culture spirituality depends on one's understanding of the nature of salvation that God is working in and around us. In God's comprehensive salvation, shaping the Christian mind is not an intellectual appendix to spiritual transformation or an option for the Christian life. The thinking faculty is essential for human existence and an integral gift for human living. The mind is to be restored by faith to serve its unique work.

Personal pious spirituality

In this section we will discuss how the biblical history of salvation shapes spirituality within given cultural context. An interesting study compared the spirituality of the 16th-century Reformer Calvin and that of the 19th-century Kuyper. Calvin and Kuyper agreed on the continuing effects of justification through the working of the Holy Spirit, but they expressed different emphases on how justification works in the present age. In the unstable European context, religiously and politically—where Calvin lived most of his adult life as refugee—Calvin assumed believers' paradoxical status, paradoxical in the sense that while they are justified, their life remains still sinful. He considered believers as pilgrims in the world. Suffering and hope for future full salvation characterized believers' present life. Kuyper, though not denying the present life's paradoxical character, emphasized believers' status as affecting the present world. Kuyper saw the Holy Spirit renewing and quickening life so that believers could enjoy the glory of God and live out the regenerated life in the world.[12]

While Calvin characterized the present Christian life as a spiritual journey to future full-salvation, he by no means advocated the soul-winning idea of salvation or escapist view of spirituality. We may find a fuller view of his spirituality by looking at his understanding of the present Christian life at the stage of salvation. Calvin stressed integrity of life—"sincere simplicity" of life in the world: "it [salvation] must enter our heart and pass into our daily living, and so transform us into itself that it may not be unfruitful for us." Christian life takes "the whole soul," the whole human self and life. Calvin tirelessly emphasized the transformation of life, thus highlighting sanctification.[13] Calvin's emphasis on spiritual journey is to be understood within such a framework of Christian life and is not to be limited to the spiritual realm. Calvin did not spiritualize the Christian life by way of a narrow view of salvation or escapist spirituality; instead, he argued that spirituality must permeate and affect believers' daily living.

Calvin identified the present spiritual journey with the marks of self-denial and cross-bearing. These seemingly pessimistic spiritual marks were required for believers to engage the sinful world. For Calvin, self-denial meant emptying the heart of worldly self-love and filling it with gratitude, humility, and cross-bearing—a voluntary suffering for the service of God and neighbor. The spiritual marks for Calvin are not signs of a begrudging obedience to God or pessimistic withdrawal from social living; instead, they are signs of engagement in social life. These spiritual marks serve as God's school for believers. Suffering may lead believers to resist pride, persevere with patience, and trust God so that their hope for future salvation may be strengthened. By leading believers to take up their cross, "the heavenly physician," through his "fatherly chastisement," corrects and matures them to a godly life.[14]

Calvin placed the personal Christian calling within the progress of salvation, as effected by Christ's saving work in the past and its effect continuously working in the present challenging world, allowing the Christian to persist with hope for its eschatological fulfillment. This spirituality for the present time, though with an emphasis on the personal life, does not imply a pilgrimage from earthly life to spiritual blessing; rather, looking to the future actively motivates present Christian living:

> … we are in preparation, so to speak, for the glory of the Heavenly Kingdom, for the Lord has ordained that those who are one day to be crowned in heaven should first undergo struggles on earth… [;] we begin in the present life, through various benefits, to taste the sweetness of the divine generosity in order to whet our hope and desire to seek after the full revelation of this.[15]

The marks of Calvin's personal piety—self-denial and taking up one's cross out of genuine humility—encouraged many believers to sustain Christian identity and persevere in a faithful life, even within the context of suffering.

World-affirming spirituality

In the wake of the 19th-century human-centered culture and a liberal theological trend, churches turned the power of the gospel to an introverted spirituality and became inactive in society. Kuyper identified the challenge of the modern age as a full-blown conflict between two "life-systems," between the modern mode of life and the Christian mode of life. The challenge was not limited to a churchly or doctrinal matter. Kuyper believed that Christians were already engaging in a mortal combat against the modern life-system.[16]

Kuyper was convinced that church reform against modern secular culture should start with the recognition that faith serves as the principle of shaping all of life. All of human life, including religion, politics, science, and work, at both personal and communal levels, must be coherently inter-related under the lordship of Christ. Any form of dualism that separates the religious realm from the public realm must be rejected. The domain of faith shaped his public and spiritual dynamic, a creative application of the gospel to all of life.

What shaped Kuyper's dynamic spirituality? Calvin applied justification in the context of believers' progressive sanctification. In pursuit of complete sanctification (even with his unswerving assurance of believers' salvation), Calvin emphasized the spiritual struggle in the sinful world. Kuyper, however, under a similarly challenging situation, located spirituality in the renewed identity of believers as the effect of justification: "Our status before God is that either of the just or of the unjust... [;] a man's status depends not upon what he is, but upon the decision of the proper authorities regarding him; not upon what he is actually, but upon what he is counted to be."[17] For Kuyper, Christians' spirituality is to live out with joy what God graciously empowers them to do.

Kuyper grounded his dynamic view of spirituality on the Holy Spirit's regenerating work in the world. The Holy Spirit, who quickened and sustained life in creation, works as the agent of generating new life in redemption today. Redemption to him means re-effecting the original creation by reversing the effects of sin in it. The regenerating work of the Spirit is not limited to humans but includes all creatures, "animate or inanimate, organic or inorganic, rational or irrational." The Spirit's work means re-creation of all so that each creature may perform with unique energy and power in God's kingdom.[18]

Kuyper's broad, world-affirming spirituality is based on the idea of salvation as analogous to creation. Bavinck, Kuyper's colleague, elaborated on the creational structure of salvation: "With his creation the Father lays the groundwork for the work of re-creation and leads toward it. With his work, on the other hand, the Son goes back deeply—as far as sin reaches—into the work of creation."[19] Salvation does not simply return the damaged creation to the originally created status, but makes the re-creation reach its intended fulness. In the grand drama of salvation, Christian individuals are not lost; instead, their existence is highlighted, for they were created with the calling of cultivating the world. Whatever they do affects the destiny of the world. Thus, regeneration of sinful humans takes the central place in God's drama of salvation. With his work of regenerating humans, God re-establishes them in the world with renewed joy and expectation.

Within this comprehensive act of God's creation and re-creation, each believer finds his/her story. God's salvation story allows room for each so that their common Christian disposition may work in the way that fits their situations. The common Christian disposition of comfort and joy may work for some by empowering the spirit of perseverance and hope for the future, and for others by motivating them to engage in daily life. Calvin urged believers to the calling of self-denial and cross-bearing in pursuit of sanctification in challenging life situations. Kuyper and Bavinck urged them to the calling of living the new life in reconciling the world to Christ. Either way, or in any creative way between the two, believers are called to live out the new life in the world.

Discussion Questions:

1. What ground or reason can you present for your faith? What success or drawback do you think the argument for faith entails?
2. Share how your spirituality may be reshaped and matured by the biblical story of salvation.
3. What do you think are the most required Christian characteristics in modern culture?

Endnotes

1. C. S. Lewis, "Is theology poetry?" in *Weight of Glory* (New York: HarperOne, 1980), p. 140. Lewis' thesis, that the Christian view of creation and redemption may contain science, art, and morality, while they, as transitory and fragmented views of reality, cannot contain the whole, may provide a helpful perspective to modern Christian thinking.
2. John Calvin, *Commentary on the gospel of John*, on 6:69 and 17:8.
3. John Calvin, *Institutes*, I.iii.1.
4. John Calvin, *Institutes*, III.ii.14.
5. Abraham Kuyper built his idea of Christian science upon the Calvinist shape of the mind in faith, in chapter four of *Lectures on Calvinism*. There he explains four points: "first, that Calvinism fostered and could not but foster love for science; secondly, that it restored to science its domain; thirdly, that it delivered science from unnatural bonds; and fourthly, in what manner it sought and found a solution for the unavoidable scientific conflict."
6. William Kingdon Clifford, "The Ethics of Belief," *Contemporary Review*, 29 (1876, Dec-1877, May), p. 295.
7. Alvin Plantinga, "Reason and Belief in God," in Alvin Plantinga and Nichoas Wolterstorff, eds, *Faith and Rationality: Reason and Belief in God* (Notre Dame: University of Notre Dame Press, 1983), pp. 55-63.
8. Alvin Plantinga, "Reason and Belief in God," pp. 64-65. Italics added.
9. Alvin Plantinga, "Reason and Belief in God," p. 79.
10. Calvin, *Institutes*, I.xiv.20-21.
11. Alvin Plantinga, "Reason and Belief in God," p. 81.
12. Willem van Vlastuin, "Kuyper's Spirituality in Its Calvin-Context," in *Church History and Religious Culture*, vol. 101, 2021, pp. 526-545.
13. John Calvin, *Institutes*, III.vii.4.
14. John Calvin, *Institutes*, III.viii.1-8.
15. John Calvin, *Institutes*, III.ix.3.

16. Abraham Kuyper, *Lectures on Calvinism* (Grand Rapids: Eerdmans, 1931), p. 11.
17. Abraham Kuyper, *The Work of the Holy Spirit*, tr. Henri De Vries (New York: Funk & Wagnalls, 1900), p. 361.
18. Abraham Kuyper, *The Work of the Holy Spirit*, p. 46.
19. Herman Bavinck, *Reformed Dogmatics*, vol 3, p. 470.

CHAPTER 19

Practicing spirituality and worldview

In the previous chapter, we discussed how faith makes sense and shapes Christian spirituality and worldview in modern secular, scientific culture. The modern culture's demand for rational and scientific evidence for faith exposes its reductionism and falls short of describing full human existence. We have attempted to present faith as meaningful in itself—instead of seeking the evidence that modern culture demands—by appealing to humanity's fundamental epistemological condition; that is, humans are created to know and live by faith. Faith here refers to the universal human condition of trusting. Life by faith involves dedication of heart and will, more than intellectual scrutiny.

In this chapter, we will move on to living the Christian spirituality and worldview. Paul suggests the following instruction on living the spiritual life:

> Therefore, I urge you, brothers, in view of God's mercy, to offer your bodies as living sacrifices, holy and pleasing to God—this is your spiritual act of worship. Do not conform any longer to the patterns of this world, but be transformed by the renewing of your mind. Then you will be able to test and approve what God's will is—his good, pleasing and perfect will. (Rom. 12:1-2)

Here, Paul expands the spiritual principle to the whole human life. Forms of ascetic spiritualism may have some benefits for certain limited and temporary uses. However, any form of escapist spiritualism or supernaturalism would not square with Paul's admonition of the holistic spiritual life. The key for living the holistic spiritual life is the integrated mind and body; the integrated mind and body is made possible by renewal of the mind and is completed with dedication of the body. Human bodily acts fulfill the "spiritual act of worship." Paul uses three adjectives—living, holy, and pleasing—to describe the bodily dedication as sacrifice to God. The Christian life is to be a living sacrifice in that as their old life dies, they dedicate their new life to God (Rom. 6:4). The new life compels believers to conform to their new spiritual status by living a morally upright life. The conforming Christian life is pleasing to God. Just as the Old Testament sacrifice, as whole and blameless, pleased God, so the Christian life must be in accord with God's will.[1]

How shall we dedicate our life as a living sacrifice to God in our sinful world? Paul's answer carries a double edge: not to conform to the sinful pattern, but to be transformed "by the renewing of your mind." Transforming the mind is necessary, for the mind serves as a bridge to the new life of fruition. Both the negative and positive charges are written in the present tense, signifying ongoing actions. A new mind is not shaped overnight: the regenerated mind may catch spontaneous spiritual insights and get motivated accordingly, but a process is needed to settle the mind into a thinking habit. After all, human culture has been formidably shaped by sin over centuries, and the mind has been set under its influence. We are called to acquire a new thinking habit.

I suggest the following aspects of the renewed mind as pertinent to today's Christian life:

- The joy of loving is the motivating power.
- Its reward spurs one into a holy life.
- Christian freedom is the means of practicing love.
- The world is to be sacramental, or holy evidence of God's salvation.
- Evangelism is to manifest the faithful existence of the church and to present the the gospel.

This list is not a complete list of Christian subjects, nor does it suggest any order of importance among them. The aspects are interrelated and work together. Each believer is called to live out holistic salvation, and the priority is to be discerned individually. On the Sabbath day, Jesus saved lives, healed the sick, fed the hungry, ate at the house of a sinner, cleansed the temple of the merchants, conversed with an afflicted woman, reasoned with law teachers, and preached in the synagogue. The diversity of his acts reflects his holistic ministry, with each act materialized according to his determined goal for the needs of the situation. Such a principle should apply to today's life.

Joy of loving

In the bottom of the heart is the desire for joy. Each person is motivated by and pursues joy. The question is, what joy? Christ advises the Christian rule of joy:

> "As the Father has loved me, so have I loved you. Now remain in my love. If you keep my commands, you will remain in my love, just as I have kept my Father's commands and remain in his love. I have told you this so that my joy may be in you and that your joy may be

complete. My command is this: Love each other as I have loved you." (John 15:9-12)

Christ begins with his love for us. It is very good to know that we are loved. Christ loves us, even continuously. How would we "remain" in his love? By keeping his commands. Are we loved because we obey his moral mandate? Do we earn his love by our legal merit? By no means! Christ clarifies the nature of his obedience by his Father's love for him: "as the Father has loved me." We know what a tremendous sacrifice he made in obedience to the Father. Voluntarily Christ obeyed the "commands." It was a loving obedience, never a grudging legalistic obedience. Love exists first, and it motivates loving obedience; a loving act does not earn love. Christ was loved first, and then he acted in loving obedience. That is the pattern of Christ's calling us to the Christian life. Knowing Christ loves us brings us joy, the deepest joy that humans can cherish. Christ desires our joy to be "complete" as our joy joins his joy. By presenting his love of us as a reflection of love among the trinity, Christ calls us to join God's joy.

Joy may explain the reason for God's creating and redeeming acts. God did not have a necessary reason to create or redeem any. His desire for a loving relationship probably led him to create. His joy is relational, reaching out his internal love and fellowship to creatures. When God created humans in his image, he was pleased to extend his perfect trinitarian love and fellowship to humans. When God created humans as male and female, he envisioned humans to reflect the trinitarian love among themselves. The archetype of God's love and fellowship was to be realized in the basic human unit, man and woman, and from there to be extended to all human relationships. The ruling mandate was to be accomplished in accordance with the purpose of their life—to rule by loving.

The joy of being loved by God motivates the Christian life. The first question is this: are you loved by God? The second question follows: how then will you live his love? For those who are loved, loving is a joyful responsibility—a response to God's love. One of the painful areas that want loving action is broken relationships. Remember: love is relational. When a relationship remains broken, we continually reproduce the brokenness. Prejudice and hatred are prevalent, while understanding and sympathy are scarce. Justice is more often paired with vengeance than with restoration. What loving acts can believers proactively do in broken contexts, such as racism, gender inequality, and cultural prejudice? One act might be promoting the benefit that diversity could bring to society. This line of thinking contends with individual interest for broadening the idea of community. We all seek communities that we deem like-minded so that we can easily identify with them. With the progress in technology, people are now given more opportunities to participate in fragmented communities, including virtual reality. The problem arises when each person seeks like-minded communities out of self-centered interest and excludes others.

God created the world as a community, and a community is characterized by diversity. The Creator intended the world as his cosmic house, with the aim of consecrating all constituents to live in shalom. In fact, God himself is a community of three persons. The purpose of a community is achieved when its diverse members live organically with one another. Diversity is not a problem or obstacle to unity; instead, it is a condition for healthier living in unity. Paul's analogy that one body has many parts beautifully describes the benefit that may be cherished in a diversified community; for each part works for the common good. When a part is damaged by hatred or prejudice, not only terrible injustice is done to the part, but also the community loses the benefit that the part was supposed to contribute. A fundamental argument that promotes diversity is based on creation. Gender, skin color, and ethnic background are fundamental aspects of human existence, thus an undeniable and irrevocable endowment of the Creator to each person. They are God's gift to each person. Nobody should suffer for God's endowment. The flipside of it is also true: nobody should use God's endowment for a reason to be proud. When we see our life within God's community, we may stop producing ugly prejudices and be able to promote fair understanding and sympathetic concern for others.

Reward

Christ promised reward to all believers. How would believers take the promise of reward in their life situations? In the modern economic setting, reward is a just, required compensation for services provided, often offered in terms of material benefit or promotion. Applying such a modern materialistic idea of reward distorts the intended use of reward in the Bible. What is the point of Christ's promise of the reward? How does the reward work in the present life and after it?

Reward is promised in return for diverse good acts. Just a few include loving one's enemies (Luke 6:35), serving the needy (Matt. 6:1 and Mark 9:41), prayer and fasting (Matt. 6:6, 18), strong faith (Heb. 10:35), seeking God (Heb. 11:6), and, most prominently, faithful works (parable of talents in Matt. 25 and parable of *minas* in Luke 19). Characteristics of reward are also given: our reward is stored in heaven until it is publicly revealed at Christ's return (Matt. 5:12); also, the reward will be justly given—"and then he will reward each person according to what he has done" (Matt. 16:27, Rom. 2:6, 1 Cor. 3:10-15). However, his judgements, shown in reward and punishment in the present age, do not exactly match the virtue of individual acts. Some wicked seem to prosper while some righteous suffer. God's present rule hides his providential judgment. Christ's use of rewards is to be recognized within the eschatological progress from his cross to his return. Meanwhile believers are called to faithfully live out their salvation and humbly seek the future reward in the context of suffering.

The two teachings of the Bible, namely giving reward in proportion to individual acts and receiving salvation by grace through faith, lead to the conclusion that though salvation is commonly granted to all believers, reward may vary, depending on the quality of their lives.[2] Reward diversity is determined by a test. Paul describes the test with the analogy of fire in 1 Corinthians 3:13-15. The quality of the Christian life is measured more by heart-motivation than by material quantity. The parables of talents and *minas* highlight a faithful attitude toward life, and the criterion by which Jesus separates sheep and goats is a compassionate attitude toward others.

The required good works, which we have discussed, are the result of justification and sanctification. Being justified and living out the new life are integrated in the believer's life. In fact, the whole course of God's action, from creation to re-creation, means that humans owe all to God. Existence itself, including all the endowed blessings of humanity, and the redemption of sinful humans are both granted by our gracious God. Our conscience agrees that the consequential holy life, if any, is the work of the Holy Spirit. As a result, we humbly concur with Luke, who says, "so you also, when you have done everything you were told to do, should say, 'we are unworthy servants; we have only done our duty'" (Luke 17:10). Good works are a responsibility, not a merit. In heaven, where believers' rewards are stored, the twenty-four elders fall prostrate before God and cast their crowns before him. The heavenly scene underscores that all "glory and honor and power" should be solely dedicated to God (Rev. 4:10-11). There is no sign of justifying reward, but only humble gratitude and worship. No good work should be regarded as meritorious.

Then, what is the reward for? Calvin wrote,

> ... yet those good works which he has bestowed upon us the Lord calls "ours," and testifies they not only are acceptable to him but also will have their reward. It is our duty in return to be aroused by so great a promise, to take courage not to weary in well-doing..., and to receive God's great kindness with true gratefulness.[3]

The reward in the Bible is God's perseverance-project for believers who are suffering in the world. The reward is promised with the goal of equipping them to live a holy life for the present, in anticipation of the future full blessing. Calvin continued, "he wills that we be trained through good works to meditate upon the presentation or fruition, so to speak, of those things which he has promised, and to hasten through them to seek the blessed hope held out to us in heaven."[4]

What does diversity in reward imply? Does it imply difference in affluence, honor, or power of any kind so that believers would be compared to one another? By no means! All the biblical passages that pertain to the reward reject such an idea. Bavinck understood the reward diversity in terms of different functions that each member has in Christ's body, appealing to Romans 12.[5]

A personal understanding of the diverse appreciation of gifts was offered by Hoekema. He described the reward "not in a mechanical but rather in an organic way." He used the example of diverse appreciation of music. Some may not be deeply appreciative of music; others are eager to enjoy it in person at a concert; others enjoy attending concerts and playing instruments or singing. The same may apply to Christian attitudes toward the gospel. Some may appreciate it for a self-centered concern, while others may be burning with desire for the sake of others. Hoekema said, "our devotion to Christ and to service in his kingdom increases our capacity for enjoying the blessings of that kingdom, both now and in the life to come."[6] The reward-as-incentive results in joy of living a godly life. A joyous experience of loving others and serving God produces deeper appreciation of the benefits of the Christian life and generates further motivation to do more. Such joy increases here and now and continues to life in the new heaven and the new earth.

There are significant motives for a rewarding life. First, Christ rewards the faithful work done with a voluntary and humble attitude. Second, reward does not aim at providing personal gain. The parable of the ten *minas* in Luke 19 is popularly used to promote the certainty of reward. The point of the parable is found in the king's judgment: "because you have been trustworthy in a very small matter, take charge of ten cities" (v. 17; see also the parable of the talents in Matt. 25). Indeed, reward is given in the form of happiness. However, the happiness that is promoted here is not personal gain. It is given in the form of getting more work. The whole point of these parables of reward is faithful responsibility. The reward consists not of idle rest but of increased service. And increased service often means unrecognized suffering and pain in actual life. You have to come out of your comfortable, self-centered cocoon, have sympathetic concern for others, and sacrifice your freedom and right in order to serve God and his people. With the promise of rewarding with increased service, Christ invites us to suffering, which is the way he serves us. The paradoxical joy that is granted by way of suffering is the true mark of imitating Jesus.

Practicing Christian freedom

Freedom, in our modern political context, is the individual right to think and act as one pleases without interference. While freedom is also an integral aspect of salvation in the Christian religion and, thus, must be cherished by God's free people, the way of cherishing it is uniquely different in the Christian life. Believers are called to freely sacrifice freedom for the sake of others, which may sound like negating freedom itself. Christ urges his people to use freedom for the sake of loving others.

Christ introduced the source of freedom: "if you hold to my teaching, you are really my disciples. Then you will know the truth, and the truth will set you free (John 8:31-32). The truth to which Jesus referred is the way of salvation, and the freedom is the consequential state of salvation. The exodus of the Hebrews serves as the preamble to Christian freedom. God set his people free from the bondage of the Pharaoh. God led his freed people into the wilderness and shaped them under his law. The freedom that the exodus account anticipated has been fulfilled by Christ's salvation. Consequently, believers are no longer cursed and mastered by evil but are indeed free. The freedom under God's law explains the nature of the freedom that God gives his people. Christian freedom does not mean the right to do whatever one pleases. It is the power to live the Christian life, characterized by Christ's love for us.

Paul, in his first letter to the Corinthian church, raised the issue of practicing Christian freedom—specifically about eating meat dedicated to idols. In the then pagan culture that included animal sacrifice, would believers be free to eat the meat that was religiously misused? There seemed to be diverse views on this issue in the early church. The disciples admonished the newly converted to "abstain from food sacrificed to idols," just as they admonished them to abstain from sexual immorality (Acts 15:20, 29). This admonition sounds different from Paul's instruction in 1 Corinthians. The difference was probably made more for pastoral reasons than theological ones. The new Gentile believers had long been accustomed to a pagan culture; as a result, the disciples judged that they needed a radical transformation to a Christian way of thinking and living. The Gentile converts were situated where the law of Moses was continuously in effect. By comparison, the Corinthian context shows evidence of Christian knowledge, which Paul took for an occasion to teach a more mature Christian lesson.

Paul offers two principles for practicing Christian freedom: the principle of truth and the principle of love. The principle of truth has to do with Christian knowledge. Truth serves as the source of freedom, as we discussed above. Regarding sacrificed meat, Paul claimed that since knowledge about God and salvation sets believers free, they may confidently consume the meat. There is one true God, and others who claim to be gods have no power over God's rule. Thus, any meat offered to idols would still be meat, though misused. Use of food does not affect believers' status before God (1 Cor. 8:8). Conscience may be firmly anchored in the truth, and believers may act according to their conscience.

The principle of love is more compelling, for life does not always run with the truth. Though the truth is one, its knowledge and expression vary. While some are confident with their knowledge of the truth, others may lack that confidence when faced with living it. It is noteworthy that Paul's advice was given to believers who had firm knowledge, not to those who did not share it and had a tender conscience. Paul advised believers to be sympathetic to others' conscience and address them with Christian love.

Paul did not disprove knowledge in extending Christian ethics to loving; rather, he offered a Christian way of practicing knowledge with love. In another place, Paul says, "nothing is unclean in itself. But if anyone regards something as unclean, then for that person it is unclean" (Rom. 14:14). Paul did not suggest situational ethics or base ethical principles on personal preference. Rather, he emphasized the importance of the individual believer's conscience for making decisions. Sin is committed when one is deceitfully or boldly heartened to act against one's conscience. In the case of eating meat offered to idols, sin could emerge when someone saw someone else acting from his conviction of knowledge without concern for others, that is, without love—creating a stumbling block. Paul harshly accused those who had knowledge without love; he did not accuse those who lacked knowledge and thus had a weak conscience. He also did not advise those who lacked firm knowledge or conscience to go and learn the truth.

In sum, freedom is given not for taking advantage of living a freer life, but for freely sacrificing one's freedom for the sake of serving others. Sacrificing one's freedom freely for others is living a freer life. That is the best way of fulfilling Christ's commandment—to love others as we love ourselves (Gal. 5:13-14). And that is the most honorable way of practicing our freedom, for it is the way that Christ exercised his freedom for our sake.

A couple of comments on the principle of living freedom are noteworthy. First, in the text, Paul dealt with indifferent matters—non-essential to the Christian confession, matters that are not explicitly encouraged or forbidden by God's law. Regarding those matters, Paul assumed the diversity of knowledge and conscience in the Christian community. The Christian community should be inclusive, meaning that individual believers' situations and character are accepted and are not to be denied for the sake of unity. Paul advised, "Therefore, let us stop passing judgment on one another. Instead, make up your mind not to put any stumbling block or obstacle in your brother's way" (Rom. 14:13).

The second point pertains to the assurance of individual freedom. When individual believers are assured of their freedom and renew their minds through it, they are able to practice self-sacrificial freedom. Considering the formidable effect of sin on the human mind, it is not strange to see that the new life does not automatically transform the mind, and believers do not automatically bear fruits in their lives. In such a context, God matures their faith and renews their mind so that they may be freed from the grip of stereotypical judgments of the culture. We see how biblical figures came out of their cultural ways of seeing the world and consequently treated one another with loving kindness in their otherwise conflicted relationships. When Peter, in Acts 10, was bound by the law's limited understanding, he was not free to see the new reality that Christ had brought in. With his vision of clean and unclean animals, which symbolically indicated equality of humans, his mind was set free from the grip of favoritism, and his conscience was assured of the new reality, allowing him to confidently associate with the Italian officer, otherwise the Jews' chief enemy. The believers in Galatians 3 had a similar experience of freedom when they heard all are equal in Christ—Jews and Greeks, slaves and free men, and men and women. The issue of meat dedicated to idols invited the believers in Corinth to be freed, first, from the grip of idols, and then, from self-love.

The issues dealt with in these episodes, even after two-thousand years, are relevant to our life. Oftentimes our mind is bound by the rules of our culture, and the freedom with which Christ blessed us is choked under their grasp. The power of Christian freedom may work in our relationships with others, in our habit of spending money and time, and even in our prayers.

The world is sacramental.

The world we are living in is God's creation and object of his care. The first humans during the innocent stage must have directly experienced the world as God's creation under his ruling. Now believers experience the world differently from that. The world is found in the two-stage kingdom structure. Though the world is still corrupted by sin and causes human suffering, we are called to see it from the future perspective of its full restoration. The world is the object of God's redemption and thus sacramental, as the history of salvation makes clear. Sacrament refers to a visible sign of a spiritual reality and thus serves as a channel for God's grace. The water of Baptism and the bread and wine of the Lord's Supper point beyond themselves to the spiritual reality of Christ's saving act. We can see how such mundane matters as water, bread, and wine are used to relay the spiritual message. Similarly, the things of the world, natural and cultural, reflect the salvific and providential care of God. They remind us of God's existence and faithful work of salvation in the busyness of our life. The world as the object of redemption and its consequent sacramental character helps us reshape our understanding and attitude toward the world. It also helps us shape our identity and calling in the world so as to promote responsibility for exploring the world and using its knowledge for the kingdom's sake.

When Abraham and Sarah struggled in their faith, God placed helpers in the sky and on earth to assure them of his promise. God instituted the law in the form of physical signs so that the Israelites could learn the true idea of the holy life. The physical differences among animals corresponded to spiritual holiness and unholiness. God also put the marks of holiness and unholiness on the human body. For example, a mother who gave birth to a son was considered unclean for seven days. When the seven-day requirement was met, on the first day of her receiving cleanness, the boy was to be circumcised (Lev. 12:1-3). Consider how the Israelites learned the godly life at the initial stage of shaping God's people. God used physical signs. Regarding circumcision, God said "it will be the sign of the covenant between me and you…. My covenant in your flesh is to be an everlasting covenant" (Gen. 17:11-13). With the physical signs Israelites were able to appropriate the holy reality in the ordinary world.

The ordinary physical world reminds us of God's existence and workmanship: "The heavens declare the glory of God; the skies proclaim the work of his hands" (Psa. 19:1). God also used the ordinary physical phenomena to teach spiritual lessons. Christ instituted the sacraments of baptism and the Lord's Supper (1 Cor. 10:1-13), with Israel's past experience of cloud, sea, food, and drink as background. The Old Testament experiences serve as "examples" for present believers. Moses, into whom Israel was baptized, is the type of Christ. The cloud and sea, in which they were baptized, point to Christ's blood. The food and drink they ate and drank in the wilderness symbolize Christ's body and blood. God places those helps before our eyes in the structure of progressive fulfillment so that our faith gets persuaded and nourished.

The ultimate sign that God provided is the incarnate Son. Jesus as Immanuel, "God with us," is, in fact, more than a sign, for a sign points beyond physical reality to the spiritual reality. Jesus is the spiritual reality of mysterious incarnation. Jesus directly reveals God in his human form. The human body is the means of God's revelation in the world. Our body, as a sign, reminds us of Christ's identity and works.

Now, when we combine the marks of God in the world and the biblical use of the natural phenomena for spiritual signs, we have a strong argument that the world is sacramental of God's acts. In modern culture, where secularized scientific worldview is prevailing, believers do not readily recognize the benefits that the sacramental character of the world offers. Calvin acknowledged that the world is the theatre of God's glory and thus our school: "let the world become our school if we desire rightly to know God."[7] It has been pointed out that the physical world reflects God's workmanship and providential ruling. The cultural transformation should also be included as God's acts, for the Christian life affects the world. The opposite signs—the signs of sin in the world—should not be neglected. Believers struggle with injustice, corruption, and hatred, but their promotion of justice and love reflects Christ's reconciliation ministry in the world.

As the natural relates spiritual reality, the natural and the spiritual are to be viewed from the vantage point of faith. The miracle is popularly defined as a performance that works contrary to natural laws. This definition is made from the naturalistic standpoint, which considers natural law as the normal way of the world. Faith sees that the Creator is the Lawgiver, who governs the world in diverse ways, for he created the world as a community of diversity. He is the source of all the good, the true, and the beautiful. Considering natural law as the normal viewpoint for interpreting reality of the world is helplessly reductionistic and cannot handle reality in its fullness. There is another reductionistic viewpoint, which is seeing the world only from the spiritual standpoint, as if the spiritual is more valuable than the physical. Reductionistic views make value distinctions. Putting a value distinction either between naturally normal and miraculous from the naturalistic standpoint, or between God's supernatural acts and natural acts from the spiritual standpoint, is misleading. Both the natural and spiritual are true and real because of the creational ordinance, and God in his providential care holds both laws in the world. It is a wrong dichotomy to postulate that faith deals with spiritual matters while science deals with natural matters. Rather, faith deals with the whole of reality, from God's standpoint, and science deals with reality in its unique physical way.

The sacramental view of the world redefines the Christian attitude toward scholarship, education, and work, which deal with knowledge of the world. Knowledge of the world is integral for living human life in the world, even more so for practicing the cultivating mandate. Then, exploring the world is God's work. Learning can be done out of joy, first born out of the gratitude of personal salvation, then motivated by realizing the mandate for cosmic reconciliation. As God is the source of all truth and rules over the whole of reality, theology and science may not be seen in conflict. Rather, they are called to serve God's kingdom in their unique roles. Pertinent to establishing the proper relationship between the two, among others, is to restore the position and role of science from the bondage of the modern reductionistic ideal. Stek suggested a "charter" of science in general:

> From this word [the Bible] concerning God, humanity, and world comes the charter for our pursuit of knowledge about the world, including the development of science. Science belongs to humanity's vocation as God's royal steward of the creation. That this pursuit of knowledge has not been fruitless is grounded in our human capacities as God's image-bearers and stewards, the intelligibility and integrity of the creation, and the continuing effectuation of God's benediction upon his steward.[8]

Science is a divine calling to serve the world according to the Creator's will. By exploring the world, scientists come to know the laws of the natural world and use its results to help the world flourish to its creational potential, which God had originally intended.

Mission and evangelism

The primary means of evangelism resides in the church's faithful existence in the world, as some of its characteristics are discussed above. Witnessing reflects what the church believes and the way she lives her faith in the world. Existence precedes and shapes ministry. The joy of salvation and evangelism reinforce each other. Our missional God sent his church into the world as a mission agent. In that sense only are mission and evangelism ministries of the church. The church does not own or practice them as part of her ministry. The church itself is on a mission, as Christ stated:

> "You are the light of the world. A city on a hill cannot be hidden. Neither do people light a lamp and put it under a bowl. Instead they put it on its stand, and it gives light to everyone in the house. In the same way, let your light shine before men, that they may see your good deeds and glorify your Father in heaven." (Matt. 5:14-16)

Christ rooted the church's mission in the church's identity. The church, individually and communally, is the light of the world. The church is in the world and a public figure there. See Christ's words on the identity of the church in the world: "of the world," "… cannot be hidden," "on its stand," "it gives light to everyone," and "let your light shine before men." The analogy of the light, as drawn from the Old Testament mission of Israel toward nations, demands the church's pure confession, faithful living, and completion of its mission in the world. The oral presentation of the gospel best works when it agrees with the faithful existence of the church.

Christ gave the well-known great commission:

> "Therefore, go and make disciples of all nations, baptizing them in the name of the Father and of the Son and of the Holy Spirit, and teaching them to obey everything I have commanded you. And surely, I am with you always to the very end of the age." (Matt. 28:19-20)

Though simple, Christ's great commission is loaded with meaning. Christ commanded making disciples, not simply presenting the gospel; baptizing them in the name of the triune God, not just helping them to believe in Christ; and teaching them to live out the gospel, not simply believing it. This mission mandate aims at equipping believers to undertake a holistic mission, the idea of mission that has been shaped throughout the history of salvation. If you are mindful of Christ's commission, know that Christ wants to shape your mission and evangelism by the whole story of God's salvation. If you realize that mission and evangelism are daunting tasks, know that you are not alone, but are with Christ, who has "all authority in heaven and on earth" (v. 18). With the supreme divine authority, Christ commissioned you and promised he will be with you to accomplish your mission.

Joy is the profound motivation for the Christian life. Aesthetic and emotional desire coupled with freedom from sin's bondage attain to the genuine worship of God. Christian freedom serves as the means for loving acts and shaping a healthy community. Loving others, serving the community, and worshipping God may sound like a grudging duty, something that conflicts with individual freedom. A misunderstanding of the gift of freedom, i.e., being shackled by the individualistic and consumeristic culture, forfeits joy and the opportunity of living a holy life. The joy of living a holy life is also augmented by Christ's promise of reward. Reward is Christ's gracious incentive for living a faithful Christian life, promised in the form of reward even for an unmeritorious life. It helps believers persevere in the challenging life and gives hope for the future. Salvation affects the things of the world, and thus things of the world reflect salvation. The joy of living a holy life is intensified by recognizing that knowledge of the world means responsibility for believers. In fact, knowing the world is as holy a matter as is worshipping God. For the knowledge of the world includes the proper way of serving it. The oral presentation of the gospel takes a significant role in the Christian life, but it works most effectively when accompanied by all of these acts of the Christian life.

Discussion Questions:

1. What are most challenging factors in your pursuit of living Christian life?

2. Share how God helps you continue and mature your faith in a challenging life.

3. In what sense are loving acts commanded in the Bible? See how the joy of salvation and the use of freedom are related to living out loving actions.

4. Share how you can serve God's kingdom through your work or education.

Endnotes

1. John Calvin, *Commentary on Romans* (Grand Rapids: Baker, 1981), on 12:1-2.

2. Herman Bavinck, *Reformed Dogmatics*, Vol. 4, p. 236. Louis Berkhof, *Systematic Theology* (Grand Rapids: Eerdmans, 1996), pp. 733-734. Anthony A. Hoekema, *The Bible and the Future* (Grand Rapids: Eerdmans, 1989), pp. 262-264.

3. Calvin, *Institutes*, III.xv.3. The reformer's idea of the reward is well captured later in the Belgic Confession, art. 24., which reads, "…Rather, we are indebted to God for the good works we do, and not God to us…. Yet we do not wish to deny that God rewards good works—but it is by grace that God crowns these gifts."

4. Calvin, *Institutes*, III.xviii.3. Bavinck writes on the goal of the reward, "he does that to spur on, to encourage, and to comfort his children," in *Reformed Dogmatics*, Vol. 4, p. 265.

5. Bavinck, *Reformed Dogmatics*, Vol. 4, pp. 728-730.

6. Hoekema, *The Bible and the Future*, p. 264.

7. John Stek cites the following from John Calvin: "For God… clothes himself, so to speak, with the image of the world, in which he would present himself to our contemplation…. Therefore, as soon as the name of God sounds in our ears, or the thought of him occurs to our minds, let us also clothe him with this most beautiful ornament; finally, let the world become our school if we desire rightly to know God." *Commentary on Genesis* (Grand Rapids: Baker, 1981, in Argument), p. 60.

8. Stek, "What says the Scripture?" p. 263.

CHAPTER 20

Foretasting the eternal life here and now

In this final chapter, we discuss what Christ will bring to the world with his return and how that affects our present Christian life. As salvation is described in terms of restoration of the created world, Scriptures implies both continuity and discontinuity between the present world and the restored world. As much as the present world is completely purged of its sin and God's kingdom is fully established in it, the restored world will be new and different from the present world. As much as the present world is still the same domain of God, the restored world will accomplish God's intension of the original creation. Scriptures do not provide detailed information about the time of Christ's return or the state of the renewed world. The message of the eschatological teaching does not fasten us to the future so that we should look up to the sky and neglect the present godly life; instead, it equips believers to live faithful Christian lives in the present age with hope of the future. Matthew calls the lesson "therefore, keep watch." In the sense that the scriptural lesson on continuity and discontinuity shapes our understanding of Christian identity and calling in the world today, the scriptural teaching on the future is a very significant feature for the Christian life.

The unique two-stage structure of God's kingdom creates a tension between the "already" aspect of our salvation and "not-yet" aspect of it. We have already discussed the conflict that believers may experience between assurance of salvation and shortcomings of godly life in the sinful world. The conflict, often accompanied with suffering, serves as a school for the maturing of believers. God chose the best way to bring us back to him. His aim is not simply to make sinful humans believe or let them suffer as redeemed people, but to shape the redeemed as full humans in genuine gratitude and in living life.

Another tension may be raised, by the two-stage salvation, between living eternal life and fear of death. Our sinful life, the old self, has been crucified with Christ, and we have been risen with him into a new life. We have become new people and are living the born-again new life. But we die. Does the universal death mean we are still under the curse of death? How is our present new life related to the accomplished new life in the new heaven and new earth? These tensions lead us to see our present life with the eschatological hope of future completion.

Before we move to the biblical teaching on the future, let us take a brief review of the nature of salvation that God has wrought so far. First, the Bible reveals the drama of cosmic salvation, in which are found the place and meaning of personal salvation. Salvation in the Bible is not limited to rescuing individuals from the human predicament, and the present life is more than a waiting period before one is transferred to heaven. By forgiving sins of humans, God re-establishes them in the world so that through their godly life he transforms all of creation.

The second issue is the holistic view of the world. Since God is the sovereign Creator and Redeemer and Lord over all, any form of dualism in God's world should be rejected, especially between the spiritual and the physical. If the popular saying of "going to heaven" refers to the transfer from the present physical reality to future spiritual reality of heaven, it does not reflect the biblical teaching of the world. God's people do not escape the sinful world and go to a spiritual realm for eternity. Rather, the world is purged of its evil, thus renewed, and becomes united with heaven. As the world is renewed, God's dwelling merges with the human dwelling. Heaven and earth are bound to one another; they are to be united so that all becomes God's kingdom. Though the future state seems to be quite new, it is not totally new, for the new heaven and new earth will accomplish God's intension of the original creation.

The third issue is the nature of the present Christian life in its relationship to the future completed kingdom. The continuity and discontinuity between the present stage and the stage to come raise the sense of Christian responsibility for the present living to a higher level, with a longing hope for the completed future. Whatever believers do as kingdom citizens here and now will be remembered in the completed kingdom. The Christian responsibility does not mean that we bring in the completed kingdom with human ability. The responsibility is parallel to the new life that we receive from Christ. As the necessity of Christ's giving new life to us implies, the transformation of the world from the present to the future depends totally on God's authority. We do not contribute to our new life per se, but we join with Christ by living the new life. Living Christ's life means joining his transforming work. The Christian responsibility implies a joyful partaking rather than a triumphant pride or burdensome duty.

Christ is returning… and then what?

All the future events hinge, and take place, on Christ's return: the end of the present stage, the general resurrection, the final judgment, and transition to the new heaven and new earth. Jesus explained, in Matthew 24 and 25, the end of the world "ahead of time" so that the church would know what to expect and how to prepare for it (24:25). He illustrated the signs of the present world's end, such as the appearance of false teachers; apostasy; and great tribulations like hatred, wars, famine, earthquakes, and persecution. There will be spiritual and moral challenges and natural disasters. These signs have been routinely repeated in the world. Jesus did not intend to relate any of these troubles to particular historical events. The signs were given as a general indicator of the end time, not for marks of particular historical or supernatural incidents. A commentator wrote on the nature of the signs, "he [Jesus] does not want his church to do apocalyptic calculations, to read runes, to have gnostic inside dope on the end of the world."[1]

As the signs have triggered fear among believers, Christ's reference to the labor pains (24:8) points to the intended goal of hardship—to equip the church for the coming hardship. Christ provided the church with signs of the end (ch. 24) and of the consequent judgment (ch. 25) so that she may faithfully pass through the hardship.

The Bible teaches that Christ's return is a sure thing. There seemed, however, to be some confusion about it in the early Christian community. Peter cited a doubt about Christ's return: "Where is this 'coming' he promised?" The ground for their unbelief sounded scientific, for they reasoned that "everything goes on as it has since the beginning of creation" (2 Pet. 3:4). Nature works in an orderly way, and an incident like Christ's return is unprecedented in the orderly world. Thus, his return is impossible to believe, concluded the doubters. Peter replied to them by pointing out God's sovereign lordship over nature and history. As God cleansed the earth with water in the past, he will cleanse it with fire at the time of Christ's return. Once the doubters believed in God's providential sovereignty that was acted out through the flood, which they believed because they were part of the church, argued Peter, then they must also believe God's act through Christ's return.

Jesus' teaching moves to the time of his coming: "No one knows about that day or hour" (Matt. 24:36). He will come "like a thief." He will come suddenly and unexpectedly when all people would consider they are safe. Jesus' teaching, "you know the signs" but "you do not know the time," shapes the Christian perspective of seeing the future. As long as the signs are given, his return may not be imminent, but as he will come like a thief, his return will be sudden. This idea of the future characterizes the Christian life with "Therefore, keep watch" (24:32).

Life after death

Why is it that we are dying even if we are living eternal life? What happens after a believer dies? The first mention of death in the Bible is found in Genesis 2-3. There was potential for the human race to live eternally. God said, after Adam and Eve's eating of the forbidden fruit, "the man has now become like one of us, knowing good and evil. He must not be allowed to reach out his hand and take also from the tree of life and eat and live forever" (Gen. 3:22). The text implies that God intended for humans to mature and to eventually be allowed to reach to the tree of life and live eternally. Before the disobedient act, God threatened death— "you will surely die"—if they ate of the forbidden tree. Adam and Eve, however, were not struck dead right after their disobedience. Their spiritual death, that is, separation from the source of life, started to dominate their life until their physical death. Death became a universal human reality. Death was not inherent in human nature; it was brought upon humans as consequence of their sin.

Since mortality was not a part of human nature, it may be cured. When Christ overcame the power of death, he could have set his people free from the curse of death. However, Jesus' death and resurrection did not return humans to their original provisional state of Genesis 2; instead, it made possible the envisioned state of the fullest human potential, that is, eternal life.

Christ's victory over death reverses the curse of death. His own resurrection and his miracles of raising the dead to life prove the newly brought reality of eternal life. But believers are still dying physical death. Death serves as the final procedure that leads our physical existence to its completed level. Through death, God accomplishes his creational purpose for human existence by uniting the renewed body with eternal life. Death that believers die is not a judgment of sin; that is, they do not die because of their sin, since Christ already died for their sins. Death is the way God prepared for our passage to complete life, following the pattern of Christ's death and resurrection.

What, then, should be the Christian attitude toward death? Fear of death may be overcome by joy over the glory of Christ's resurrection and hope for our resurrected eternal life. Satan is falsely claiming his power over death and deceiving humans with it. He cannot hold humans under its curse, for Christ has overcome its power of death. Hope for the resurrected eternal life brings significant meaning for the present life. Believers are now living the life that belongs to the age to come. They are here and now foretasting the future-age blessings. John witnesses to the present blessing of eternal life: "a time is coming and has now come" (John 5:25). The future lives in the present. Every day is a tribute to eternal life and remembrance of overcoming death.

Where do "we" go when we die?[2] At death, the body decays, but some of the human person survives physical death. Paul provides a future picture of human existence between death and resurrection: "We are confident, I say, and would prefer to be away from the body and at home with the Lord" (2 Cor. 5:8). What part of the human person is with the Lord after death? Many have tried to answer the question with a holistic personal existence rather than a partial human ego such as soul, spirit, or heart. The "I" who is with the Lord after death is able to experience blessed fellowship with God. The episode of the dead Lazarus, who was carried to "Abraham's side," implies the retention of self-identification and the personal experience of the Lord's blessing. It is biblical to conclude that a "core" personhood that retains the self-identity with memory of earth exists in the post-mortem period, rather than one part of the person, such as soul or spirit: "Persons can exist without earthly bodies.... I—my essential selfhood or core personhood—must survive physical death. The being or entity who I am must continue to exist."[3]

Where do we "go" when we die? The Bible does not provide detailed information about the whereabouts. The New Testament employs diverse terms to refer to believers' post-mortem existence, such as Abraham's side, paradise, or heaven. We may conclude that the deceased believing person is transferred to heaven, for heaven refers to the presence of God. There they stay, resting and comforted. The unbelieving persons experience separation from the Lord of life in suffering. The state between death and resurrection is considered the intermediate state, for it is not the final home of God's people. Though there the deceased believers experience blessed rest and comfort, their human life is still incomplete. When Christ returns and confirms the judgment of each human, the core human person will be united to the resurrected body in the new heaven and new earth. The new heaven and new earth is the final home for God's people, where they will enjoy the fully achieved human life as God intended.

New heaven and new earth

It is no coincidence that the Bible begins with the creation of the world and humanity in it and ends with the hope of the new creation and restored humanity in it, when we consider that the biblical history of salvation aims at completing the Creator's intention of his creation. When we compare the description of the creation account of Genesis 1 and 2 to that of the new heaven and new earth in Revelation 21 and 22, we find, first, a progressive correlation between the creation and re-creation and, second, a correlation that attests to God's fulfillment of cosmic restoration by way of human salvation.

While the creation was described as a garden, the new heaven and new earth is described as a city, "the new Jerusalem." It is "coming down out of heaven from God... [, after which] the dwelling of God is with men, and he will live with them" (Rev. 21:2-3). God's presence is coming down to dwell with humans; believing humans do not go up to heaven to meet God. Heaven coming down is God's gift, not a human achievement. We are not earning this hope; we are given this hope. A progression is found from the garden to the holy city. While in the garden "streams" came from the ground and rivers nourished the garden, in the city "the river of the water of life" comes from God's throne and nourishes the whole city. While the tree of life was kept from humans in the garden, in the city "the tree of life" planted by the river nourishes and heals the nations with its fruits and leaves. In the city there will be "no more death or mourning or crying or pain." There the human potential, implanted as the image of God, is fully cultivated to eternal life. The radical comfort we find there is that we will never be separated from God. The old promise of salvation, "I will be your God and you will be my people," is accomplished. This progressive parallel is also found between the orders of the heaven and earth and the new heaven and new earth. In the creation account, God separated light from darkness, and water from dry land. In the new heaven and new earth, there will be no night or sea, signifying the non-existence of evil power. (See the extended spiritual meanings of light and water that were developed in the history of salvation.) The new city is full of light, decorated with precious stones that symbolize light. There will be no need for the sun, moon, or temple, for the significance of them has been achieved by God himself.

The completed people of God are described as "a great multitude," composed "from every nation, tribe, people, and language" (7:9). There, "the nations will walk by its light, and the kings of the earth will bring their splendor into it.... The glory and honor of the nations will be brought into it" (21:24-26). The "nations" are God's people out of all nations. Isaiah long ago envisioned the nations glorifying God. The nations and their kings will bring "the riches of the nations" to serve Zion: "You [Zion] will drink the milk of nations and be nursed at royal breasts. Then you will know that I, the Lord, am your Savior" (60:16). People of Egypt, Assyria, Moab, and all neighboring countries will worship God with the Israelites. While worshipping God in unity, they will enjoy reconciliation of all the conflicts and struggles they had among themselves. This unity of God's people invites us to envision the reconciliation of the conflicts that we experience today among nations and cultures. Our personal struggles will also change to loving and serving one another.

The way God creates the new heaven and new earth has long captured the theological imagination. And the divine means of creating it determines the way believers are to live in the present time. God's sovereign intent for salvation has been shown in that he preserves his creational cause by eradicating the evil from his creation. Peter explained that the eradication of evil will take place by means of fire. Fire will consume the sinful effects in the world, not the world itself, for judgment is on the evil: "for the day of judgment and destruction of ungodly men" (2 Pet. 3:7). The role of fire is attested as revealing the quality of life, as Paul teaches that "his work will be *shown* for what it is, because the Day will bring it to light. It will be *revealed* with fire, and the fire will test the quality of each person's work" (1 Cor. 3:13). The verbs "showing" and "revealing" are also used by Peter when he teaches, "the heavens will disappear with a roar; the elements will be destroyed by fire, and the earth and everything in it will be *laid bare*" (v. 10). The physical description of fire should be read for a theological meaning. By using fire, God will reveal how each human lived life by testing the quality of his/her life by the criterion of faith.

Keep watch

If things are taking place in that way, "what kind of people ought you to be?" Peter answered, "You ought to live holy and godly lives as you look forward to the day of God and speed its coming… [;] we are looking forward to a new heaven and a new earth, the home of righteousness" (2 Pet. 3:11, 13). Peter asked the question of how we shall live here and now with the hope of future renewal of the world, not the question of how we shall prepare ourselves to go to heaven.

Peter's call for the "holy and godly life" is captured in Jesus' teaching, "keep watch."

His teaching of "keep watch" is illustrated in the following parables: ten virgins, the talents and minas, and the sheep and goats. In all these parables, Jesus assumed a period between his going away and returning. The lapse of time is the present age, situated between his ascension and his return. When Christ returns, he will demand an account of each person's life. It is good not to know the time of his return, but it would be tragic not to know that he returns and judges.

The parables call the readers, on the one hand, to discern the significance of the present age. The present age is for refining their faith and living out the new life, and, through faithful living, for preaching the gospel. On the other hand, the parables call readers to take moral responsibility in everyday life. It warns against a complacent attitude toward the doctrine of justification. Justification by faith implies neither that once you believe you will always believe, nor that faith is only a spiritual matter.

The parables teach that every human will receive either reward or judgment, depending on the quality of their lives. Reward and judgment are dreadfully different. Reward is described as joining God's joy and inheriting the kingdom, while judgment as being thrown into darkness, weeping, gnashing of teeth, and fire (See Matt. 13:40-42). The words of judgment are hard to swallow. Believers face both joyous assurance of reward and fear of God's judgment. Bruner comments on the text: "Yes, the two are entirely compatible—every true believer has both and knows this coexistence in experience. 'There is forgiveness with thee, that thou mayst be feared' (Psa. 130:4)."[4] Fear of God's judgment, to believers, does not imply his threat of destruction. Rather, it results in a deep personal piety that runs into reverence of God. As long as believers have faith, they are given the promise of salvation and may boldly seek reward in God. At the same time, as long as believers fail to give the due honor to God, they face the just God and humbly seek for his grace. Christ does not apply a mechanical measurement for an accounting of believers' life, as if human acts earn salvation. In deep gratitude and fear, believers are called to dig deeper into the cause of salvation. God gives us the talents and mercifully deems our lives as faithful as if they are.

The biblical teaching on the future culminates our reading of the history of salvation. Biblical teaching about the future does not simply show what will be at the end of this age, as if, for that reason, it takes the last couple of pages in Scripture. Rather, the whole Scripture is structured with a future-oriented viewpoint. All God's acts in Scripture are arranged—from creation through Christ's redemptive acts—to point progressively toward the goal of the new creation. God's acts of salvation are creational, as he accomplishes his intent for creation, and are eschatological, in that his salvation is accomplished in the new creation. In the movement from Christ's redemptive work toward the new creation is found our identity and calling as the church. Finding our present place and mission of life within the grand drama of salvation is an important factor for living the present life. Within God's grand story we find a coherent story of ourselves, why and how we were created and placed in the world, why and how we became sinful and are suffering in the world, how we are saved through Christ, how our salvation will culminate in the new creation, and finally, how we ought to think and live in the present life. Otherwise, our stories are lost in the fragmented pieces of salvation's story. All human acts we do in church and at home, in schools and in workplaces, are to be guided by this eschatological insight.

Discussion questions:

1. Share the implication for the Christian life in Jesus' teaching about his return—that we are given the signs, but we do not know its time.
2. What should be the Christian attitude toward death?
3. In what way does the promise of the new heaven and new earth promote Christian education or work?

Endnotes

1. Frederick Dale Bruner, *Matthew: A Commentary*, vol 2 (Dallas: Word Publishing, 1990), on 24:25.
2. There has long been a confusion between the ancient Greek idea of immortality and biblical idea of the human soul. If immortality of the soul is de-

fined as an inherent human nature that automatically makes all dead human souls survive physical death and enjoy eternal life, it is not found in the Bible. Immortality is not an inherent human nature, but a gift of God endowed to his people.

3. John Cooper, *Body, Soul and Life Everlasting* (Grand Rapids: Eerdmans, 1989), pp. 162-164.

4. Bruner, *Matthew: A Commentary*, vol 2, on 24:40.

CHAPTER 21

Epilogue: My story in God's story

Some studies of salvation history have emphasized God's work for human salvation at the disregard or expense of creation theology. Supporting such an argument, some have pointed out that while the Old Testament maintains a distinct concern for the creation, the New Testament lacks that concern and focuses only on human salvation.[1] In this view, which seems to assume a modification in God's working of salvation between the two Testaments, Christ's salvific work is limited to redeeming sinful humans out of the sinful world. This emphasis on personal salvation, in reading the Scripture, has been intensified in modern culture, where religion is considered a personal matter. People are urged to accept Christianity for the sole purpose of obtaining the personal benefits of salvation, out of fear of death and sin, and thereby following the utilitarian lead of culture. Much of the academic and popular writing about Christianity reinforces this emphasis on personal salvation, an emphasis that keeps Christians from living out the full benefits of salvation.

The Scripture, read as an integrated history of salvation revealed in a progressive way, shows that God's work of salvation is analogous to the eschatological force of his creational ordinance, in that God pursues the completion of his creation. Creation theology is not an isolated or passing theme in the Bible and, thus, should not be reduced to a subordinate context for redemption or an appendix to the redeemed life. Rather, the divine creational ordinance guides the purpose and nature of redemption. The Creator God is the Lawgiver. Through his ordinances, the world came into being, with his laws implanted in it—spiritual, natural, and moral. Without the creation-based normative laws, no meaning of human acts is discerned. The criterion that distinguishes right and wrong, and which later determines the nature of sin, is found only in the creational norm. The purpose of creation and the nature of redemption are found in God's sovereign and gracious providence for the created world.

Reading the Scripture is a discipline that aligns our faith and thinking in accord with God's work of salvation. The big picture of God's salvation provides us with a guide to the meaning of history and prayer and is a means of discernment for the Christian life.

History reflects divine providence in a doxological way. God's providence is the remedy for the fear of oblivion of any meaning in history. The divine wisdom in God's acts of creation, redemption, and present ruling remains a mystery and compels our worship. In that mystery, however, God covenants with us to communicate his will for creation and re-creation. In the progress between the two—creation and re-creation—is found the meaning of history, in that God restores the sin-corrupted world. Until the world becomes restored to God's original intention, all of creation is judged *abnormal*. The abnormal status works most acutely in recognizing truth. Humans pursue the ways of whatever they deem true and right. However, history is not open to, or dependent on, their ideas and acts; rather, their acts *react* to God's creational norm. God guides history to its eschatological goal—the re-creation. The gracious God, who sent his Son incarnated, proved that he is tenacious in his ruling.

As history progresses toward the goal of re-creation, what affects the Christian life the most is the tension between the "already" and "not-yet" of God's redemption. The tension explains moral struggles that we experience—joy and freedom on the one hand and conflicts and doubts on the other. Christ's Spirit, who comforts and strengthens the church, uses hardships as opportunities for maturing the Christian's faith. The maturing process implies God's high expectations for his people as they are established anew to serve as salt of the earth and light of the universe. A prominent characteristic of the Christian life, that has been overlooked in the modern pleasure-seeking culture, is suffering. Christ's kingship is characterized by his suffering, and he calls us to imitate him. Wanting reconciliation and justice in our society demands our suffering. For instance, we are often victims of our own bigotry. Enslaved by our bigotry, we become blind to others. But through suffering, we learn to see our story within God's story so that we may align our view with Christ's. We are to make friends with people not of our kind, not just lament over the news of hate-crimes. We are to be sensitive to people's situation around us and try to be compassionate with them. Each of these acts for reconciliation and justice, however small it may be, requires a bit of patience, sacrificed freedom, and suffering. Christ calls us to suffer by giving us the vision of participating in his joy. Joy and suffering are a perfect duo in the Christian life.

Prayer is also a necessity for the Christian life. Prayer, being a petition to God born out of our need, reflects our view of the Christian life. Christ taught us how to pray through the Lord's Prayer. That is, he taught us his view of the Christian life. It begins with praising God, which is followed by four petitions. The first petition is "your kingdom come, your will be done on earth as it is in heaven." This petition, born out of the harsh Christian experience that motivates the next three particular requests, guides our attention to God's will. Christians are not to try to sway God to satisfy their needs, but instead they are to seek after the way of life that is in accord with God's will. God's will is indeed revealed through Christ's salvation work. The point of the Lord's Prayer is that Christians trust God to bring his kingdom to their life. Christians are assured that they will not be left in hardship, but instead will be under God's providential care. God's salvation, they trust, is now working in their reality and will be completed. With their minds set on God's will, Christians may plead that God will satisfy their particular needs—and all for God's glory.

Endnote

1. Charles H. H. Scobie, *The Ways of Our God*, pp. 182-184.

www.ingramcontent.com/pod-product-compliance
Lightning Source LLC
Chambersburg PA
CBHW050816090426
42736CB00022B/3473